MW01383660

For Professor Charles Rearick, with thanks for all your
help –

Andrew Jones
January 1999

Opera, State and Society in the Third Republic, 1875–1914

Studies in Modern European History

Frank J. Coppa
General Editor

Vol. 23

PETER LANG
New York • Washington, D.C./Baltimore • Boston
Bern • Frankfurt am Main • Berlin • Vienna • Paris

André Michael Spies

Opera, State and Society in the Third Republic, 1875–1914

PETER LANG
New York • Washington, D.C./Baltimore • Boston
Bern • Frankfurt am Main • Berlin • Vienna • Paris

Library of Congress Cataloging-in-Publication Data

Spies, André Michael.
Opera, state and society in the Third Republic, 1875–1914 /
André Michael Spies.
p. cm. — (Studies in modern European history; 23)
Includes bibliographical references (p. ****) and index.
1. Opera—Social aspects—France—Paris—19th century. 2. Opera—Political
aspects—France—Paris—19th century. 3. Opera—Social aspects—France—
Paris—20th century. 4. Opera—Political aspects—France—Paris—20th
century. 5. Music and state. 6. Opéra–Comique (Paris, France)—History.
7. Opéra de Paris—History. I. Title. II. Series:
Studies in modern European history; vol. 23.
ML1727.8.P2S78   792.5'0944'36109034—dc20   96-35897
ISBN 0-8204-3696-8
ISSN 0893-6897

Die Deutsche Bibliothek-CIP-Einheitsaufnahme

Spies, André Michael:
Opera, state and society in the Third Republic, 1875–1914 / André Michael
Spies. –New York; Washington, D.C./Baltimore; Boston; Bern;
Frankfurt am Main; Berlin; Vienna; Paris: Lang.
(Studies in modern European history; Vol. 23)
ISBN 0-8204-3696-8
NE: GT

Cover design by James F. Brisson

The paper in this book meets the guidelines for permanence and durability
of the Committee on Production Guidelines for Book Longevity
of the Council of Library Resources.

Printed in the United States of America.

Dedicated to the

Faculty of the University of

North Carolina

PREFACE

This work is intended for musicologists, historians of the Third Republic in France, and scholars interested in the relationship between cultural and social phenomena. I have tried to write in such a way as to make it accessible to opera buffs as well.

I expect none of these groups will be entirely satisfied. Historians might complain that I have included some previously unpublished material on the administration of the Opéra and Opéra-Comique even when it is not strictly relevant to my thesis. On the other hand, musicologists who benefit from this material may find the thesis itself irrelevant. I have chosen to provide brief identifications of prominent composers and historical figures, which will be superfluous to scholars in the relevant discipline. I hope that everyone will blame the flaws in the work on the requirements of scholars in fields other than their own.

It is a pleasure to be able to thank publicly many benefactors and colleagues who have contributed over the years to my professional development or to the improvement of this work. I owe a particular debt to Professor Emeritus Edward Fox of Cornell University, whose example convinced me, even in 1969, that an academic career was compatible with the utmost personal integrity and kindness. At the University of North Carolina, I benefited greatly from the guidance of Professor Joan Scott. Professors David Griffiths, Donald Reid, Lloyd Kramer and Lamar Cecil, all at one time connected with the UNC History Department, contributed valuable suggestions to this work. Thanks also to Professor Cecil for taking an interest in my prose.

It gives me great satisfaction to acknowledge the contributions to this work of scholars from other disciplines. Musicologists have been generous to this interloper in their field; in particular, Dr. James Haar of the University of North Carolina Department of Music was extraordinarily forthcoming when, as an obscure graduate student in history, I solicited his help. M. Michel Bouille, Documentaire-Archiviste aux Archives Nationales in Paris, provided invaluable lexicographical assistance. The remarkable Faculty Writing Workshop at Hollins College, consisting of colleagues from a variety of fields, helped me clarify both my ideas and my writing.

These scholars' willing assistance should be not construed as an endorsement of my conclusions.

Hollins College reference librarian Elizabeth Doolitle, along with my student assistant Somer Cross '98, ably checked bibliographical references. I am indebted also to Ann Mansfield for expert proofreading. Dr. Heidi Burns at Peter Lang Press has been a patient and accommodating editor. I am, of course, solely responsible for any errors in the text.

A grant from the Lurcy Foundation, distributed by the University of North Carolina, and a Sowell Grant from Hollins College made research abroad possible.

Finally, I wish to thank my wife, Wendy Zomparelli, for immeasurable support — financial, logistical, and emotional — throughout the process.

ACKNOWLEDGEMENTS

Portions of Chapter III appeared in Essays in European History 2 (1996) under the title "The French Revolution and Revolutionary Values in Belle Epoque Opera." This material is reprinted here with permission of University Press of America. All rights reserved. Some of Chapter IV appeared as "Lohengrin Takes on the Third Republic: Wagner and Wagnérisme in Belle Epoque Paris" in the journal Nineteenth Century Studies 3 (1989). Reprinted here by permission of the editors. All rights reserved.

Book design by M2 Studio, Moneta, Virginia.
Principal type is Bembo.

TABLE OF CONTENTS

Chapter I

Introduction

In the introduction to Volume I of his *Soirées Parisiennes* (1875), "Un Monsieur de l'Orchestre"[1] reported the results of his recent survey of Philippe d'Ennery's dramatic works. He claimed to have counted 84 male orphans and 112 female orphans, 60 blind persons and 10 feigning blindness, 93 young women abducted, 22 fratricides, 8 parricides, 2 cases of incest, 145 found children, 162 lost children, 116 stolen children, 124 substituted children, 212 overturned wills, 216 stolen briefcases, 198 sword fights, 168 gunfights, 8 knife fights, 2 sabre fights, 13 arsonists, 123 shootings, 136 poisonings, 46 drownings, 26 guilty convicts, 62 innocent convicts, 80 liberated convicts, 35 escaped convicts, 17 falsely accused adulterers, 77 asphyxiated persons, 64 rapes, 115 escapes, 206 kidnappings, 40 cases of violent madness, 39 cases of benign madness, 62 cases of cretinism, 28 cases of feigned madness, 113 spouses deceived before the marriage, 105 during the marriage, and 41 before and during. I took this list to be simply a clever *blague* until I encountered one of d'Ennery's works myself. His libretto for Gounod's opera *Le Tribut de Zamora* (O–1881)[2] features one foundling, one sword fight, one suicide pact, one rape, one shooting, 20 virgins (female) abducted by Saracens, and a mad woman who recovers her sanity whenever she hears the name Zamora.

While bizarre librettos like d'Ennery's undoubtedly contribute to opera's charm, they also seem to validate the traditional emphasis of opera scholars and aficionados on music and *mise-en-scène*. Since musicologists have increasingly come to accept the notion that music can convey ideas, and that it has ideological content, even scholars interested in the social context of the opera have turned to the music as fruitful ground for their research. The argument of this work, in contrast, takes as its starting point opera's capacity for conveying social and political messages through the dramatic action. But my interest in the librettos of the late-nineteenth-century French operas is emphatically not based on any conviction of the unimportance or irrelevance of the music or staging to its social context, or of the impossibility of interpreting its meaning.

When this was still a matter of debate, I found the rather limited conclusions of Peter Kivy convincing.[3] His argument was that music can express emotions through imitation of speech patterns, or through accumulated conventions, but that such emotional content can best be identified when it comes into relation with text. My subsequent encounter with the work of Wolfgang Burde[4] demonstrated to my satisfaction that sophisticated analysis of operatic music in relation to text can help to reveal the social consciousness of the composer. Since the publication of Leppert and McClary's collection of thoughtful essays,[5] and Paul Robinson's influential *Opera and Ideas*,[6] the notion that music can convey ideas may be considered to have entered the mainstream of musicological thought. The recent, comprehensive work of Anselm Gerhard[7] leaves no doubt of the capacity of operatic music to bear the burden of ideology.

If a historian has any unique contribution to make to the study of opera, however, it is more likely to derive from the application of our characteristic techniques to texts written in words. Irritating as opera librettos can be to work with, they have the advantage of being extremely limited in the subtlety and sophistication of the ideas that they are able to convey. In comparison with poetry, the novel, and other forms of literature and drama, not to mention music or the other constituent arts of the opera, the process of identifying patterns in their librettos' ideological content is enormously simplified, making it possible to deal with large numbers of texts over a long period of time.

The analysis of opera's content that follows is based on 138 full-length French operas that had premieres at the Opéra and Opéra-Comique during the forty-year period from 1875 to 1914.[8] "Full-length" is understood to include only operas of three acts or more, and "French" means that the libretto was written originally in French. The controversy over Wagnerian imports was substantial, and receives extended treatment below, but my principal emphasis is on operas written specifically for the late-nineteenth-century Paris audience. Such works accounted for more than half of the total performances at the Opéra-Comique and a bit more than one quarter at the Opéra, where the traditional repertoire of July Monarchy and Second Empire classics was firmly entrenched. Since most critics believed that the music and *mise-en-scène* counted for much more than the libretto in the success or failure of each individual opera, and did their best to reinforce that point of view, I have been unwilling to assume that the frequency of performance of individual operas is an indicator of audience reaction to the librettos' content. Until the role of the libretto in the success or failure of particular operas becomes clear, until we know how anticipated audience response to ideological considerations affected librettists' decisions, the many obscure failures among these 138 operas will hold as much interest as operas that have survived in the repertoire, or those that have been revived from time to time.

Now that we have reached a stage where even music is accepted as representing ideas, it would hardly seem necessary to address the declining body of opinion that continues to maintain, like nineteenth-century audiences, that opera can be only amusing or beautiful. A German sociologist of music, however, has recently revived some of the traditional arguments against social interpretations of opera. Ch.-H. Mahling[9] claims that the music limits too severely the number of words available to carry any substantive message, and also keeps the audience from following any that might creep in. He therefore denies to opera in general any capacity for explicit social commentary or even for *Selbstdarstellung*, the unselfconscious representation of contemporary social reality. Mahling might have cited in support of his position Saint-Saëns' bitter complaints against opera subscribers who boasted of never paying the least attention to the words. And the composer Alfred Bruneau estimated that Opéra audiences understood only one syllable in ten of Wagner's *Siegfried*, even in French translation.[10]

Opera's ability to communicate ideas through the dramatic action has not, however, depended on conscious assimilation of the words, as Mahling seems to assume. On the contrary, the July Monarchy Opéra director Véron asserted that the action of an opera should be comprehensible to the eyes alone.[11] For example, during the period of my study, Barbier's and Carré's adaptation of Dante's Francesca da

Rimini story raised the question whether extenuating circumstances could ever excuse adultery. The librettists' last-act tableau, which portrays Beatrice assuming Paolo and Francesca into heaven, implicitly condoned the illicit lovers' affair. The composer Gounod, who had commissioned the work, rejected the finished product precisely because of the ethical content of the plot, opting instead for a different libretto by the same writers about the Christian martyr Polyeucte.[12]

The light comedies preferred by Opéra-Comique audiences were equally adaptable to didactic purposes. The many plots revolving around arranged marriages must have been particularly interesting to young women exhibited in Opéra-Comique boxes for the approval of prospective husbands' families. Some of these seventeen-year-olds undoubtedly faced the dilemma of the young heroine of Membrée's *La Courte Echelle* (OC-1879): whether to resist her parents' plans or submit to a "life of tears and memories" (Act II:Scene ii). Librettists who approved in principle of the *mariage de raison* could easily combine the acquiescence of their heroines with a happy ending (for the Opéra-Comique), or filial revolt with tragic misfortune (for the Opéra). Proponents of romantic love and personal choice would, of course, reverse these plot resolutions. These alternatives and their consequences required no extensive verbal elucidation. And far from obscuring the librettist's point, the music fortified it with emotional effects capable of reducing whole audiences to tears.

The simplest means of introducing social commentary into librettos was to reinforce certain attitudes or types of behavior by identifying them with obviously sympathetic characters. Conversely, the librettist intent on discrediting a particular point of view chose a villain or buffoon for its champion. In the book for Bruneau's *Messidor* (O-1897), one of Emile Zola's characters advocates violence as a response to an industrial dispute. His surly, vindictive nature contrasts unfavorably with the gentle magnanimity of the hero, who stolidly attends to his daily labor and eventually defends the factory owner — and his beautiful daughter — from the mob's attack. In the last act, Zola completely undermines the moral authority of the agitator by exposing him as a thief and a murderer.

Adopting this approach to analysis of operatic action, innovative opera historians of past generations — Bekker, Combarieu, Crosten — discovered abundant references to current political events in the early-nineteenth-century French Grand Opera that was their subject matter. From this evidence, they argued for the social relevance of the genre: Scribe's and Auber's portrayal of a revolutionary situation in *La Muette di Portici* was so timely and potent that an 1830 performance in Brussels triggered the successful Belgian revolution; Meyerbeer's operas referred to the socialist ideas and religious controversies that arose during the July Monarchy through historical parallels in *Le Prophète* and *Les Huguenots*. Bekker goes so far as to say that in the Grand Operas of Auber, Rossini, and Meyerbeer, "with their basis in revolutionary, political and sociological ideas, actuality is intensified until it becomes unqualified up-to-dateness."[13]

Some limitations of this approach to a social history of opera have since become apparent. In contrast to Bekker, Theodor Adorno suggested that Meyerbeer's librettists had systematically neutralized the ideological content of their historical plots by confining them to the purely personal level. *Les Huguenots*, for instance, reduced the St. Bartholomew's Eve Massacre to a matter of personal vengeance on the part of a Catholic nobleman whose daughter had been seduced by a Protestant.[14] Adorno concluded that the relationship between opera's content and its social context was a more complicated one than earlier scholars had realized: that the trivialization process revealed more about the July Monarchy than the specific political content of the individual librettos did. What Adorno failed to appreciate was that the technique of reducing history to the level of personal conflict actually operated in reverse. The writer with an agenda invested the standard thwarted-love-affair plot with social significance simply by manipulating characters and action to make his point. This mixing of personal and public themes in historical operas, moreover, perfectly matched the outlook of the *grands notables* who were their chief patrons. Reducing the great events of the past to the personal level did not trivialize history, as Adorno suggested; on the contrary, it reinforced the audiences' belief in the capacity of individuals — as opposed to social forces — to make history.[15]

Though they rejected Adorno's theoretical lead, a team of German sociologists led by Heinz Becker[16] nevertheless agreed that the topical references in French Grand Opera required more sophisticated explanations. They accumulated evidence suggesting that librettists chose historical settings and social situations not for their ideological potential, but primarily as vehicles for "local color," intended for the inspiration of costumers, set designers, composers and choreographers. While exhibiting the mode in clothes and furniture, librettists sometimes incidentally amused their audiences by referring to fashionable intellectual motifs or introducing chic ethical dilemmas. Thus a critic described the Renaissance, very much in vogue on Parisian operatic stages during the late eighteen-seventies and early 'eighties, as "interesting for its subjects, its costumes, even its morals."[17] According to this view, topical references that scholars mistook for social commentary had been merely ornamental. Aesthetic considerations, rather than ideological ones, had determined the shape and substance of Scribe's efforts. Mahling, as a participant in Becker's project, even described Gustave Charpentier's *Louise* (OC-1900), one of the most controversial works of the Belle Epoque for its contemporary working-class setting and advocacy of free love, as merely a late manifestation of the continual search for novel local color.[18]

But local color itself had profound social and political implications, as the director Carvalho's initial reaction to *Louise* demonstrated. When the composer/librettist first brought the opera to the impresario, the latter suggested transporting the action to the eighteenth century so that the characters could be dressed in Ancien Régime styles. The staging would gain in magnificence, the director asserted, and the drama in profundity, if it were generalized by a century or two. To Charpentier it was apparent that Carvalho believed that the vulgarity of the costumes and language in the original version would offend the public, but that the same drama in eighteenth-century guise would upset neither their expectations nor their peaceful digestion. The composer preferred to keep his opera off the stage entirely, rather than have its impact diluted and its message undermined by Carvalho.[19]

Obviously the conventions of the opera provided innumerable occasions for expressing ethical, social, and political opinions indirectly. Indeed, the means of conveying ideas through operatic drama were so varied and so potent that social and political messages routinely crept in without the conscious intention of librettists or composers. Only those operas were truly devoid of meaning in which characters acted so inconsistently or unintelligibly as to preclude any coherent interpretation of their behavior, and those in which the intervention of chance removed the crucial questions from the moral to the metaphysical plane. Such operas were exceptional, however, and opera's capacity for conveying ideas cannot seriously be doubted.

Taking for granted the presence of implicit messages in operas, contemporary scholars have developed sophisticated techniques for the deconstruction of these complex texts. Catherine Clément makes effective use of "Freudian-Lacanian pyschoanalytic models."[20] Jane Fulcher mines a broad range of French Grand Opera materials for layers of meaning that illuminate the political history of the July Monarchy. She demonstrates that the political implications of operatic plots, costuming, and staging were widely discussed among both supporters and critics of the government, to the extent that some productions came to be perceived and evaluated as reflections of "the nation's image."[21] Anselm Gerhard's brilliant exposition of some of Rossini's innovations in *Le Siège de Corinthe* and *Guillaume Tell* vindicates Paul Bekker, leaving little doubt that the composer was aware of and did his best to reinforce the ideological content of his operas.[22]

Fulcher's work appeared as I was engaged on an earlier version of this project; I recognized that her explanation of opera's relationship to state and society might be applicable to the Third Republic. I knew that the state regularly justified its subsidies and administrative control of the opera by referring to the moral benefits of exposing the population to its exalted sentiments. Moreover, the various governments of the pre-war Third Republic had every power necessary to ensure that these sentiments were exalted: They not only appointed and dismissed the directors who selected the repertoire, and determined the provisions of their contracts, but they could withhold or increase subsidies, select specific operas for performance on official occasions, and censor or ban offensive works. There is, in addition, plenty of evidence from the librettos themselves to suggest that the state took an active role in defining the content of the opera repertoire.

Operas from the first years of the Third Republic — the so-called "Republic of the Dukes" dominated by competing factions of reactionaries — disseminated a distinctively aristocratic point of view. They featured heroes who were invariably either monarchists or *frondeurs* who resisted encroachments on the privileges and power of the nobility. Peasant choruses introduced for local color rejoiced in festive celebrations, identifying their own prosperity with that of the nobility. Family tradition shaped the political opinions and motivated the actions of the heroes. Librettists regularly arranged marriages for their characters for dynastic reasons, and these marriages turned out well. Catholic dogma defined the ethical norm. Except for the important aberration of *Carmen* (OC-1875), the second opera house of Paris, the Opéra-Comique, shared the predilection of the Opéra for historical operas with royal or noble heroes during the first decade of the Third Republic.

After about 1879, however, the social and political messages emanating from the two stages diverged. Heroes of new *opéras-comiques* began to subordinate personal honor to the national interest. Devotion to the state, usually a republic, supplanted allegiance to local or royal dynasties. In the 'nineties, Opéra-Comique librettists even rehabilitated the French Revolution and championed the ideal of social equality. Typical heroes were leaders of peasant revolts who fell in love with *seigneurs'* daughters, or aristocrats' sons who joined the republican army when their fathers refused to let them marry peasant girls. The new orientation of the Opéra-Comique coincides precisely with the conquest of the Third Republic by republicans, marked by the election of Grévy as president in 1879. But while the Opéra-Comique's ideological content began to correspond closely to the political interests of the republican parties in power, the values implicit in the Opéra librettos continued to respond to the preoccupations and concerns of its anti-republican, anti-democratic, aristocratic clientele. This divergence between the operas at the two state opera houses shows that their social and political content could not have been the simple product of state intervention. Persuasive as Fulcher's explanation might be for the period of the July Monarchy, her model does not apply to the subject of my research.

The following work focuses instead on the correspondence between the content of the librettos and the changing class relationships of the pre-war Third Republic. This era is exceptionally fruitful for such an exercise in the social history of ideas — though the July Monarchy arguably has more significant opera — because momentous social changes were compressed into a relatively brief span of time. And one of the advantages of opera as an object of this sort of study is that in comparison with other forms of art, and especially literature, the audience is relatively discreet and comparatively easy to identify. It is even possible to some extent to assess the particular tastes and interests of the various social components of the clientele. I will argue that while the composition of opera audiences changed very little over time, the tastes and expectations of the different elites represented in the audience varied according to shifts in their status within French society as a whole.

The values implicit in many of the operas that had premieres during the eighteen-seventies and 'eighties may be imputed to the *grands notables* not because they dominated the government, but because they made up the bulk of the Opéra subscribers and set the tone for the Opéra audience during this period. Comparison of the two opera houses' administrative histories and clienteles after 1879 shows that differences in the social composition of the Opéra and Opéra-Comique audiences provide the key to ideological differences in their respective repertoires. While at the Opéra-Comique the increasingly self-assertive republican bourgeoisie celebrated the First Republic's centenary with an orgy of French Revolution operas, aristocratic Opéra audiences abandoned historical themes for the fantastic and mythical settings of *Wagnérisme*. As we might expect from reactionary elites suffering a decline in their political position, they responded favorably to librettos featuring beleaguered, heroic outsiders in hostile social and political environments. Later still, when the residual *notable* aristocracy had definitively been displaced by the bourgeoisie, the latter also lost interest in historical opera. The critical, subversive potential of democratic and revolutionary themes, realized so effectively in the battle against incumbent aristocrats, became not only superfluous, but dangerous, to the newly won hegemony of the bourgeoisie. After 1900, bourgeois Opéra-Comique audiences embraced *faits divers* opera — working-class dramas that expressed a suitably conservative approach to class relations.

Though my primary concern is to draw conclusions about the social function of French opera, the changes in opera's content that I identify depend on and in turn corroborate a particular interpretation of pre-war socio-political developments, which needs to be made explicit. The opera librettos reinforce Arno Mayer's emphasis on the lingering power of the nobility in late-nineteenth-century France,[23] which retained an influence out of proportion to its numbers in local politics, diplomacy, and the arts. An important turning point in the displacement of this residual aristocracy by a class of people with different ideas and interests occurred in 1879 when the French bourgeoisie, predominant in economic and cultural life at least since the revolution, captured control of the political apparatus as well. With it came control over the opera, which was subsidized and supervised by the state.

Except for the short-lived, aberrant, radical republican ministry of Léon Gambetta, which threatened to radicalize the opera as well, the next decade was a period of consolidation of power. Bourgeois leaders demonstrated that a republic could be stable as long as it was conservative. At the end of the 'eighties, successful deflection of General Boulanger's threatened right-wing coup d'état vindicated their approach; successful negotiation of an alliance with Russia shortly afterwards crowned their accomplishment with international respectability. This second decisive juncture in the life of the regime also had important repercussions at the opera. Resolution of the Dreyfus Affair around the turn of the century may be taken as the third great turning point in the life of the pre-war Third Republic. Having survived this latest threat from the right, the bourgeoisie felt able to redeploy its resources, making use of the state and its cultural apparatus as strategic strongholds for repressing emerging lower classes while co-opting their radical republican and reformist socialist leadership.

If aristocratic subscribers to the Opéra preferred operas with noble heroes expressing anti-democratic values, how did they arrange to get them? In the absence of documentary evidence for direct state manipulation of the repertoire, the more general question becomes: Who determined the content of the repertoire and how? The answer requires an exploration of all the institutional channels — the opera administration, the government's Ministry of Public Instruction, the highly influential "Tout-Paris of the Opera," the press, and the composers' and librettists' professional organization — through which various groups could manipulate the content of the opera, and an assessment of their capacity to do so. For example, an important leadership role in the Tout-Paris naturally devolved to members of the government, who insinuated into this coterie friendly critics and artists, and prominent socialites attached to the ruling parties. The substantial influence over audience opinion that resulted enabled supporters of the government to exercise informal influence over the opera, which compensated for the official restraint of the ministry. At the same time, the Tout-Paris helped co-opt the radical republicans among them into the established system of elites. Generally speaking, the complex nexus between government and audience attitudes provides the key to defining opera's ideology.

The process is complicated, however, by traditions and initiatives peculiar to the institution and to the operatic arts. The repercussions of aesthetic changes, which developed relatively autonomously, according to a separate logic, and the convictions of individual composers and librettists, also contributed to opera's changing ideology. The writers' social origins, and the necessity most were under of earning a living through literature or otherwise, gave them an outlook different from that of the audience, thereby skewing the content of the repertoire in some interesting and important ways. The bohemian style of life embraced by many nineteenth-century aspiring writers in the early stages of their careers informed many of their librettos with an ideology critical of bourgeois values and assumptions. General disgust with Third Republic politics became the characteristic feature of the bohemian writers' political outlook. This effect must not be exaggerated; the socialization process that reproduced the pool of acceptable potential writers, including the perquisites dangled before them, constrained most writers to avoid sentiments offensive to the audience by catering to established canons of taste.

On the other hand, due largely to the efforts of the remarkable Société des Auteurs et Compositeurs Dramatiques, one of the most effective professional organizations of all time, Belle Epoque composers and librettists enhanced not only their material wealth and social status, but also their autonomy. These developments encouraged writers such as Maeterlinck and Charpentier to challenge established myths of social relations. In admiration for the works of Richard Wagner, Opéra audiences and librettists found common ground. In his prose works, librettists found their alienation from mainstream political processes incorporated into a theory of culture that bolstered the prestige of opera librettists among artists while exalting artists in general as saviors of society. Their promotion of *Wagnérisme* further increased their independence by raising their status and fostering their self-esteem. By reproducing the principles of Wagnerian idealism for their elite patrons, the librettists also contributed to a general *fin-de-siècle* assault on French positivism.

Impresarios had some leeway for introducing counterhegemonic works into the repertoire because articulate elements within the audience consistently refused to acknowledge that librettos had any social and political content. One of the more striking contrasts between July Monarchy and Third Republic opera is the penchant of leaders of public opinion during the later period for drawing attention away from the social and political implications of the operas presented to them. Theatre critics regularly discouraged librettists' attempts to address social issues overtly; to introduce controversial ideas of any kind was in bad taste. The critics', composers', librettists', and government administrators' resistance to the idea that opera either should, or did, or could have ideological content is an important indicator of opera's social function. Cultural hegemony theory[24] provides the theoretical context for my explanation of the sources and institutional channels of opera's ideological content.

Belle Epoque opera did not merely passively reflect social attitudes; it also helped to define and propagate ideas and values that were useful to the dominant elites. This is not to say that they used the opera in any obvious, conspicuous way to "educate" the audience to a different way of thinking. Overt manipulation of the repertoire would have been self-defeating; by alerting the audience to opera's didactic potential, it would have reduced the opera to a mere instrument of propaganda. Informal influence by dominant elites was therefore much more effective than official government interference in the repertoire as a means of propagating values. But neither did the opera function as an "ideological apparatus," deliberately and systematically manipulated by hegemonic elites who conspired to hide their activities from the public. The opera of the pre-war Third Republic is rather an interesting example of a truly hegemonic institution, characterized by the self-deception of the beneficiaries.

This self-serving self-deception could be maintained because the implicit messages in apparently uncontroversial, frivolous, aesthetically pleasing operas appeared to be ideologically neutral — that is, they reproduced the prejudices of the dominant groups. In the absence of petit-bourgeois and working-class opera lovers, who were routinely excluded from the audience, subordinate fractions within the dominant groups themselves must have been the chief victims of this hegemonic activity. In order to participate fully in the distinction — as Pierre

Bourdieu applies the term[25] — that attendance at the opera imparted, these subordinate fractions had to accept that opera was ideologically meaningless. Interest in opera's ideas, they were told, led down the slippery slope of derogation, as the left's indecent preoccupation with the social content of art demonstrated. These patrons therefore had no choice but to accept uncritically, as common sense, the values of the dominant fractions that were implicit in the librettos. Opera reviewers helped by promoting as conventional wisdom the notion that opera conveyed no ideas whatever.

Notes on Terminology

For convenience, I apply the term "Belle Epoque" in its loosest sense, to the era of the pre-war Third Republic. In occasional, more specific references to the period 1890–1914, or to the particular cultural content of that era, I sometimes employ the term "Belle Epoque proper."

Some readers might find my use of the term "local color" idiosyncratic; if I use it where "exoticism" or "ambience" might seem more appropriate, I do so in order to bring my argument into relation with the work of Becker et al. referred to above.

The argument that follows does not depend on any technically precise understanding of the term "ideology." In my view, the best discussion of the concept is to be found in Erica Harth's *Ideology and Culture in Seventeenth-Century France*.[26] While I endorse her conclusions, I use the term in its everyday meaning in this work.

Notes to the Introduction

1 Un Monsieur de l'Orchestre, *Soirées Parisiennes*, 11 vols. (Paris, 1875), 1:25. "Un Monsieur de l'Orchestre" was a *nom de plume* of Arnold Mortier.

2 The parenthetical notations following the names of operas that had premieres during the period covered by this study refer to the place and date of the premiere. "O" designates the Opéra, and "OC" the Opéra-Comique.

3 Peter Kivy, *The Corded Shell: Reflections on Musical Expression* (Princeton: Princeton University Press, 1980), 111. Brigid Brophy's impressive article entitled "Figaro and the Limitations of Music," *Music & Letters* 51 (1970) restricts music's conceptual potential even further. Cf. also Catherine Clément, *Opera: or the Undoing of Women*, Betsy Wing trans., (Minneapolis: Virago Press, 1988), 15f.

4 Wolfgang Burde, "Analytische Notizen zum gesellschaftlichen Gehalt und Standort von Musikwerden" *Zeitschrift für Musiktheorie* 2 (1974). The article includes an excellent discussion of the theoretical difficulties involved, and also of the social utility of the whole proceeding.

5 Richard Leppert and Susan McClary, eds. *Music and Society: the politics of composition, performance and reception* (Cambridge: Cambridge University Press, 1987).

6 Paul Robinson, *Opera and Ideas* (New York: Harper & Row, 1985).

7 Anselm Gerhard, *Die Verstädterung der Oper: Paris und das Musiktheaters des 19. Jahrhunderts* (Stuttgart, Weimar: Verlag J.B. Metzler, 1992).

8 Librettos or full scores are available for these 138 at the Bibliothèque Nationale or at the Music Library in the rue Richelieu. I have excluded from consideration two additional operas that fit my criteria — Paladilhe's *Diana* (OC-1885) and Missa's *Ninon de Lenclos* (OC-1895) — because the librettos are unavailable and the scores do not include the spoken dialogue.

9 Ch.-H. Mahling, "Selbstdarstellung und Kritik der Gesellschaft in der Oper? Bemerkungen zu Opern von Mozart bis Dessau," *Bericht über den Internationalen Kongress Bonn 1970* (Kassel, 1971), 232, 234.

10 Alfred Bruneau, *Musiques de Russie et Musiciens de France* (Paris, 1903), 124ff.; Camille de Saint-Saëns, "Lettre de Las Palmas," *La Nouvelle Revue* 30 March 1897 [available also in Bibliothèque de l'Opéra (henceforth cited as B.O.), Dossier d'Artiste: Saint-Saëns].

11 Gerhard, *Die Verstädterung der Oper*, 134.

12 Arthur Heulhard, "Revue Musicale," *La Chronique Musicale* 3e. année, 9 (July–September, 1876), 284. The libretto that Gounod abandoned appeared eventually in Ambroise Thomas' *Françoise de Rimini* (O-1882).

13 Paul Bekker, *The Changing Opera*, Arthur Mendel trans., (N.Y., 1935), 149f.; William L. Crosten, *French Grand Opera: An Art and a Business* (N.Y.: King's Crown Press, 1948), 94f.; Jules Combarieu, *Histoire de la Musique*, 3 vols. (Paris, 1923), for example 3:25. Cf. Jules Massenet, *My Recollections* (Boston, 1919) H. Villiers Barnett, trans., 7; Gustave Bertrand, *Les Nationalités Musicales* (Paris, 1872), 229f., 237f.

14 Theodor Adorno, *Klangfiguren: Musikalische Schriften* I (Berlin: Suhrkamp, 1959), 40. Cf. Jane Fulcher, *The Nation's Image* (N.Y.: Cambridge University Press, 1987), 91. The ideological resonance of some historical incidents was so powerful that it survived the most shameless attempts of the librettists to trivialize them: *Les Huguenots* aroused passions to such a pitch in the religiously divided city of Nîmes, that the Third Republic had to ban performances there. See below, Chapter V, p.127f.

15 Gerhard, *Die Verstädterung der Oper*, 274f.

16 Heinz Becker, ed., *Die "Couleur locale" in der Oper des 19. Jahrhunderts* (Regensburg: Bosse, 1976). See in particular the editor's article entitled "Die 'Couleur locale' als Stilkategorie der Oper." In the discussion of his paper "Giacomo Meyerbeer's Mitarbeit an den Libretti seiner Oper," Becker calls local color "the essence of French opera," *Bericht über den Internationalen Musikwissenschaftlichen Kongress*, 162.

17 Edouard Noël and Edmund Stoullig, *Annales du Théâtre et de la Musique*, 40 vols. (Paris, 1875-1914) (henceforth cited as *Annales*), 8:122. On fashions in intellectual topics, cf. Pierre Martino, *Parnasse et symbolisme 1850-1900* (Paris, 1925), 198; Romain Rolland, *Musiciens d'aujourd'hui*, 2nd. ed., (Paris, 1908), 271. Bertrand, *Les Nationalités Musicales*, 237f., hints at the same idea.

18 Ch.-H. Mahling, "Selbstdarstellung und Kritik," 233.

19 André Himonet, *'Louise' de Charpentier* (Paris, 1922), 24. For an even more persuasive example, see the description in Chapter III, p.64f. below, of Carvalho's argument with Zola and Bruneau over the director's decision to transpose *l'Attaque du Moulin* to a Revolutionary War setting.

20 Susan McClary, "The Undoing of Opera: Toward a Feminist Criticism of Music," "Foreword" to Clément, *Opera*, xiv.

21 Jane Fulcher, *The Nation's Image*, passim.

22 Gerhard, *Die Verstädterung der Oper*, 59, 71, 84-87, 91, 116. Otherwise, much of the contemporary work on opera's social revelance has concentrated on Italian opera. See Klaus–Dieter Link, *Literarische Perspektiven des Opernlibrettos: Studien zur italienischen Oper von 1850 bis 1920*, Abhandlungen zur Kunst, Musik und Literaturwissenschaft, Band 173 (Bonn: Bouvier,1975), and Maryse Jeuland-Meynaud,"Légitimité de la Librettologie," *Revue des Etudes Italiennes*, Nouvelle Série XXII (1976).

23 Arno J. Mayer, *The Persistence of the Old Regime* (NY: Pantheon Books, 1981).

24 The pioneering effort towards formulation of a theory of cultural hegemony is Antonio Gramsci, *Selections From the Prison Notebooks*, Quintin Hoare and G.N. Smith, eds. and trans.,(New York: International Publishers, 1971). More recently, Raymond Williams, *Marxism and Literature* (Oxford: Oxford University Press, 1977). Cf. Thomas L. Haskell, "Capitalism and the Origins of the Humanitarian Sensibility," *American Historical Review*, 90 No.2 (April 1985); Louis Althusser, in *"Lenin and Philosophy" and other essays*, Ben Brewster, trans., 2nd. ed. (London: NLB, 1977).

25 Pierre Bourdieu, *Distinction*, Richard Nice, trans., (Cambridge, Mass.: Harvard University Press, 1984).

26 Erica Harth, *Ideology and Culture in Seventeenth-Century France* (Ithaca: Cornell University Press, 1983).

CHAPTER II

THE ADMINISTRATION OF THE OPERA

The Opéra and Opéra-Comique of the pre-war Third Republic owed their administrative structure to the July Monarchy of the "Bourgeois King," Louis-Phillippe of Orléans. Whereas previously the Bourbons had administered the opera as part of the king's household, in 1831 the new regime began appointing, supervising and subsidizing impresarios who exploited the opera for their own profit or loss during seven-year renewable terms.[1] This combination of private enterprise and state control was an immediate success, contributing greatly to the flowering of the art that became famous as French Grand Opera. Aside from a brief reversion to the Bourbon model of administration during part of Louis-Napoléon's regime, the mixed public and private system continued intact through the end of the Second Empire and into the Third Republic until after the war.[2]

With the exception of a few shows chosen by the government for performance on special occasions, the repertoires of the Opéra and Opéra-Comique were selected by the impresarios appointed and subsidized by the state. Known as directors, these entrepreneurs combined the roles of producer and director. They had formal responsibility for choosing the operas to be produced, and they could also foster or frustrate the success of works that they had accepted by the manner in which they produced them. They evaluated the various characteristics of librettos that they might eventually produce, and since these were only working texts, they could also modify them substantially in the process of bringing them to life on stage. In addition, directors allocated the resources in time, effort, and enthusiasm that would be committed to various productions, which greatly affected their initial reception and the length of their run. Their autonomy was limited in many ways, however. They were squarely in the middle of a complex struggle for power and influence, mediating constantly between the state, which claimed the right to supervise the daily activities of its appointees; the audience, who provided the receipts vital to the directors' solvency; librettists and composers committed to the integrity of their individual works; artists and performers with varying degrees of leverage; and financial backers with a variety of individual and corporate axes to grind.

Besides a substantial state subsidy, the two major sources of revenue available to the directors were yearly subscriptions from the elite audience of the boxes and orchestra stalls, which provided a stable financial base, and box office receipts from casual customers whose frequency of attendance spelled the difference between short-term commercial success and failure. While changing patterns of receipts alerted the directors to long-term changes in audience taste and enabled them to adjust the content of the librettos accordingly, the Tout-Paris of the opera played the crucial role of keeping opera management abreast of audience reaction to individual works. This powerful coterie decisively influenced public reception of new operas, so its judgments had extensive repercussions in the subsequent calculations of directors and dramatists as well. Impresarios had in addition to consider the opinions of *commanditaires* — investors who helped subscribe the substantial working capital necessary to commence operations — and of critics who could influence the rate of audience attendance. Some directors made a fortune, but the potential for rapid and complete failure was equally great. Though they determined the content of the repertoire, they seldom had sufficient leeway to impose their own tastes and prejudices on the opera in opposition to any of these groups.

Heinz Becker's description of the normal procedure for obtaining librettos at the time of Meyerbeer, during the second quarter of the nineteenth century, applies equally well to the Belle Epoque:

> It was traditional at the Paris Academy that an opera libretto was solicited by the director. He then gave the libretto to the composer of his choice to be set to music. This did not preclude composers and librettists from working together in advance and obtaining the opera director's blessing afterwards.[3]

On the other hand, composers who found librettos on their own risked having directors dismiss their operas even before hearing the music, as in the case of Halanzier's reaction to *Sigurd* (0-1885), discussed below (Chapter IV). In their contract with the composer Victorien Jonçières, the directors Bertrand and Gailhard explicitly stipulated their right of prior approval of the book: "It is agreed that a full-sized work of three acts with music by M. Jonçières will be performed at the Opéra two years after the reception of a libretto which must be mutually acceptable."[4] Impresarios had to take particular precautions with composers who were notoriously incapable of judging a libretto for themselves: "... not a single scene that hasn't been passed through the sieve," complained Saint-Saëns on one occasion.[5]

The directors' discretion in accepting or rejecting librettos was severely limited in practice. In his discussion of July Monarchy procedures, Becker points out that in the case of a successful and independently wealthy composer such as Meyerbeer, the director's approval of the libretto had a purely formal character.[6] During the Third Republic, independent composers and librettists whose names generated good receipts sometimes arrived at a position of comparable autonomy and command. At the turn of the century, for instance, the Opéra-Comique director Albert Carré accepted Alfred Bruneau's *L'Ouragan* (OC-1901) sight unseen because it had a libretto by Emile Zola. Such librettos could be the means of introducing idiosyncratic, even subversive, ideas into the repertoire.

Both directors and composers were constantly on the lookout for good subjects, and they sometimes accepted unsolicited manuscripts. A newly appointed director was "quickly surrounded by a court of authors, every one of whom has something in his pocket."[7] Carré said that he regularly spent the midnight hours after a performance searching in books and manuscripts for suitable material. He claimed to have read every manuscript submitted to him and to have returned the rejects with an explanatory letter.[8] It is impossible to estimate the proportion of completed librettos that were actually produced, but considerable numbers of writers thought it worthwhile to write scenarios and even complete librettos on speculation, hoping to interest a director or composer. Massenet found the libretto for *Le Jongleur de Notre Dame* (OC-1904) in his mail one morning, sent to him by a young student, and the composer Hüe came across *Le Roi de Paris*

(O-1910) in a trunk ten years after the death of its author.

Impresarios could recommend particular librettists to composers, or bring prospective collaborators together socially. As a condition for accepting a piece, they sometimes even insisted that an author work with a collaborator designated by themselves. Impresarios actively solicited librettos on behalf of promising novice composers, and occasionally for veterans as well. The following letter from the Opéra director Ritt to the rising young writer Jean Richepin documents an attempt to obtain his story of "Le Mage" for Massenet, the most prominent contemporary composer:

> I hear from mutual friends that you are working on a poem which they say would make a good opera. We have been wanting to do something by you. Do you know Massenet? We are sure you two would get along. We are also very anxious to know whether the subject suits our style. Please write back right away, and if you can, send a detailed scenario, so we can judge the piece as a whole. If you could come and read us your play, then we could tell right away what we have to deal with.[9]

Librettists expected that composers would alter their products substantially, of course, but directors and even performers often took a hand as well. It was common for directors to dictate changes to be made in librettos as a condition of their reception. Afterwards, for modifications made during rehearsals, the consent of the librettist was nominally required. But many were unwilling or unable to stand up for their works, even when changes suggested by the directors fundamentally altered the author's conceptions. The following passage recounts the composer Saint-Saëns' experiences with the Opéra-Comique impresario Carvalho, notorious among directors for tinkering with plots; it represents what might be called a worst-case scenario.

> He wanted to collaborate himself in every work he staged. If even works hallowed by time and success had to bear his mark, how much more vulnerable was a new one! He would suddenly tell you to change the period or the country where the action took place. He tormented us for a long time to make the leading role, a dancer, that of a singer, so that his wife could take it. Later on he wanted to introduce a second dancer as well. ... He took upon himself to invent the most eccentric innovations. One day he suggested that I introduce wild animals. Another time he wanted to cut out all the music with the exception of the choruses and the dancer's part, leaving the rest of it to be played by actors. Later when

it was rumored that the Opéra was rehearsing a water scene for *Hamlet* he wanted to send Madame Miolan-Carvalho to the bottom of a river. ... Two more years were spent in these idiocies.[10]

Much of the directors' real authority derived from their ability to influence audience appreciation of specific works by the care and effort they put into production. Librettists submitted to the tyranny of impresarios such as Carvalho because, as Hofmannsthal commented to his composer Richard Strauss, the essential prerequisite for success was that the musical and theatrical management at the highest level be really well-disposed toward a work. French librettists agreed that the initial audience reception of an opera depended largely on the director's attention to staging. It takes some time to get used to new music, asserted Carré, who was by turns librettist and director, but the spectacle can hold the interest of the audience until the music eventually becomes familiar. "If the director secures the premiere, the composer secures the hundredth [performance]," he wrote, quoting the composer Auber.[11]

Directors had a variety of other means for influencing the tastes of their public as well. Occasionally they "primed the pump" by temporarily subsidizing operas that they hoped would eventually find a regular audience. Carré persevered with Debussy's *Pélléas et Mélisande* (OC-1902) for two weeks in the face of scorn from the Tout-Paris of the premieres, generally hostile press reaction, an audience charivari, and very sparse houses, before the opera showed any signs of its ultimate triumph. Carvalho felt that he could guarantee the eventual success of any work he chose simply by presenting it often enough: "The crowd grows accustomed to a title as to anything else and succumbs to its attraction," he said.[12] There are many examples, from a variety of motives, of directors' maintaining in the repertoire works incapable of paying their own way. The Opéra-Comique impresario Du Locle continued to produce *Carmen* after its crushing rejection by the Tout-Paris of the opera because, having invested everything in its success, he had nothing else to offer in its place. A later director of the Opéra, P.-B. Gheusi, claimed that he and Gailhard produced *Ariane* (O-1906) fifty times in one year to reward its composer Massenet for giving the prestigious Prix de Rome to Gailhard's son.[13]

It was even easier to sabotage an opera that the director did not intend should be a success, such as one of the works by novice French composers imposed on the director by the government. Inferior or inappropriate casting or staging were most damaging to a new opera's prospects, but even the timing of a premiere could have a decisive adverse effect. The government would have had to carefully supervise the number, the time of year, and the days of the week of these performances, in order to prevent the directors from negating the prescriptions of their *cahiers des charges*, wrote a former Director of Fine Arts. Gheusi accused the impresario Carvalho of ruining the prospects of his *Guernica* (OC-1895) simply by introducing it at the very end of the season.[14] Directors who developed eccentric or inexplicable prejudices against individual works could simply decline to produce them at all. Paravey of the Opéra-Comique had no confidence in Massenet's *Manon* (OC-1884); he refused to produce it despite the noteworthy achievement of seventy-five performances in its first year. At the hands of Paravey's successors, it became the second most frequently produced *opéra-comique* to have its premiere during the Belle Epoque.[15]

Librettists and composers attempted to protect themselves from the worst abuses of directorial authority through their professional organization, the Société des Auteurs et Compositeurs Dramatiques. Towards the end of the century, as the Société became increasingly powerful, and as the prestige and importance of the librettist's role grew, more writers succeeded in impressing their views on opera impresarios. This trend culminated in a successful lawsuit brought by Maurice Maeterlinck, the most intransigent of the Belle Epoque librettists, which guaranteed them legal recourse if directors' decisions undermined the integrity of the librettists' artistic conceptions. These issues are discussed in greater detail in the Epilogue, below. Ultimately, however, writers' and composers' challenges to directorial authority remained severely limited, since the selection of new operas, and their further production after a minimum run of three performances, continued subject to the directors' discretion. The Opéra-Comique's refusal to produce Fauré's *Pénélope* in 1912, "because of the expenses entailed by the *mise-en-scène* and the engagement of the artists designated by the composer," suggests that authors with ambitious plans and artistic integrity were most vulnerable.[16]

In the long run, the extent to which the artists could impose their ideas on management, and defend the integrity of their texts against directorial meddling, depended on the character and status of the individuals concerned. The power of the directors grew in proportion to the length of their tenure, which often was considerable. Pedro Gailhard, with a series of partners, ruled the Opéra for twenty-two years, from 1885 to 1907. Except for a three-year hiatus, Léon Carvalho dominated the Opéra-Comique from 1877 to 1897; his successor, Albert Carré, stayed until 1913. Louis Gallet, the most successful and sought-after of all Belle Epoque librettists, summed up their attitude towards the directors, in his inflated librettist's style: "All of them, good, bad, or mediocre, exercised without resistance this sovereign, occasionally tyrannical, power that bent before them both spirit and character, and gave them such complete disposition over the material destinies of works, that the author sometimes disappeared..."[17] If the most successful writers and composers customarily bowed before their impresarios, imagine the diffidence of the novice when things began to go badly in rehearsal, and he was confronted with the recommendations of a successful, experienced director.

If, in relation to composers and librettists, the impresarios were sovereign autocrats, they were at the same time servants of the state and slaves to financial necessity. In consequence, although they had considerable control over the repertoire's content, and even some capacity to influence the tastes of their audiences, they were rarely in a position to indulge their own tastes or propagate their own opinions. All directors produced a range of different types of opera, and, until at least 1913, ideological shifts in the opera repertoire did not coincide with changes in administrative leadership. Directors gained some room for maneuver from the universal unwillingness to acknowledge or discuss the social and political content of the opera. But the case of *Carmen* shows what befell the only director, during the pre-war Third Republic, who deliberately tested the limits of his autonomy. *Carmen* was the first new work to appear during the period of my study, and, measured in terms of frequency of performance, ultimately the most successful. Its production history, exceptionally well documented in Mina Curtiss' *Bizet and His World,* serves as a colorful entrée to the complexities of opera production and administration, and to the network of influences impinging on the formation of the opera repertoire.

In defiance of all precedent, and over the objections of his advisers, his partner, and his well-respected and experienced librettists, Camille Du Locle persevered in producing a work whose success, he hoped, would lead to a complete regeneration of the Opéra-Comique repertoire. When *Carmen* made its debut on 3 March 1875, the opening night audience, consisting of critics and other journalists, theatre people, and leaders of fashion, known collectively as the "Tout-Paris of the premières," proclaimed the piece to be shocking and scandalous.[18] No character had ever been murdered on the Opéra-Comique stage before; nor had any of its heroines worked in a factory, exhibited such earthy exuberance, or claimed and exercised complete freedom over the disposition of her affections. The pitiless rejection of Bizet's and Du Locle's challenge to accepted canons of taste and propriety was an example to all future directors of the penalties for ignoring the various constraints that they operated under, including especially the financial pressures exerted by influential leaders of the audience.

The audience reaction was predictable; the puzzling aspect of the story is that such an eccentric opera should have come to the stage in the first place. It could not have happened without a thoroughly committed composer — later in the century, librettists could play the same role — and a director willing to risk his short-term financial interests for his artistic vision. For a young composer, even one with Bizet's sound academic credentials, penetrating the repertoire of the Opéra or the Opéra-Comique was extremely difficult. At one point in the composer's career, the Imperial Ministry of Public Instruction demonstrated its repressive approach to modern opera by prohibiting those houses from producing works by untested composers. Since new productions of any kind entailed considerable investments for impresarios, who were personally interested in the finances of the houses they administered, they willingly acceded to the audiences' apparent preference for old favorites from the traditional repertoire. As a Prix de Rome winner, Bizet was entitled to an Opéra-Comique libretto to set to music, and the directors of the house eventually assigned him the book to *La Guzla de l'Emir*, by a prominent team of Second Empire librettists, Jules Barbier and Michel Carré.[19] But this emblem of his success entailed no commitment to produce the resulting opera, which never saw the stage. Because remuneration for the writers and composers was based entirely on receipts, the effort earned nothing for any of the three collaborators.

Bizet's persistence and musical genius earned their due reward when the third opera house of Paris, the progressive Théâtre Lyrique, took an interest in his work. Léon Carvalho, its colorful, maverick director, was notorious for perennial financial difficulties (which eventually ended in a crashing bankruptcy), for hiring the friends of important officials as singers and dancers, and for tinkering with the plot of every opera that came into his hands. He subsequently gained a reputation, during a long run as director of the Opéra-Comique, as unsympathetic toward younger, untested composers, but early in his career Carvalho was "ready for every kind of audacity."[20] Hoping for a brilliant success that would reestablish his finances, he offered the young Bizet *Les Pêcheurs de Perles*, a book by Michel Carré and Eugène Cormon, and, what was more, committed himself to a production date. In the early stages of his career, a composer commonly had little control over the content of his librettos; in this case Bizet suffered greatly from the poor quality of the material presented to him. Cormon afterwards admitted that he and his co-author would never have given him "that white elephant" (*Les Pêcheurs de Perles*), if they had recognized Bizet's talent as a composer. The work had such obvious flaws that Carvalho and the librettists continued to make changes in the plot, some of them drastic, even while rehearsals were in progress, up until a few days before the premiere.[21]

Increased stature as a composer enabled Bizet to work much more closely with his next librettist, Louis Gallet. This writer had recently made his reputation by having a libretto chosen as the subject for a state-sponsored contest for opera composers. Having established his political credentials, he enhanced his position by willingly subordinating his role to those of the composer and director. The consummate hack, Gallet went on to become the most successful of all Belle Epoque librettists, writing or collaborating on nineteen different full-length works produced at the Opéra or Opéra-Comique, more than twice as many as any rival. His first meeting with Bizet was contrived by the far-sighted Opéra-Comique director, Camille Du Locle, who placed the two next to each other at dinner one night. Du Locle even retrieved a Gallet libretto — eventually known as *Djamileh* — from another, procrastinating composer in order to present it to Bizet. Although Gallet had completed the work some time previously, Bizet at least had the opportunity to discuss his interpretations with the librettist.

Before *Djamileh* went into production, the pair began a second collaboration on a work commissioned by a star Opéra performer, the baritone Faure. Supremely conscious of his public image, and banking on the audiences' propensity to confuse the performers with the characters they portrayed, Faure asked Bizet and Gallet to create for him a hero of impeccable nobility and outstanding moral character. "Not only must he be great, handsome, generous and strong, but also his praises must be sung even when he is offstage," commented Bizet on the singer's expectations.[23] The two writers, for their part, hoped that Faure had sufficient influence with Opéra management to get the work accepted for production. Bizet soon found a suitable subject in *Don Rodrigue*, based on the early career of the Cid, and subsequently worked closely with Gallet in the elaboration of plot, character, and atmosphere. As was the rule in such collaborations, the librettist finished his part before the composer began. Afterwards, Bizet would occasionally ask for changes dictated by the requirements of his music — for a few verses of a particular number of feet, for instance. Letters between the two are full of detailed discussions of the poetic or dramatic effect of various individual passages. Administrative dislocations resulting from an Opéra fire caused Bizet to abandon *Don Rodrigue* before its completion. *Djamileh*, meanwhile, had run for a meager ten performances, but most critics attributed this failure to the dearth of dramatic action and the weakness of some leading singers rather than to the score.[24]

Bizet's contribution won critical acclaim from many of his colleagues and a second commission from the Opéra-Comique, this time for a full-length, three-act opera on a libretto by the prominent playwrights Meilhac and Halévy. After some research and discussion of alternative subjects, Bizet and his new librettists settled on Prosper Merimée's story of Carmen. This daring choice revived a deep-seated conflict within the management of the institution. While the progressive director Du Locle, an early Bizet supporter, readily approved, his partner DeLeuven had much more conservative taste. *Djamileh* had left him cold, but *Carmen* appalled him, as his protest to the librettist Ludovic Halévy demonstrates:

> Carmen! Merimée's Carmen? Isn't she killed by her lover? — And that background of thieves, gypsies, cigar-makers! — At the Opéra-Comique,

a family theatre! The theatre where marriages are arranged! Every night five or six boxes are taken for that purpose. You will frighten off our audience. — It's impossible.[25]

Unable to dissuade his colleague from supporting the project, DeLeuven resigned from the partnership before *Carmen's* premiere.

In principle, almost any theme could be adapted to the conventions of the Opéra-Comique. It would have been within the tradition of the repertoire to marry Carmen off to Escamillo. If she had to die, her death might have been made to function as a just punishment which reinforced ethical norms by implicitly threatening a similar fate to any young girl tempted to imitate her licentious behavior.[26] Abetted by the singer Galli-Marié, Bizet chose instead to portray Carmen as a proud and unrepentant character who consciously sacrificed her life for her libertarian principles: "Free she lived, free she will die," she says of herself in the last act (IV:ii). Carmen not only flouted conventional morality, but compounded the sin by affirming an alternative, anarchic code: "For a country, the universe; for a law, her will" (II:iii). This presumptuous proclamation of a subversive ideology by a lower-class, female character was bound to exacerbate the hostility aroused by Carmen's deviance from the behavior of traditional comic-opera heroines.[27]

The librettists Meilhac and Halévy made serious efforts to temper the violent emotions and action of the Merimée original. Like most Opéra and Opéra-Comique composers and librettists, Meilhac and Halévy regularly attended rehearsals of new works in order to help settle technical problems, judge the effectiveness of various interpretations, and, in some cases, defend the integrity of their works from the whims or prejudices of directors. During this process, they greatly expanded the role of frail, pious, demure Micaela, thus creating a typical Opéra-Comique heroine, according to Halévy. To mitigate the disreputable, even threatening behavior of Carmen's criminal associates, Meilhac introduced comedy to the gypsy scenes.[28] It gradually became clear nonetheless that, despite the best efforts of the librettists, DeLeuven's fears might be well-founded. Both Bizet's music and the leading singers' performances seemed to accentuate those aspects of *Carmen* likely to offend the traditional Opéra-Comique audience. As a result, Du Locle found himself in the middle of a dispute between, on the one hand, Bizet and the leading singers who sympathized with his conception of the work, and, on the other hand, the librettists who thought its scandalous aspects compromised the opera's chances for success.

The motives of the principals in this backstage drama were complicated and diverse. In objecting to the supposed excesses of Carmen, Meilhac and Halévy genuinely believed that a milder interpretation of the main character would better conduce to Bizet's prestige and profit. The success or failure of *Carmen* mattered least to these two partners, who had already reached the summit of their careers as collaborating dramatists. They had provided numerous librettos to Offenbach, the king of the Second Empire operetta, including *La Grande Duchesse de Gerolstein*, credited with undermining the Imperial regime by ridiculing the stupidity and incompetence of its military leadership. More recently, the partners had conquered the theatre of the boulevards with a series of dramatic works, of which *Froufrou* was the best known.[29] Like many other librettists, they were successful and conscientious playwrights who approached libretto-writing as a potentially remunerative but frivolous and uninspiring sideline. They chose not to invest too much pride or effort in works destined to be submitted unconditionally to a musician, then perhaps mutilitated beyond recognition by the frustrated creativity or venal calculation of a powerful director. But if Meilhac and Halévy had little personal stake in the success or the aesthetic integrity of *Carmen*, they had great sympathy for Bizet. The composer was particularly closely connected with Halévy, whose cousin he had married and whose uncle had acted as his mentor at the Conservatoire. Halévy wrote:

> His interests alone matter in this instance. The thing has little importance for Meilhac and me. If *Carmen* does open on Wednesday we shall have a premiere and a hundredth performance on the same night, *Carmen* and *La Boule*.[30]

The librettists' opinions were well-informed; their success depended on intimate understanding of the social milieu and outlook of their audience. Ludovic Halévy's family came from the well-to-do Orléanist bourgeoisie. His father was a habitué of the Opéra, where Ludovic's uncle, the composer Fromenthal Halévy, had had many works produced. Ludovic's family introduced him at an early age to the coulisses, where prominent subscribers hobnobbed with the stars and made assignations with upwardly mobile dancers. Devoting himself to an administrative career, he eventually obtained the position of secretary to the Duc de Morny, the powerful Imperial Minister of the Interior and half-brother of the emperor. In this office, in company with his illustrious patron, he wrote vaudevilles on official state paper, launching a literary career that culminated in election to the Académie.[31] His partner Meilhac, who eventually joined him there, was a gambler and boulevardier rather than a respectable family man like Halévy. Together, they compassed the outlook of the prosperous men of the world who dominated opera audiences.

Bizet was at home in such circles as well, as his marital alliance with the Halévys demonstrates. But in his aspirations and convictions he was closer to the world of bohemians and struggling artists. Having acknowledged that Carmen was his last chance for popular success, he staked everything on the triumph of a new aesthetic ideal. He could not have begun to realize his ambition without the connivance of a sympathetic, reckless director like Du Locle, however. Unlike other impresarios of his time, he was willing to gamble that the merits of the work would overcome the conservative prejudices of his audience. Mina Curtiss suggests that Du Locle's radical initiatives owed more to bravado and dilletantism than to any deep-rooted conviction. But he had always favored younger composers such as Bizet, who supported his attempts to reconstruct the repertoire of the Opéra-Comique. Du Locle continued to innovate in advance of audience taste even when financial reverses began to undermine his health and threaten his position. That he lost his nerve in the end, when the full impact of Carmen became manifest, should not detract from his initial enthusiastic support for the opera or from his reputation as a bold, progressive impresario.[32]

Pressure to soften Carmen's effect mounted when an outside consultant, the former Opéra-Comique director Emile Perrin, who was Du Locle's father-in-law, joined with those who predicted certain failure for the opera. Du Locle finally gave in; finding the second act duet "too naturalistic," he requested, but in vain, that the composer shorten it and introduce appropriate occasions for applause.[33] Meilhac and Halévy continued to criticize Galli-Marié's interpretation of Carmen because she persisted in emphasizing her character's sensuality, assertiveness, and self-assurance, in defiance of current notions of respectable feminine deportment. But Bizet had firm and powerful allies in the most bohemian, and the most independent, of all the elements connected with the production. As a later director of the Opéra-Comique put it, "without the insistence of Galli-Marié and Lhérie, who created Carmen and Don José, Carmen would likewise have ended with a double marriage: José-Micaela and Carmen-Escamillo, because Bizet had nearly succumbed to the pressure from his directors."[34] The singers' refusal to accept these changes forced Du Locle either to submit or to lose all of his investment in the project.

In retrospect, it appeared to the librettists that there had been a concerted campaign against Carmen among some of the most important newspapers which, as if by signal, published malevolent advance notices of the planned production.[35] There is little doubt that the Tout-Paris of the premieres, which included opera critics among its most influential members, was sharply critical of the music, of the libretto, and of Galli-Marié's frank and unblushing sensuality. On the other hand, one veteran observer of the Parisian stage suggested that the regular Opéra-Comique clientele of bourgeoisie and provincials might have supported Carmen if the more sophisticated audience of the premieres had not condemned it in advance. Having heard about the inauspicious opening, he was surprised to find that the second-night audience, which saw Carmen before any published reports appeared, responded warmly to the opera.[36]

According to Halévy, Carmen continued to play to numerically respectable audiences, generally better than the rest of the repertoire, and the number of admirers of the work gradually grew. The opera reached the considerable total of fifty performances in its first season, leading to some confusion about the actual degree of its success or failure; such a long run normally signified respectable receipts because impresarios could not afford to sustain continued losses. Curtiss very plausibly theorizes that Bizet's publisher De Choudens subsidized many performances of Carmen. She points out that even the appearance of success would have greatly increased the demand for his published scores.[37] In any case, Du Locle probably lacked both the resources and the stomach for a new mid-season production. Though he continued to present Carmen for several months, receipts never covered expenses; ultimately, everyone involved in the production acknowledged that it had been a commercial failure. In the short run, the influence of official and unofficial critics was too strong. The Tout-Paris of the opera, as unofficial, self-appointed censors responsible for defending traditional morality, enforced with self-conscious severity an ethical code that had little reference either to their own private practice or to the sensibilities of the regular opera public. Du Locle retired as director of the Opéra-Comique the following year, and Bizet also succumbed to the barrage of adverse reaction; the opera public recognized his genius only after his premature death.

Soon after the disastrous Paris opening, foreign opera houses began adapting *Carmen* to their own requirements. Normally, they transformed it into a grand opera, with a ballet that interrupts the last act and recitatives that "falsify the psychology of the characters [and] render the plot almost unintelligible."[38] In the grand-opera version, the character of Carmen is less sympathetic than in Bizet's original, making it easier to reject her claims to personal autonomy based on a universal principle. When foreign and provincial productions turned out to be highly successful, Parisian agitation for a revival quickly became irresistible; government officials, including the director of fine arts, added their persuasive voices to the clamor.[39]

Memories of the critics' animus caused profound modifications in the 1883 Paris revival of *Carmen*, however. Carvalho, the former Théâtre-Lyrique director who succeeded Du Locle at the Opéra-Comique, had been as staunch an early supporter of Bizet as his predecessor. But he felt compelled to bastardize the composer's masterpiece in response to criticisms of the work that Bizet himself had consistently rejected. The director deleted much of the violent action, transformed the disreputable tavern into a typical Opéra-Comique inn, and rehabilitated the gypsy dancers as ballerinas. He also chose a leading lady who would play the part of Carmen with "bland restraint."[40] Such precautions proved superfluous, however; the next season the opera returned in all its original integrity, with Galli-Marié in the title role, to the acclaim of critics and audiences alike.[41] The firmness with which it maintained a prominent place in the repertoire in subsequent years suggests that the malice of the Tout-Paris had not originated in any deep-seated or widespread public revulsion against the work. Subsequently, the Opéra-Comique presented a total of 1338 performances of *Carmen* before the Great War, 300 more than its closest rival, Ambroise Thomas' *Mignon*.

The production history of Bizet's opera is illuminating because it shows an ideological controversy manifesting itself in a backstage power struggle. But this case study is interesting and useful because it is exceptional rather than typical — because *Carmen* illustrates the limits of the directors' autonomy rather than the norm. Only the unique combination of a composer and a director committed to an aesthetic principle with revolutionary implications was capable of bringing to the stage a work that challenged the values of the audience elites. The combination remained unique because it became clear, after Du Locle's fiasco, that the opera establishment would ruin such a director.

Later in the century, when increasingly independent librettists were the vehicle for introducing radical challenges to established audience opinion, it was the role of the directors, as servants of audience elites and of the state, to resist the librettists' pretensions. The dominant social elites subordinated directors to their will through a variety of formal and informal pressures. The most important were government authority — close daily supervision of impresarios' activities backed by threats of dismissal or promises of reappointment — and market forces reflecting audience tastes. These were important in varying degrees at different times; usually they reinforced each other.

The directors' sensitivity to financial exigencies was heightened by a record of wide variations in the success enjoyed by state theatre directors: While Ritt of the Opéra and Carré of the Opéra-Comique retired as wealthy men, Vaucorbeil at the Opéra and Du Locle and Paravey at the Opéra-Comique suffered complete disaster. It was said that the staircase of the new Opéra house, the Palais Garnier, made the fortune first of the architect Charles Garnier, and then of Olivier Halanzier, who was director when it opened in 1875. From that time until the end of his regime in 1879, Halanzier cleared somewhat more than Fr.300,000 per year, an income sufficient to maintain the highest standard of aristocratic life. In contrast, Halanzier's less fortunate or less astute successor Vaucorbeil lost, after the state subsidy was figured in, an average of Fr.50,000 per year.[42]

To some extent, prosperity depended on minimizing operating expenses consisting of lighting and heat, the remuneration of choruses, musicians and principal performers, the royalties due to authors for the use of their work, and administrative costs. Ritt and Gailhard, who succeeded the hapless Vaucorbeil, increased receipts at the Opéra only marginally — about .1 percent. But by reducing expenses more than 10 percent, the new co-directors managed to turn their predecessor's crippling deficit into a substantial profit of almost Fr.200,000 per year.[43] On the other hand, no amount of care in the limitation of expenditure could save directors who persistently alienated their chief sources of revenue. Opera finances circumscribed the autonomy of the directors by subjecting them to the dictates of their primary sources of funds. The following passage from the memoirs of Carré reinforces the idea that even the boldest of Belle Epoque directors was constrained by financial considerations to look after the interests of his financial backers, and that their interests dictated that he should maximize receipts by catering to the tastes of the audience:

> The Opéra-Comique is a repertory theatre. The repertory, which supports the Opéra-Comique, always makes the maximum receipts, and everyone knows that with all the expenses that burden it, every theatre, and even more so, a lyric theatre, needs, in order to survive, to make the greatest receipts possible. In order for a new work, consequently — once past the activity due to curiosity — to supplant, in a limited number of performances, a work from the repertory which is sacrificed to it, it must justify itself by bringing in, like the latter, the maximum receipts. The director can help a work at its debut, and he owes it such aid. But he is not a Maecenas, and he is obliged also to consider the financial interests consigned to him.
>
> That is why, *whatever it costs him*, he is obliged to bow before the verdict of the public which, ultimately, is the only one that counts.[44]

It is clear that directors thought, at any rate, that they were responding to the preferences of the audience in selecting the works that they produced. With the exception of Du Locle, in his original production of *Carmen*, directors who appeared to be defying audience prejudices acted in response to undisclosed marketing considerations, or to outside pressures more significant than a temporary loss of receipts. Some new directors deliberately introduced shocking works in hopes that a *succès de scandale* would attract attention to themselves and to their houses. Thus Léon Carvalho, just appointed to the Opéra-Comique after acquiring a reputation as a daring and innovative Théâtre Lyrique director, "wanted to impress public opinion with an audacious coup." He chose Bruneau's opera *Le Rêve* (OC-1891), based on a story by the *enfant terrible* Emile Zola, who collaborated on the libretto himself.

Likewise the startlingly unorthodox *Louise* of Gustave Charpentier was the first *opéra-comique* that Carré introduced on his own initiative after his appointment in 1898. The librettist Robert de Flers described the strategy behind such choices in the following terms: If the director can make the public think

> no, this is impossible, we can't permit it, this upsets our logic, our principles, our prejudices, our tastes, our hypocricies, our customs, everything we are accustomed to put on when we go the theatre, then as one by one these fears disappear, the public is captivated by delicious perils, the rather breathless satisfaction that is the welcome product of an escape from danger. The dreaded scandal gives place to the most brilliant and complete success.[46]

Carré also willingly sacrificed receipts to subsidize the occasional *succès d'estime*, as long as other works in his repertoire continued to draw well. "I'm going to revive the *Ariane et Barbe-Bleue* of Dukas, which is a masterpiece," he wrote to critics who complained of frequent productions of popular Italian works. "If you like, I will send you the receipts of *Ariane et Barbe-Bleue* with the figure of my resulting losses, and let you see the receipts of *Tosca* and *Madame Butterfly* which re-establish the average that I require."[47] Similarly, because "many musicians requested it," Messager and Broussan produced Rameau's *Hippolyte et Aricie* at the Opéra in 1908, even though the public predictably failed to appreciate it.[48] Such ventures as *Ariane et Barbe-Bleue* and *Fidelio*, which Carré also presented at a financial loss, had the important side-effect of promoting the prestige of the house and of its administration. His genuine conviction of the merit of the controversial but enduring works that he sponsored cannot be disputed, but directors who produced works that enjoyed critical rather than popular success also intended to satisfy public demand. They simply recognized that the public included constituencies, such as the artistic cognoscenti, whose importance was out of proportion to the price of their admission.

This informed public, whose respect was indispensable to the long-term health of the Opéra-Comique especially, demonstrated in the case of Olivier Halanzier that they could arrange for the dismissal of a director who did not, in their view, reinvest enough of his profits in Art. Halanzier's productions filled the Opéra regularly during the first decade of the Third Republic; he established the house on a firm financial footing while accumulating a substantial personal fortune. He was at the height of his success in 1879, when Minister of Public Instruction Jules Ferry came under pressure to replace him. The influential subscribers among the deputies and in the press who agitated for his dismissal made no objection to Halanzier's choice of operas. His competence as a director was not at issue either, though critics attributed his success to the novelty of the Palais Garnier, the spectacular new opera house that opened in 1875, rather than to the merit of his productions. Their criticisms focused chiefly on Halanzier's scorn for the rhetoric of aesthetics and the irreverence of his attitude toward Art. He referred to composers as "song merchants," for instance, and dismissed Saint-Saëns' *Samson et Dalila* (0-1892), requested by the subscribers, because he "didn't like pieces in which they cut the tenor's hair."[49] Halanzier's offense lay in his plebian origins and uncultivated manner: He was the son of an actress and a captain of dragoons; he had been educated on stage since the age of four, and he was sometimes found in his shirtsleeves, helping to unload scenery. Simon Boubée, opera critic for the reactionary *Gazette de France*, refers to him as an "*industriel.*" The aristocratic subscribers were all the more resentful, perhaps, since he was clearing Fr.300,000 per year.[50]

In addition to audience receipts, the directors' other vital source of revenue, one which likewise subjected them to limitations on their freedom to choose the repertoire, was the subsidy provided by the state. Upon appointment to a state theatre, the director and his backers put up a sum of money — in the case of the Opéra, a minimum of Fr.800,000 during most of this period — half as a security deposit for the protection of the state, and half as operating capital. The government then provided its impresarios with yearly subsidies, subject to the approval of the Assemblée Nationale. For the Opéra, the level was fixed at Fr.800,000, somewhat more than one-fifth of the gross receipts; the relatively insignificant Opéra-Comique subsidy rose from Fr.100,000 to Fr.300,000 in 1885.[51] The two houses and their directors also benefited from the prestige that went with their official standing.

State subsidies, ostensibly designed to free directors from financial worries so that they could base decisions concerning the opera on purely artistic grounds, did not, and logically could not, have that effect.[52] By increasing the directors' working capital, subsidies enabled them to offer productions of sufficient opulence to attract customers. But since state subsidies did not eliminate the profit motive, directors continued to behave like any other theatrical entrepreneurs: They collected revenues and paid operating expenses, pocketing the excess — or distributing dividends to their backers — and making up deficits from their accumulated resources.

The government had wide latitude in dismissing directors whenever they "ceased to direct the Opéra with the dignity and éclat appropriate to the foremost national lyric theatre,"[53] though in practice they never exercised this option. Each new or renewed appointment was the occasion for renegotiation of the *cahiers des charges*, which defined the general nature of the relationship between the state and the director, and the specific terms of each concession, including the genres of works that might be presented. The state then closely monitored the directors' conformity with the provisions of these contracts through the offices of the Ministry of Public Instruction (sometimes called the Ministry of Public Instruction and Fine Arts):

> The Commissaire du Gouvernement près les théâtres subventionnés is charged with overseeing every aspect of the administration of the Théâtre de l'Opéra-Comique, including fulfillment of the *cahiers des charges*.... He will send the Minister reports on all new works, revivals, debuts; on the manner in which business is conducted, on infractions of the *cahiers des charges* which might have been committed, and in general on all incidents which he feels should be noted.[54]

The close correspondence between the social and political content of the opera and the interests of the governments in power, documented in the next chapter, implies that some form of supervision, whether institutional or informal, was highly effective.

Directors naturally resisted the interference of the government to the greatest extent possible. Productions of works by young French composers required by statute invariably failed because directors skimped on production costs. One such composer complained that whenever the choice of the government was not in accord with the personal preference of the director, "the musician imposed by the one [was] fatally sacrificed by the other."[55] This cannot be taken as the expression of a general rule, but it accurately reflects the limitations on the government's attempts to manage its directors' decisions. Directors also exploited divisions within the government in order to carve out for themselves spheres of relative autonomy. Through judicious distribution of favors and patronage, the tenured impresario of established reputation could build a political base to counterbalance that of the director of fine arts.

After twenty years in office Gailhard easily prevailed over a fledgling ministry reluctant to count Gluck's eighteenth-century opera *Armide* as one of the new works that the director was required by statute to produce. Gailhard's successful mobilization of friends in the cabinet, along with threats of parliamentary intervention conveyed by a sympathetic senator, sufficed to put the director of fine arts in his place; he agreed to accept *Armide* if receipts failed to meet the costs of production.[56] The extraordinary diplomatic maneuvering surrounding the *Armide* incident testifies also to Gailhard's extremely careful concern for the financial well-being of his enterprise, a sign of the fragility of the directors' financial position; to the serious repercussions of introducing a single work outside the main current of taste; and to the state's own preoccupation with the financial side of the operation.

1 The important texts for opera administration, including its relationship to the state, during this period, are: Pierre Bossuet, *Histoire des Théâtres Nationaux: Les Théâtres et l'Etat* (Paris, n.d.); Paul Dupré and Gustave Ollendorff, *Traité de l'Administration des Beaux-Arts*, 2 vols. (Paris, 1885); Paul Pelissier, *Historie Administrative de l'Académie de Musique et de Danse* (Paris, 1906); Raymond de Pezzer, "L'Opéra devant la loi et la jurisprudence," Thèse pour le Doctorat, Faculté de Droit de l'Université de Paris, 1911.

2 Though opera's administrative structure is not her primary concern, the best starting point for the earlier period is Fulcher, *The Nation's Image*, 12f., 54ff., 57f. Cf. Crosten, *French Grand Opera*, 17f. Fulcher's work also contains a useful bibliography.

3 Becker, "Giacomo Meyerbeer's Mitarbeit," 155. Cf. Gerhard, *Die Verstädterung der Oper*, 39.

4 "Bertrand and Gailhard to M. Joncières, 11 November 1893," B.O. Fonds Rouché, Pièce 120, no.110.

5 "Saint-Saëns to director of the Opéra, 8/28/1886," *France. Archives Nationales* (henceforth cited as *A.N.*) Dossier AJ XIII (1098-99).

6 Becker, "Giacomo Meyerbeer's Mitarbeit," 161.

7 Escudier in *L'Art Musical* (12 October 1876), quoted in Rouxel, *L'Etat et Les Théâtres* (Paris, 1877), 16.

8 Albert Carré, *Souvenirs de Théâtre* (Paris: Plon, 1950), 333, 420. The highly unsuccessful novice Opéra director Vaucorbeil, in writing such a rejection notice to Louis Gallet for *Le Chevalier Jean*, subsequently produced at the Opéra-Comique in 1885, documented in laborious detail the inconsistencies and improbabilities of the plot, the lack of motivation for various actions, and the repetition of devices from previous operas. His preoccupation with these irrelevant issues probably explains his failure as a director. Though the opera in question was not, in the event, particularly successful, Gallet built a brilliant career supplying librettos of exactly this type. Vaucorbeil's untitled memorandum is available in *A.N.* AJ XIII (1197).

9 "Ritt to Jean Richepin, 17 July 1888," B.O. Fonds Rouché, Pièce 119, no. 236; Louis Gallet, *Notes d'un librettiste* (Paris, 1891), 7ff., 116; Adrien Peytel, "Jurisprudence: Le Théâtre et les Auteurs," *Encyclopédie de la Musique* (Paris, 1931), 3879.

10 Quoted in James Harding, *Saint-Saëns and his Circle* (London: Chapman and Hall, 1965), 99. Directors had much less freedom with regard to pieces by deceased authors and composers, being restricted to the last text published during the author's lifetime. In practice, however, custom sanctioned many alterations, especially omissions, that had been made regularly over a long period of time. See De Pezzer, *L'Opéra devant la loi*, 84, 136f.

11 Carré, *Souvenirs*, 220; Richard Strauss and Hugo von Hofmannsthal, *Correspondence*, trans. Hanns Hammelmann and Ewald Osers (London: Collins, 1961), 24.

12 Quoted in Bruneau, *Musiques de Russie*, 132f.; Carré, *Souvenirs*, 280ff.; Carré's rival Gheusi suggested that Carré's musical director Messager and "a few aesthetes" persuaded the impresario to produce the Debussy opera against his better judgment and despite strong personal distaste, but Gheusi's career is characterized by jealousy and spite. P.-B. Gheusi, *Cinquante Ans de Paris*, 4 vols. (Paris, 1940), 3:330f.

13 Gheusi, *Cinquante Ans*, 3:246.

14 Gheusi, *Cinquante Ans*, 3:33; Joseph Paul-Boncour, *Art et démocratie* (Paris, 1912), 126.

15 After *Carmen*. *Mignon* also had more total performances than *Manon*, 1035 to 811, over the whole period, but many of these occurred before the premiere of *Manon*. Figures on frequency of performance here and below are derived from yearly totals for the Opéra and Opéra-Comique published in the *Annales*. Noël and Stoullig report Paravey's aversion to *Manon* without speculating on the reasons for it: *Annales*, 17:128.

16 Victor Debray, "A L'Opéra-Comique: La Danseuse de Pompéii," *Courrier Musical*, 15e année n.22 (11/15/1912), 604.

17 Louis Gallet, "Quatre Directeurs de l'Opéra," *Revue Internationale de la Musique* v.1 no.4, 208f.

18 Mina Curtiss, *Bizet and His World* (New York: Knopf, 1958), 389-392.

19 *Ibid.*, 107.

20 Armand Silvestre, *Au Pays des Souvenirs* (Paris, 1887), 279. Cf. Harding, *Saint-Saëns*, 99; Curtiss, *Bizet*, 135ff.

21 *Ibid.*, 135f., 131.

22 Gallet, *Notes*, 12.

23 *Ibid.*, 62f., 83. On the tendency of the audience to confuse actors with the roles they played, see Théophile Gauthier, *Souvenirs de Théâtre, d'Art et de Critique* (Paris, 1883), 183f.

24 Curtiss, *Bizet*, 325ff.; Gallet, *Notes*, 75-82, passim, 85. Cf. Meyerbeer and Scribe in Gerhard, *Die Verstädterung der Oper*, 281. Cp. a description of the method of collaboration between the composer Léo Delibes and the librettist Phillippe Gille in Tout-Paris, "La Journée Parisienne," *Le Gaulois* (3/9/1880).

25 Curtiss, *Bizet*, 351, 329.

26 And it could easily be misinterpreted this way, either willfully or through wishful thinking. See, e.g. Ernest Reyer, "Revue Musicale," *Journal des Débats* (3/14/1875).

27 Adolphe Jullien, "Revue Musicale," *Le Français* (3/15/1875).

28 Curtiss, *Bizet*, 378f., 382f.

29 Besides the standard biographical references, such as G. Vapereau and L. Guitane, *Dictionnaire Universel des Contemporains* (Paris, 1870-1873), cf. Curtiss, *Bizet*, 264f., 371-378, passim.

30 Quoted in *Ibid.*, 373, 383.

31 Henri Roujon, *Artistes et Amis des Arts* (Paris, 1912), 244. Cf. André Bellessort, *Les Intellectuels et l'Avènement de la Troisième République* (Paris, 1931), 92; Eric C. Hansen, *Ludovic Halévy: A Study of Frivolity and Fatalism in Nineteenth-Century France* (Lanham, MD: University Press of America, 1987), 58. Halévy's intimate knowledge of the Opéra sub-culture later became the basis for *La Famille Cardinal* (Paris, 1883), a widely read series of revealing vignettes dealing with backstage mores.

32 See Georges Bizet, *Lettres à Un Ami: 1865-1872* (Paris, 1909), 176. Cf. Edmond Genêst, *L'Opéra-Comique: Connu et Inconnu* (Paris, 1925), 193. Later, Du Locle wrote *Sigurd* (O-1885), a radical departure from the traditional libretto in both form and content. At first rejected by director after director, the opera by Reyer eventually inaugurated the *Wagnérisme* that dominated the Opéra for the following twenty years. See E. Reyer, "Revue Musicale," in *Journal des Débats* (6/21/1885). It is noteworthy also that the source that Curtiss relies on to impugn Du Locle's convictions also credits the impresario with refusing to engage in the traditional practice of bribing critics even though it might have hurt *Carmen's* chances for initial success. See Curtiss, *Bizet*, 319f., 379, 393. For the bohemian influences on Bizet, *Ibid.*, 105f., 122f., 245.

33 *Ibid.*, 383.

34 Carré, *Souvenirs*, 236.

35 Ludovic Halévy, "La Millième Représentation de *Carmen,*" *Le Théâtre*, 1905 no.1 (January-June), 8.

36 Curtiss, *Bizet*, 393f.

37 *Ibid.*, 415; Halévy, "La Millième Représentation," 10.

38 John W. Klein, "The Two Versions of 'Carmen,'" *Musical Opinion* (March 1949), 292f.

39 Curtiss, *Bizet*, 426-432. Cf. Halévy, "La Millième Représentation," 12.

40 Curtiss, *Bizet*, 432ff.

41 *Ibid.*, 434.

42 "Moyennes comparatives des Recettes et des Dépenses par Direction et par représentation," *A.N.* AJ XIII (1202). The figures from this document must be multiplied by the total number of performances per year, which can be compiled from figures for individual operas in each issue of *Annales*. On the reasons for Halanzier's success, see Ernest Reyer, *Quarante Ans de Musique* (Paris, 1910), 43. Cf. "Rapport de la Sous-Commission sur la question du Théâtre Nationale de l'Opéra," *A.N.* AJ XIII (1202). This profit was in addition to his annual salary, which, if comparable to that of directors for whom this information is available, was in the neighborhood of Fr.20,000-30,000. See, for example, Chambre des Députés, Session Extraordinaire de 1888, "Rapport de la Commission du Budget 1889; Ministère de l'Instruction Publique et des Beaux-Arts," *Journal Officiel*, 19. Vaucorbeil's losses amounted to more than twice his salary. Cf. "Budget 1883-1884," B.O. Opéra-Comique Arch. 19e. Siècle, no.79. An income of Fr.300,000 francs permitted a family to maintain a country estate while living in the Fauborg Saint-Honoré, with all that such a style of life implied, including, *de rigeur*, a place at the Opéra for all three nights of *abonnement*. For a complete description of this syle of life, Gaston Jollivet, *L'Art de Vivre* (Paris, 1887).

43 See, e.g., the budget for the year 1896 in *A.N.* AJ XIII (1202). Another important outlay was not subject to control: the City of Paris collected the *droit des pauvres*, a luxury tax on theatrical performances, at the rate of 9.09% of gross receipts. See Jules Martin, *Nos Auteurs et Compositeurs Dramatiques* (Paris, 1897), 603. It is interesting to note that this tax reduced net subsidies from the state by almost half in the case of the Opéra, and much more in the case of the Opéra-Comique, without any

corresponding reduction of state responsibility or influence. For the receipts and expenses of various directorial regimes, "Moyennes comparatives." Ritt's and Gailhard's increase in receipts would have been greater if, like Vaucorbeil, they had been permitted to dispense with lower-priced shows introduced to democratize the Opéra clientele. For a useful chart of yearly expenditures and receipts of the Opéra, Jean Gourret, *Ces Hommes qui ont fait l'Opéra* (Paris: Albatros, 1984), 216-226.

44 Carré, *Souvenirs*, 310 (his emphasis). Whereas in his memoirs Carré proclaimed the director's obligation to earn the maximum receipts possible, in the letter quoted below, p.37, which was intended for immediate public consumption, he claimed only a "necessary average." Complaining about his receipts, he asserted that maximum receipts were, in fact, the minimum necessary for survival. Elsewhere, however, he admitted that his financial backers made money, even if he himself did not: *Ibid.*, 222.

45 *Annales*, 17:119. Cp. Camille de Saint-Croix, "Tribune Littéraire: Opéra-Comique," *Le Paris* (7/8/1896) (also available in B.O. Dossier d'artiste/ Carvalho).

46 Leon Treich, ed., *L'Esprit de Robert de Flers* (Paris, 1928), 40f.

47 J. G. Prud'homme, "Albert Carré, 1852-1938" (Milano, 1939) (extract from *Rivista Musicale Italiana* Anno XLIII, fasc. 3-4), 4. Cf. Carré, *Souvenirs*, 316f.

48 Untitled report of the 1908 meeting of *commanditaires* of Messager and Broussan, *A.N.* AJ XIII (1187). For the similar case of Fidelio, see Carré, *Souvenirs*, 245.

49 Reyer, *Quarante Ans*, 43. Cf. Gallet, "Quatre Directeurs," 215f.

50 *Ibid.*, 214. Cf. Georges Maillard, "M. Halanzier-Dufrenoy," *Revue du Monde Musical et Dramatique*, 1e année no.2 (11/23/1878) (available also in B.O. Dossier d'artiste/ Halanzier); Simon Boubée, "Musique," *Gazette de France* (4/12/1877); Louis Laloy, "L'Opéra," Rohozinski, ed., *Le Théâtre Lyrique et la Symphonie de 1874 à 1925* (Paris, 1925), 19; "Rapport de la Sous-Commission sur la question du Théâtre Nationale de l'Opéra, 11/27/1878," *A.N.* AJ XIII (1202).

51 Pelissier, *Histoire Administrative*, 162, 175; Dupré and Ollendorff, *Traité de l'Administration*, 2:384; Laloy, "L'Opéra," 26. The director of the Opéra also used the Palais Garnier rent-free, along with the costumes and scenery of the current repertoire. The director of the Opéra-Comique, on the other hand, not only paid rent for the privately-owned Salle Favart, but he had

to purchase costumes and scenery from his predecessor. See Carré, *Souvenirs*, 220; Adrien Bernheim, *Trente Ans de Théâtre*, 4 vols. (Paris, 1903), 1:99.

52 Ortolan, "Rapport à l'Assemblée Générale," 6.

53 Quoted in Dupré and Ollendorff, *Traité de l'Administration*, 2:380.

54 "Théâtre Nationale de l'Opéra-Comique, Cahier des Charges 1911," B.O. Dossier P.A. 1900-1927, P.A. 1/24 mai/1911, Article 78. There is a collection of *cahiers des charges* in *A.N.* AJ XIII (1187). Cf. de Pezzer, "L'Opéra devant la loi," 84; Pelissier, *Histoire Administrative*, 152.

55 Henri Maréchal, *Rome: Souvenirs d'un Musicien* (Paris, 1904), 299.

56 Gailhard's request was not as unreasonable as it might appear; in 1882 the minister of public instruction had strongly urged Vaucorbeil to produce *Armide* under exactly those conditions. See the exchange of letters on the subject in *A.N.* AJ XIII (1194).

CHAPTER III

THE STATE
AND THE IDEOLOGY
OF THE OPERA:
Carmen or Jeanne d'Arc?

In 1875, the same year that *Carmen* made its debut at the Opéra-Comique, *Jeanne d'Arc*, with a libretto and music by Auguste Mermet, had its premiere at the Opéra. The first new work to be introduced at the Opéra during the Third Republic, *Jeanne d'Arc* was an eminently suitable projection of "the nation's image." A contemporary observer claimed that the minister of public instruction insisted on production of *Jeanne d'Arc* as a condition of Halanzier's *cahiers des charges*.[1] Deliberate official manipulation of the repertoire, such as Fulcher found to be characteristic of the July Monarchy, might be supposed to account sufficiently for the social and political content of Third Republic opera as well. The traditional ties of the opera to the sovereign and his court provided a precedent for close identification of opera's political content with the reigning ideology; under the Bourbons, and again as recently as the Second Empire, opera administration had functioned as part of the monarch's household. In this chapter — an examination of the librettos' social and political content in the context of pre-war Third Republic politics — the attitudes of various government parties towards the opera are relevant, as are the political interests of other forces capable of influencing the repertoire.

Mermet's eponymous heroine provided a wonderful example of a peasant woman, inspired by piety and patriotism, who attains to purity, chastity, and, in the interests of France, even to self-sacrifice. When Baron Mermet, son of one of Napoléon I's generals, first submitted

Jeanne d'Arc to the Second Empire Opéra administration in 1868, he probably hoped the local color of the Hundred Years' War would appeal to an audience filled with martial aspirations. By the time the piece went into production seven years later under the Republic, the Opéra public was looking for a patriotic work that would revive its pride in the military after the fiascos of the Franco-Prussian War.[2] Returning to Mermet's opera, the director Halanzier was fortunate to find what had become in the intervening period a *revanchiste* allegory. The opening act takes place in Lorraine (in Joan's birthplace of Domrémy), a setting guaranteed to stimulate interest in any theatrical piece during the pre-war Third Republic. France is occupied by foreign troops: "Heaven has condemned you, my unhappy country" (I:ii). The opera ends happily with the reconquest of the fatherland and the coronation of the rightful king who, in the best Old Regime tradition, "guarantees to everyone his exemptions [*franchises*] and privileges" (IV:iv).

These were sentiments certain to win the approval of the political leadership, which maintained monarchist political views through the early years of the republic. Bénédict, the critic for *Le Figaro*, which at that time espoused a Legitimist political position, wrote in his review of the opera: "For those who have a sense of inherited glory and of the great patriotic struggles of our country, this *fleur-de-lys*-covered mantle thrown on the shoulders of a king — even though only a stage king — was not only a memory, but a hope." The "monarchist republic" of the eighteen-seventies was a period when a Chambre des Députés speech against, say, freedom of the press, might conclude with a rousing demand for Joan's canonization. The Legitimists, especially, exploited her as a symbol of their own conception of the new regime, as when the Comte de Chambord, Bourbon heir to the throne, evoked Joan's memory in his notorious manifesto insisting on the white flag for France. [3]

Who then was responsible for the presence of the anomolous, subversive *Carmen* at the other state-subsidized opera house, at exactly the same time as *Jeanne d'Arc* was serving the "monarchist republic" so well? It is ludicrous to imagine Carmen as a contestant for the role of nation's image, and there is scarcely a hint of state involvement in the whole detailed history of the controversial production. We might dismiss *Carmen* as a temporary aberration; the fledgling republic, during the unsettled early years of its existence, was unable to exercise such strict supervision of its appointees as Louis-Napoléon's regime had.[4] But the messages disseminated at the Opéra-Comique typically continued to diverge in significant ways from those at the Opéra, complicating any interpretation of the social and political content of the opera based entirely on the premise of active state control over the repertoire. The two houses had exactly equivalent relationships to the state, but ended up with very different ideological orientations.

For at least a few years after the premieres of *Carmen* and *Jeanne d'Arc*, to be sure, what is striking about the content of the Opéra-Comique and the Opéra repertoires is how closely both responded to shifts in the political balance of power. This is especially evident in the long-term, lowest-common-denominator trends in operatic ideology, conveyed in details that probably owed nothing to the deliberations of the librettists and that certainly eluded the consciousness of the audiences. *Jeanne d'Arc* is exemplary from this point of view. In its treatment of minor lower-class characters, the opera contributed to a pattern of thoroughly undemocratic sentiments, which was the chief characteristic of both Opéra and Opéra-Comique ideology in the late 'seventies, and of Opéra ideology until the Great War. In Mermet's opera, the collectivity of common people is represented by soldiers who, in the absence of their social superiors, neglect their duty completely, drink to excess, and engage in orgies with equally dissolute village women (III:vi-vii). This theme of the unreliability — or at best the irrelevance — of the lower classes recurred in every new work that appeared at the Opéra before the end of the 'seventies. In Massenet's *Le Roi de Lahore* (O-1877), the common people desert their heroic, wounded king on the field of battle in order to follow a defeatist usurper (II:iii-v). In Gounod's *Polyeucte* (O-1878), the persecution of noble Christians arouses the indignation of the leading characters, who remain indifferent to the massacre of Christians among the "vile populace" (III:i).

At the other, family-oriented state theatre, the common people appeared in festivals rather than in battles and massacres, but the rhetorical effect was the same. After the resounding failure of Du Locle's attempts to portray the passions and ideals of more realistic common people in all their complexity, the new management of the Opéra-Comique sagely pursued the opposite course. It inaugurated its administration with Gounod's *Cinq-Mars* (OC-1877), in which a chorus of peasants joyfully celebrates the success of the nobles' hunting expedition and regrets the good old days when the nobility was prosperous (III:vii). The only individual lower-class character is an unreliable servant. The noble hero of the opera rehearses various threats to the well-being and political power of the nobility, and appeals to them to defend their interests, even by conspiracy, if necessary. August heads have been rolling, great names proscribed, and prelates outraged, he sings; "Let us save the nobility of France!" (IIB:v).

Other Opéra-Comique presentations during this period contrasted the values and behavior of the nobility favorably with those of the bourgeoisie, with financiers coming in for special opprobrium. In Paladilhe's *Suzanne* (OC-1878), an unsympathetic financier offends the sensibilities of the noble heroes by his indifference to any human suffering occasioned by the accumulation of wealth (III:ii,iv). A Jewish usurer who has been persecuting an impecunious nobleman in Membrée's *La Courte Echelle* (OC-1879) sings a ridiculous love song to gold, indulges in egregious anti-Christian slander, and ultimately abases himself before the noble hero in the most abject, servile manner (II:i, III:iii). The bourgeoisie appear *en masse* as a chorus of civil guards whose duty it is to interfere with an affair of honor; the spirited armed resistance of the noble heroes is very attractive in comparison with the submissive, literal-minded devotion to duty of this "vile populace" (II:viii). With the conspicuous exception of *Carmen*, every new opera at either the Opéra or the Opéra-Comique between 1875 and 1879 had a noble or royal hero whose virtues and abilities compared favorably with the character traits of villains and buffoons from lower social classes.

After 1880, however, new Opéra-Comique operas began to contradict in various ways the aristocratic and anti-democratic bias typical of both houses during the previous decade. *L'Amour Medecin* (OC-1880) and *La Taverne des Trabans* (OC-1881) have only bourgeois and petit-bourgeois characters. *Jean de Nivelle* (OC-1880) depicts the arbitrary arrest and harsh treatment of a peasant by a nobleman (II:iii). The triumphant return of *Carmen* to the Opéra-Comique stage in 1883 is a manifestation of the same pattern, and the trend towards more sympathetic, nuanced portrayals of the common people continued, though more discreetly, in Massenet's *Manon* (OC-1884). In a brief passage that is entirely incidental to the main action, *Manon's* librettists attribute the common soldiers' untrustworthy and cowardly behavior to the poor pay they receive from the king; the characteristic alienation of the soldiery is blamed on the indignity of their labors (V:ii). Beginning around 1883, there are signs of change at the more aristocratic Opéra as well. The bourgeoisie are still cowardly in 1882, in Ambroise Thomas' *Françoise de Rimini* (O-1882), while the "vile multitude" actually sell out to the enemy (IA:ii). But the following year, in Saint-Saëns' *Henri VIII* (O-1883), the common people play a responsible parliamentary role; in Gounod's *Sapho* (O-1884), they are heroic revolutionaries. The latter was a revised version of an opera that had run afoul of Louis-Napoléon's censorship office in 1851 because its libretto, by the well-respected republican *homme de lettres* Emile Augier, featured a republican hero and chorus who conspire against an oppressive tyrant.[5]

Further evidence of a change towards a less aristocratic, more democratic point of view, even at the Opéra, comes from Paladilhe's *Patrie!*, which was written in 1881 and had its premiere five years later. The action takes place in sixteenth-century Flanders, during the popular revolts against the Spanish regime of the Duke of Alba, and hinges on a noble hero's decision to subordinate his personal honor to the cause of political liberty and the rights of his fatherland. He refrains from calling out his wife's lover because the latter, as captain of the bourgeois guard, is indispensable to their conspiracy to deliver Flanders from oppression (IV:ii). At the end of the opera the adulterous captain redeems himself by killing his unscrupulous mistress, who had betrayed the revolution for personal advantage; he then submits to execution in company with his comrades.

Patrie! is similar to *Jeanne d'Arc* in that the revolutionaries' leader and chief martyr (though he is not an important character in the opera) comes from the common people. But for the patriots in *Patrie!* the legitimacy of the government resides in laws established by their forefathers (IV:i) rather than in a particular dynasty, and their appeal is to a Rousseauist "great soul" of the people (IV:i). The change in the political climate of the Opéra by the mid-'eighties is also evident in the anti-Catholic rhetoric that accompanies these relatively progressive political ideas. Whereas the monarchist sentiments of the 'seventies' operas were sanctioned by traditional religious beliefs, in *Patrie!* brutal Catholic soldiers thirst for the blood of the democrats "in the name of the living God" (IV:vi).

So far, the evidence of the librettos seems clear: A substantial shift toward a more democratic outlook occurred in the early eighteen-eighties, at the expense of the aristocratic values that had dominated the preceding decade. Of course this shift in operatic ideology coincided with a dramatic alteration in the course of French political life at the end of the 'seventies resulting from the electoral triumph of republican principles and personnel.[6] Although the Third Republic had been proclaimed formally on 4 September 1870, its legislatures were at first dominated by notables committed to its eventual overthrow. The republic would have been in serious jeopardy if these Legitimists, Orléanists, and Bonapartists could have united behind an alternative. But the young regime survived until its adherents won a series of electoral victories in the late 'seventies and early 'eighties, which helped stabilize the republic and led to the ultimate eclipse of monarchist hopes. This reorientation of French political life had important repercussions in cultural affairs, which, according to contemporary observers, had continued to follow Second Empire patterns through the 1870s.[7]

It should come as no surprise that the new political, moral, and aesthetic climate inaugurated along with President Grévy led directly to changes in the ideological content of opera librettos in view of the longstanding republican appreciation of the pedagogical potential of the theatre. In the eighteenth century, the ideas of writers such as Voltaire, who said that the theatre "instructs better than a large book,"[8] had led to a general recognition on the part of Enlightenment *philosophes* of opera's moralizing capacity, in opposition to the traditional Ancien Régime conception of opera as an aristocratic fête. Following the lead of their music writer, J.-J. Rousseau, the *Encyclopédistes* condemned the tradition of *"merveilleux"* opera in favor of historical subjects, which lent themselves to more didactic treatment. Republican heirs to this philosophical tradition continued to acknowledge, usually from an envious distance, the pedagogic potential of the state theatres, including the opera. Victor Hugo, that embodiment of nineteenth-century republicanism, who seemed to link the era of the revolution with the Third Republic, formulated a specific program that included more active state participation in theatre administration:

> The theatre is one of the branches of public instruction. Responsible for the morality of the people, the State should not play a negative

role. Beside the unrestricted theatres it should install theatres that it controls itself, where social ideas will be presented.[9]

Louis Blanc also, in a widely quoted passage in the *Histoire de dix ans*, called the theatre "the most efficacious and legitimate means of government," and suggested that no state should abandon the moral direction of the society through the theatre.[10]

In 1878-79, at the time of the consolidation of republican control over the new republic, the future status of the relationship between state and opera was an open question. The minister of public instruction charged a subcommittee on the "Question de l'Opéra" of the Commission consultative des théâtres with a re-evaluation of the system then in effect. While recognizing the greater efficiency resulting from management by a single individual, as well as the danger of political interference in the opera administration, — a very real one, as events soon proved — the committee concluded that completely independent private ownership was unthinkable. It reported "that the Théâtre Nationale de l'Opéra is truly an institution of State...and that it is the proper function of the State itself, especially when invited by circumstance, to take such a task in hand and to accomplish it."[11] The subcommittee eventually recommended that the government retain the system of administration then in effect, but with closer surveillance of the director's activities than had been possible during the unsettled conditions of the post-war period. Prime Minister and Minister of Public Instruction Jules Ferry confirmed this endorsement of the existing system, which continued in effect throughout the Belle Epoque.

The attitude of the Ferry regime towards the opera was more ambivalent than the committee's rhetoric suggests, however. Having committed his government publicly to the existing administrative relationship between opera and ministry, Ferry renounced any intention of politicizing the opera. In view of the potential for active state supervision of the directors' decisions with regard to the repertoire, the impact of the Ferry regime on the opera must actually be considered rather limited. His first important initiative in this regard was the selection of a successor to Olivier Halanzier, who as director of the Opéra had run afoul of the aristocratic subscribers. Ferry's choice illustrates the profound reluctance of the new government to impose an aggressively republican ethos on the opera.

One of two candidates for the position was Charles de La Rounat, who had managed the state-supported Odéon theatre for ten years. As a former secretary to the minister Albert during the Second Republic, his republican credentials were impressive. More recently, in his capacity as opera critic for Le XIXe Siècle, he had taken the lead among republican critics with a most favorable review of Carmen. Since he had been brought up "according to the tastes and customs of the aristocracy," he was immune to the sort of criticism leveled at Halanzier. But Ferry passed over the obvious candidate in favor of his wife's music teacher, Vaucorbeil, a correct and dignified composer and former instructor at the Académie Nationale de la Musique. Vaucorbeil was thought to be a republican, but having previously served the "monarchist republic" as Commissaire du gouvernement près les théâtres subventionnés,[12] he had ties to the right as well. Ferry followed up his appointment with a letter to the new director insisting that the Opéra become a "museum of music,"[13] a conception reaffirmed by all subsequent pre-war ministries.

The spectre of deliberate, overt exploitation of the opera for partisan political ends was apparently as antipathetic to Ferry and his friends, newly absorbed into the opera establishment, as it was to older members of the Tout-Paris of the opera. The danger that they anticipated was that some irresponsible group capable of capturing the state apparatus would politicize the opera. This fear was very nearly realized in 1881, when the charismatic radical republican Léon Gambetta briefly acceded to power. His supporters clearly had designs on what they considered to be a neglected pedagogical resource; part of Gambetta's plan for the "Grand Ministère" was to elevate the Department of Fine Arts to the status of a separate ministry in order to facilitate more active state intervention in matters concerning the theatre. His choice as head of the new ministry was Antonin Proust, one of his most prominent supporters, who publicly espoused the philosophy of Victor Hugo, quoted above, that the government should propagate republican ideas through the theatres. Proust advocated a change to direct state administration of the opera in order to introduce more progressive, democratic, and popular new works expressing "social thought."[14]

He never had the opportunity to implement his program, of course, because widespread opposition to Gambetta's radical initiatives — opposition in which the opera establishment undoubtedly participated — led to his early fall from power. In the aftermath of this missed opportunity (or narrow escape), aware of the need to reassure more conservative elements that the republic did not necessarily imply any radical transformation of society, Ferry and his conservative "Opportunist" successors took an even more circumspect approach to the opera. It responded with a series of works expressing ideas uncongenial to committed bourgeois republicans.

Widor's *Maître Ambros* (OC–1886), like *Patrie!*, which appeared in the same year, revolves around a popular attempt to establish representative political institutions in the Low Countries. It takes place in 1650 —the century after *Patrie!* — as all of Amsterdam "lines up under the banner of the law" (IA:i) to resist the monarchical pretentions of William of Orange. The bourgeois leaders of the citizenry have the support of the army and the common people, but many small merchants are bitter because the long siege is ruining their businesses (III:ii). One of these petit bourgeois dissidents, motivated by hatred of the bourgeoisie (IV:iii,v), eventually betrays the city to its enemies. Though the rhetorical effect of *Maître Ambros* operates in defense of the republic, the heroine of *Maître Ambros* behaves in a manner more characteristic of Ancien Régime than of bourgeois women. She not only scrambles around the town at night on a military mission (III:ix), but declares her intention of marrying whichever of her suitors succeeds in saving the cause (IV:v). Her actions demonstrate that political intrigue is more fulfilling for her than bourgeois feminine domesticity.[15] The opera also gives an ominously militaristic, nationalistic, and patriotic tone to its anti–monarchical sentiments.

The rise to prominence of General Boulanger, whose support at this early stage of his political career came from petit-bourgeois, republican heirs to the authoritarian, patriotic Jacobin tradition, coincided exactly with the appearance of the opera. During the next few years, the responsiveness of the Opéra-Comique repertoire to the short-lived but spectacular phenomenon of Boulangism was striking. As the vogue for early modern Dutch and Belgian themes continued in the late 'eighties, they took an increasingly authoritarian turn. The repertoire continued faithfully to reproduced the general's emphasis on strong military leadership, and when Boulanger's true colors began to show more white than red, the Opéra-Comique began to reassert the values of the reactionary social elites.[16] The democratic and republican ideals characteristic of the repertoire during the previous decade yielded to a more paternalistic conception of government that purported to serve the interests of the common people while excluding them from the decision-making process. The emphasis in *Egmont* (OC-1886) is on decisive leadership. Having decided that they are incapable of acting without a noble leader (I:viii), the revolutionary Flemish bourgeoisie subordinate themselves to Prince Egmont, who stresses his exalted rank at every opportunity through the rest of the opera (e.g. IV:i). In *Esclarmonde* (OC-1889), likewise, the populace is incapable of fighting the Saracens alone or under its superannuated king, and turns of necessity to Roland, invincible wielder of the sacred sword. Following *Egmont* and *Esclarmonde*, operas such as *Proserpine* (OC-1887), *Le Roi d'Ys* (OC-1888), *L'Escadron Volant de la Reine* (OC-1888), and *Dimitri* (OC-1890) also expressed aristocratic, monarchical, and religious values, which had been missing from the Opéra-Comique earlier in the decade.

These parallels between the development of Boulangism and the values propagated at the opera reinforce the idea that the librettos were responsive to political phenomena, but they provide no support for the thesis that the government dictated the ideological content of the repertoire to its opera directors. The republicans running France recognized early on that the politics of the new right were inimical to the survival of the regime; they would certainly not have actively promoted the dissemination of anti-republican Boulangist sentiments at the opera. On the other hand, the power of the reactionary elites was magnified, just at this time, by the introduction of an Opéra-Comique subscription series which gave the aristocratic element in the audience more prominence, a focus for its economic influence, and a structure for more effective lobbying in favor of certain types of libretto.[17] The social and political content of the repertoire emerged in this case as the product of some more complicated balance of power between government and opera audience.

Although the conservative republicans' policy towards the opera thus opened up the repertoire of the state theatres to anti-republican ideas, it did not have the intended effect of reassuring the right as to the pacific intentions of the republicans. It did, however, alienate the left, which proved increasingly reluctant to subsidize reactionary opera. In sum, Ferry's strategy of renouncing the use of opera as a means of public instruction was an utter failure. Legislative backing for opera subsidies eroded on both ends of the political spectrum through the 'eighties, reaching its nadir in 1890, when a motion to reduce state theatre subsidies failed by only 230-269. The gravity of this situation forced subsequent ministries to search for a different formula that would placate the right without alienating potential allies on the republican left.

In 1891, Léon Bourgeois' ministerial *circulaire* to the theatre inspectors begins with traditional republican rhetoric:

> We would like the theatre to be a school....The powerful influence of the theatre must come to our aid and second the efforts we make to instruct the common people [*le peuple*], to fortify them, to make them worthy of exercising the power that the Republic puts in their hands in order to give France the moral grandeur appropriate to a democracy.

But the next passage eschews any program for promoting republican or democratic principles at the theatre:

> To that end, with regard to policy, let us provide all the liberty compatible with the maintenance of public peace. The two principles of the Republic are: dignity and liberty.[18]

Like its predecessors, the Bourgeois ministery interpreted these principles in a way that countenanced the propagation of explicitly anti-republican doctrines. In 1891, their articulation of this approach turned the legislative tide toward a consensus of approval for state-sponsored opera. When, during the crucial debate, a former minister of public instruction attempted to argue that "the subsidies that we award to the fine arts, and in particular to our theatres, are not designed to revive hatreds and rekindle the zeal of the adversaries of the Republic," the government spokesman responded that "the State has no doctrine," and that "it is only authoritarian governments that have an official doctrine on every subject — politics, religion, philosophy, fine arts...."[19]

This rhetoric set the stage for a successful change in policy inaugurated by the Bourgeois ministry the following year, one which his successors continued during the remainder of the pre-war Third Republic. In effect, republican politicians abandoned the Palais Garnier to its aristocratic *abonnés*, while maintaining the Opéra-Comique as their own preserve. This led to the immediate introduction of the anti-republican, anti-bourgeois works of Richard Wagner and his French disciples at the Opéra, a development that served the requirements of Léon Bourgeois' domestic and international political strategy of reconciliation with the forces of reaction very well. At the same time, the Opéra-Comique introduced a series of republican revolutionary operas, which illustrated the opportunities that existed for a republican state opera. Though the interpretation of the revolution that appeared on stage in the eighteen-nineties was antipathetic to leftist Radical republicans, the rivals of Bourgeois, even they began to reconcile themselves to state opera as the chances of their own accession to power steadily improved.[20] Legislative approval of opera subsidies was never again in jeopardy during the remainder of the Belle Epoque.

After the turn of the century, when radical-socialists began to form ministries, they returned to the rhetoric of opera's pedagogic function in budget debates over the opera subsidies. Committee reports in 1906 and 1910, for example, noting Rumanian, Spanish, and in particular English and German attempts to mobilize the arts for the improvement of the population, concluded that the state opera could promote virtue among the French citizenry in a similar fashion. The authors required the arts to provide "ever more beautiful and more noble conceptions" to mankind, because the strength of a nation depended on its moral fibre as much as on its cultural heritage. But not until 1913, upon the appointment of a radical-socialist as director of the Opéra, was there any sign that this rhetoric would be implemented by any administration.[21]

As a result of the Bourgeois compromise in 1891, the Opéra-Comique's turn to the right proved to be as short-lived as Boulangism itself; during the 'nineties, this house came to serve the needs of the republicans in power more precisely than ever. Although, in 1889, at the beginning of the centenary of the Revolution, the Third Republic had survived for nearly thirty years, longer than any other nineteenth-century regime, intransigent opposition from anti-republicans on both the right and left continued to threaten its existence. A new right had reared its ugly head. The rise and fall of Boulangism seems like a comic opera in retrospect, but it was exceedingly sinister at the time, and all the elements of the Dreyfus Affair were already in place. The alliance with Russia broke France's diplomatic isolation, but the Republic continued to be oppressed by memories and fears of Prussian militarism. Under the circumstances, the centennial of the First Republic of 1793-4 was a public relations windfall. It presented the government with obvious opportunities to capitalize on a "military era that is always sympathetic, and very much *à la mode* at the moment."[22] Commemoration of the victories of those years permitted beleaguered Belle Epoque republicans to borrow some prestige from their political ancestors' triumphs over Prussia, and over domestic opponents of the republic as well. Opera was the ideal vehicle for recreating the martial music and pageantry of the era.

Beginning in 1893, inaugurated by a successful peasant revolt in Delibes' *Kassya*, a series of librettos reproduced first the social conflicts of the Revolution, and eventually its military history as well. Such topical material could have been incorporated into the opera in any number of ways; in practice, the librettists' selection of incidents and outcomes from the panorama of French Revolutionary history inevitably endorsed certain aspects of the French revolutionary tradition, while repudiating others. During the decade-long celebration, the Revolution became increasingly important and controversial symbolic ground for the discussion of contemporary political issues. Its importance as a frame of reference for discussions of contemporary political problems during this period is well-documented by modern historians. Paul Farmer, for instance, introduces his study of Third Republic historiography with the following statement:

> The controversy over the history of the Revolution is distinguished from other unsettled historical problems in that judgments on the Revolution serve as the locus of almost all the divisions of opinion in France on the problems of modern life. Historical interpretations are inseparably joined to alignments on contemporary politics, to corresponding opinions on such questions as the interrelationships of the state, the individual, religion, society, and classes, and to corresponding evaluations of nationalism, tradition and the Church. A particular position on the history of the Revolution implies a particular attitude on most other public questions, and these, in turn, are customarily referred to the Revolution as a major premise.[23]

At first, librettists refracted the socio-political content of their operas by transferring revolutionary references to other times and places. *Kassya*, for instance, which censures the aristocracy while portraying popular political action in a favorable light, takes place in mid-nineteenth-century Galicia. The countryside is being ravaged by a plague of banditry, horse stealing, and arson, all condoned by the local count. The neighboring *seigneurs* despise the peasantry and laughingly approve when the count arranges to conscript the fiancé of a peasant girl who has caught his eye (II:vi). Arrogant in their rank and position, they boast that pleasure is the only guide to their behavior (II:vii). The count raises taxes so high that the hero's father is forced off his land (III:iii). When the hero returns from the army, he leads a band of armed peasants against the chateau where the local lords have apparently been singing, drinking, and playing since the beginning of the second act. After defeating them, he assures the peasantry that it will have nothing further to fear from the nobility, who will henceforth be subject to the laws or go into exile (V:ii).

Two years later, in 1895, the Opéra-Comique produced Lalo's *La Jacquerie*, about the armed peasant revolts of the fourteenth century. A peasant hero who has been trying to better himself by acquiring learning in Paris is forced to flee to the countryside after defending a poor man mistreated by a nobleman. The futility of his love for the local *seigneur's* daughter has made him a revolutionary, and convinced him that the nobility does nothing but evil. Instead of dispensing justice, they raise taxes: "Our labor goes for nothing. They take the earth and its fruits that God gave to us" (II:i). But, he says, the hour will come when a young, ardent, strong people will break their chains; in order to obtain victory over their oppressors, they must unite like brothers, learn to sacrifice their self-interest in the interests of all the peasants of France (II:ii). The political program advanced on behalf of the Jacquerie by the librettists — the right to approve new taxes, legal equality and the renunciation of noble privileges, abolition of the *taille* and *corvée* — reproduces in every detail the revolutionary initiatives of 1789-91. But in contrast to the successful direct action in *Kassya*, the confrontation between the peasantry and nobility in *La Jacquerie* teaches the dangers of violent political activity. When, despite the hero's attempts to intervene, the peasantry murders the count and burns his chateau, the swift defeat of its just cause ensues.

Peasant heroes superseded noble heroes on the Opéra-Comique stage at a time when the perceived community of interests between the peasantry and the bourgeoisie — who dominated the Opéra-Comique audience — had become one of the foundations of Third Republic politics.[24] In *La Jacquerie*, oblique references to the Revolutionary tradition gave color and substance to a symbolic affirmation of the electoral alliance between the two groups. Librettos that drew directly on the Revolution for plots and characters, and that addressed still unresolved political issues much more explicitly, soon followed.

Godard's *La Vivandière* (OC-1895), the most successful of the French Revolutionary operas, celebrates the military victories of 1794. Act I opens with a chorus of peasants and domestics cursing the local marquis while cheering on the passing Army of the Rhine. The hero is a younger son of the *seigneur* and the only member of his family loved by the common people; having been forbidden by his father to marry a girl of no family, he leaves home to join the republican army. The soldiers' evident bravery, cheerfulness, camaraderie, and filial devotion, the mutual respect and love between soldiers and officers, and especially their success in important battles against invading Germans, all combine to show the republicans in the best possible light. The following year, Cahen's *La Femme de Claude* (OC-1896) reinforced the idea that the republican army was the guarantor of French sovereignty. When the action of the opera begins, a republican general is confidently defending Lorraine from invasion. To emphasize the inseparability of the province, the heroine sings a local folk song about Joan of Arc in Lorraine "saving the country of France" (II:i). Before the vogue for Revolutionary themes expired, Erlanger's *Kermaria* (OC-1897) introduced yet another republican army hero, this time opposed by a brutish Chouan (Breton monarchist) villain.

The rich tableau of revolutionary history held the potential for more pointed political statements as well; *La Vivandière* and *La Femme de Claude* defined for the opera public the acceptable heritage of the First Republic by carefully excluding the ideas and practices of the Jacobins. There could have been little doubt, in the era of Clemenceau, that operatic denunciations of Jacobinism represented a repudiation of contemporary Radical republicanism as well. The Radical leader, himself a prominent devotee of the opera, had made the moral character of revolutionary Jacobin rule one of the touchstone historiographical issues that distinguished Belle Epoque Radicals from other republicans by declaring that the Revolution had to be accepted "*en bloc*" — Robespierre and all. This view, well-known and often quoted as official Radical dogma, had been enunciated by the Tiger during a speech about another theatre piece with a French Revolutionary theme. Victorien Sardou's *Thermidor* had been closed by the police in 1889 after causing riots in the streets; during the Chambre des Deputés debate that followed — which has been described as the most intemperate debate of the whole intemperate Third Republic — Clemenceau's Radical defense of Robespierre almost caused a riot in the Chambre.[25]

At the Opéra-Comique, therefore, the librettists of *La Femme de Claude* could attack contemporary Radicals by portraying a heroic republican general as a victim of the Jacobins, who unjustly imprisoned him on the strength of a false denunciation. Likewise, the hero of *La Vivandière*, after participating in the triumphs of the republican armies, deplores the Jacobins' slaughter of their political opponents, while endorsing the Thermidoreans' reconciliation with defeated adversaries of the Republic. This opera ends happily with the amnesty for political prisoners that ended the Reign of Terror; among the captured Vendéens released by decree of the Convention is the hero's father, the misguided marquis. "Every eye, at this moment, turned to the presidential box, whence came the signal for the bravos," wrote the critic from *Le Gaulois*.[26] Thus the moderate republicans in power in 1893-4, by denouncing the Jacobins of 1793-4 as false and impure representatives of the French republican tradition, contrived to exclude from the reflected glory of the First Republic the Third Republic leftists who were their vocal critics and chief rivals for power. At the same time, they represented on stage a republic prepared to extend the hand of reconciliation to the heirs of the aristocratic tradition.

The staging of Alfred Bruneau's *L'Attaque du Moulin* (OC-1893), with a Louis Gallet libretto based on the work of Emile Zola, made the same point. Zola originally set the piece in 1870-71; he intended to portray the stupidity of war in general, and to humanize Prussian soldiers as sad, lonely, innocent victims of the war, worthy of the sympathy and respect of French civilians. In transposing the time of the action to 1793, and the Prussians into unspecified opponents of the revolution, the Opéra-Comique director Carvalho obviously wanted to capitalize on the interest in the Revolution at the time of its centenary. But his new version altered the political message of the work entirely:

Instead of humanizing current enemies of the French nation, as Zola had in mind, Carvalho's *L'Attaque du Moulin* put opponents of the Republic — the *emigré* ancestors of the subscribers, in fact — in the position of arousing sympathetic, fraternal sentiments from the audience.[27]

Both *La Vivandière* and *L'Attaque du Moulin* should be interpreted in the context of Solidarism — Léon Bourgeois' new broadly based strategy of a general opening to the right. Besides the conspicuous rejection of Radical doctrine at the Opéra-Comique in favor of a conciliatory approach to opponents of the republican regime, just described, the Solidarist approach to the opera manifested itself in two other ways: in the renunciation of any claim to interfere in the Opéra, chief amusement of the traditional right, which precluded the propagation of any republican ideas there at all; and in a tolerant acceptance at the same house of the *abonnés'* attraction to reactionary *Wagnérisme*. A more detailed investigation of the social composition of the Opéra audience, and of their tastes in musical theatre, follows.

1 Léon Husson, "Revue Musicale," *Le Pays* (4/4/1876); Fulcher, *The Nation's Image*, 2, calls the opera "a subtly used tool of the state," and goes on to say: "Official intervention integrally affected the formation of the genre's artistic traits, the audience's construal of their significance, and concomitantly the gradual transformation they sustained in response."

2 *Annales*, 1:17.

3 Henri Avenel, *Histoire de la Presse Française* (Paris, 1900), 652, 685; Bénédict, *Le Figaro*, (4/7/1876).

4 Commission du Théâtre, "Rapport de la Sous-Commission, Question de l'Opéra," B.O. Opéra Archives 19e siècle (321), 23f.

5 Curtiss, *Bizet*, 34. This is the story of the Greek Sapho, not to be confused with a modern-day Sapho whose story Massenet set to music in 1887. After the failure of the Gounod opera in 1851, it was substantially reworked before its 1884 revival.

6 Daniel Halévy, *La fin des notables* (Paris, 1930), 2 vols, I:7; v.II, *La République des Ducs*, 341, 381.

7 See, for instance, the librettist and journalist Louis Davyl, *Les Idées de Pierre Quiroul* (Paris, 1883), 75ff. Cf. Laloy, "L'Opéra," 23. Cf. also Daniel Halévy, *La Fin des Notables*, I:120.

8 Quoted in Bossuet, *Histoire des Théâtres Nationaux*, 19.

9 Quoted in *Ibid.*, 20, and in Antonin Proust, *L'Art sous la République* (Paris, 1892), 79. Cf. Elizabeth Guiliani, "Le Public et le répertoire de l'Opéra à l'époque de J.J. Rousseau," Mémoire de Maîtrise, Université de Paris X, 1970-71, 153, 166, 171; René Guiet, "L'Evolution du Genre: Le Livret d'Opéra en France de Gluck à la Révolution 1774-1793," *Smith College Studies in Modern Languages*, 18 (Oct. 1936-July 1937), 23, 31ff.

10 Louis Blanc, *Histoire de dix ans*, 5 vols. (Paris, 1841-44), IV:481, quoted in Nancy W. Nolte, "Government and Theatre in Nineteenth-Century France: Administrative Organization for Control of the Comédie-Française Repertoire," Ph.D. Dissertation, University of Akron, 1985, 17.

11 Commission du Théâtre, "Rapport de la Sous-Commission," 21-24 passim, 29.

12 Noël and Stoullig mention Vaucorbeil's experience in their account of the appointment, *Annales*, 5:16. The only reference to Vaucorbeil's politics that

I found was a passing one in E. Benjamin's and A. Buguet's gossipy *Coulisses de Bourse et de Théâtre* (Paris, 1882), 156. The best source for Charles de La Rounat is his *Souvenirs et poésies diverses* (Paris, 1886).

13 "Ferry to the Director of the Opéra Vaucorbeil, 7/20/1882," *A.N.* AJ XIII (1194).

14 Proust, *L'Art sous la République*, 91f., 94, 96ff.

15 The character and personal qualities of the typical Belle Epoque opera heroine developed over time in interesting and suggestive ways which elude Catherine Clément, with her synchronic approach and her disregard for all but the best known operas of the period. The heroine of *Maître Ambros*, for instance, has more in common with Jeanne d'Arc than with the frail, retiring heroines of the seventies. The strongest heroine of the earlier period is Suzanne, from Paladilhe's 1878 *opéra-comique* of the same name, but even she comes to regret her self-assurance and her temerity in attempting to acquire a Cambridge University education.

16 My interpretation of the development of Boulangism follows Frederic. H. Seager, *The Boulanger Affair* (Ithaca, N.Y.: Cornell University Press, 1969).

17 Albert Soubies and Charles Malherbe, *Histoire de L'Opéra-Comique*, 2 vols. (Paris, 1892), 2:396. See below, Chapter V. As Boulangism came increasingly to be identified with the new, proto-fascist right, its adherents demonstrated their antagonism towards the values of their former allies on the traditional, monarchist right by rioting against *Lohengrin*. See below, Chapter IV, p.87.

18 "Circulaire de M. le Sous-Secrétaire d'Etat des Beaux-Arts à MM. les Inspecteurs de théâtre, 2/26/1879," reprinted in *Société des Auteurs et Compositeurs Dramatiques: Annuaire*, 7 vols. (Paris, 1887-1915), (henceforth cited as *Société: Annuaire*), 1:139.

19 Chambre des Députés, Séance du 1/29/1891, *Journal Officiel*, 146-149.

20 Thomas J. Sudik, "The French Administration of Fine Arts, 1875-1914," Doctoral Dissertation, University of North Carolina, 1979, 31ff. Cf. "Pas-Perdus," *Le Figaro* (11/25/1890), available also in *A.N.* F XVII 2661; *Le Voltaire* (9/14/1891), available also in *A.N.* F XVII 2662.

21 See below, Chapter IV, p.91. "Rapport fait au nom de la Commission de finance," Sénat No. 111, Année 1910; Chambre des Députés, 2e séance de 2/14/1906, Comte Rendu in Extenso (also available in B.O. Dossier P.A. 1900-1927, P.A. 2/14/1906).

22 *Annales*, 8:122.

23 Paul Farmer, *France Reviews its Revolutionary Origins: Social Politics and Historical Opinion in the Third Republic* (Morningside Heights, N.Y., 1944), 2.

24 Sanford Elwitt, *The Making of the Third French Republic* (Baton Rouge: Louisiana State University Press, 1975).

25 See, e.g., David Robin Watson, *Georges Clemenceau* (N.Y., 1974), 118ff. Cf. Chambre des Députés, Annexe No.2, Enquête de 1891, Commission relative à l'abolition de la censure et à la liberté des théâtres, Séance du 1/18/1892, *Journal Officiel* (1/30/1892), 38, [available also in *A.N.* F XXI (1337)].

26 Interim, "La Soirée Parisienne," *Le Gaulois* (4/2/1895).

27 Bruneau, *A l'Ombre d'Une Grande Coeur* (Paris, 1932), 56; Cf. Jean-Max. Guieu, "Le Théâtre Lyrique d'Emile Zola," Doctoral Dissertation, University of Maryland, 1976, 47.

CHAPTER IV

THE AUDIENCE
AND THE IDEOLOGY
OF THE OPERA

The French aristocracy's continuing refusal to accept the social and political consequences of the Revolution — demonstrated once again in 1889 by its boycott of the centennial exposition in Paris — explains the Opéra management's rejection of librettos based on revolutionary themes like those typical of the Opéra-Comique. The impresario Bertrand, when he was newly appointed director of the Opéra, asked his old friend Emile Bergerat to "Bring me as soon as possible a lyric vehicle [*machine lyrique*] which I'll give to one of our younger composers." But the volatile French Revolutionary libretto that Bergerat brought back was adamantly rejected, much to his disgust, by Bertrand's co-director Gailhard, on the grounds that it was patently offensive to the aristocratic audience: "The Revolution at the Opéra? *Tricoteuses* and *carmagnoles* on the stage? Why not the guillotine? Do you want to drive away the *abonnés*?"[1] The inadmissibility of this material at the Palaïs Garnier, while Opéra-Comique librettos such as *La Vivandière* embraced the principles and accomplishments of the Thermidorean Convention, strongly suggests that differences in the social composition of the two audiences were crucial to the formation of the Belle Epoque opera repertoires.

While at the Opéra-Comique *Kassya* and *La Jacquerie* exposed the antagonism between peasantry and nobility, the aristocratic Opéra tackled the theme of class conflict very differently, pitting the interests of the peasantry against those of the industrial bourgeoisie. In the first act of Bruneau's *Messidor*, a peasant family blames its misfortunes on a factory owner who has devastated the local economy and made himself rich by diverting a vital source of water to his exclusive benefit. The librettist contrasts the greed of the wealthy entrepreneur with the generosity of the patient, understanding peasant hero who gives a glass of the precious water — carried from five miles away — to the industrialist's daughter when she is overcome with heat at their door (I:iv). Though this depiction of a struggle between bourgeoisie and peasantry could be expected to appeal to the aristocracy, the reaction to *Messidor*, when it appeared on stage, indicated that the Opéra audience considered any sort of overt class conflict an inappropriate theme. In responding to Emile Zola's proposal for an opera based on the poem "Violaine," Gailhard manifested his concern for audience sensibilities with the following reference to the *Messidor* controversy:

> The audacities of your theme would alarm a public which we have to reckon with; the precedent of *Messidor* which I produced — as you will acknowledge — with a genuine artistic enthusiasm, is always there to remind me that here we have to take into account the susceptibilities of what you refer to as "castes crazed with extravagance and greed"....[2]

Accurate assessment of the extent to which differences in the social status of the Opéra and Opéra-Comique audiences may have affected directors' decisions about the content of the two repertoires requires a careful comparison of their clienteles, juxtaposed with analysis of the social and political content of the genres — *Wagnérisme* and the *faits divers* — characteristic of *fin-de-siècle* opera at each of the two houses. The available source material permits only a limited articulation of the audiences' social composition and of the tastes of the various components, but some distinctions can be drawn with confidence nonetheless. Audiences consisted of a combination of *abonnés*, who subscribed to a box or stall at the opera during all or part of a season, and occasional patrons who bought tickets for individual performances. While the subscribers provided indispensable stability in the form of consistent long-term income, the rest of the audience determined the immediate financial success or failure of any particular work. Because revenue from the *abonnement* was constant during any given year, operas that generated the greatest receipts must have been favorites of the casual patrons. When, on the other hand, directors retained in the repertoire operas that earned mediocre receipts year after year, they did so to satisfy the *abonnés*. On this basis, it is possible to distinguish the types of opera preferred by the subscribers from those preferred by the occasional clientele.

The regular subscribers consisted of the very highest social, financial, and political elites. Noël and Stoullig, in 1887, referred to the Saturday subscription performances of the Opéra-Comique as the "accepted rendez-vous of Parisian high society," but this description fits the three days of Opéra *abonnement* even better.[3] Contemporary, impressionistic descriptions of the socially prominent subscribers are contradictory, but their names have been recorded, and standard biographical guides provide considerable information about many of them. The casual clientele is more obscure. Analysis of the Opéra price structure provides some insight into the probable lower limits of their social status, and newspaper accounts of an Opéra-Comique fire in 1887 supplement the meager literary evidence with biographical data for thirty-odd victims. There is, moreover, abundant testimony to the exclusion of certain elements of the population from regular attendance at the opera. The well-documented story of private and public initiatives to "democratize" the clientele through free or reduced-price performances, or through Théâtres Populaires that would come to the people in their own neighborhoods, is one of consistent failure.

Regular subscribers to the Opéra leased boxes or orchestra stalls for every Monday, Wednesday and Friday performance, or for one or two of these three days of *abonnement*, during the whole season — a total of 157 shows — or for three or six months at a time. Those who subscribed for all three nights were privileged with access to the backstage area, the coulisses, where they could hobnob with management and with dancers *en deshabille*. On nights when they did not care to attend, subscribers invited friends or clients to make use of their places. With the permission of the director, they could even sublet boxes or stalls for one or two nights a week on a regular basis. They could not, however, dispose of their places on the open market, since denizens of adjacent boxes were easily offended by unsuitable neighbors. In the highest social circles, to subscribe for all three nights was *de rigueur*, and directors scheduled new productions and other major attractions equally among them. None of the three nights was consistently more fashionable than the others, as Saturday was at the Opéra-Comique, or Thursday at the Comédie-Française. Instead, each night in turn had its temporary vogue, as leaders of fashion attempted to stay one step ahead of the gawkers.[4]

Elisabeth Bernard, in her article "L'Evolution du Public d'Opéra de 1860 à 1880," finds that 115 of 520 names on the list of Opéra *abonnés* for the year 1891 were titled. Through the early nineties, at least, L.A.R. the Ducs de Nemours and d'Aumâle, as well as the supreme arbiter of Parisian fashion during the early Belle Epoque, the Prince de Sagan, led the aristocratic patrons of the Opéra, while Princesse Mathilde Bonaparte frequented the Opéra-Comique. Presidents of the Republic had their own boxes at both Opéra and Opéra-Comique, which they used for official receptions of visiting royalty and lesser dignitaries.[5] Bernard points out that in addition the great aristocratic clubs — le Jockey-Club, l'Union, l'Union Artistique, le club des Mirlitons, and that of the rue Royale — took boxes which they made available to members. She concludes nonetheless that the aristocratic influence was in decline by 1891, since "bourgeois dynasties" had enjoyed numerical preponderance for a considerable period of time.[6] The freedom with which noble families and *haute bourgeoisie* intermingled in the orchestra and boxes of the opera, as elsewhere in nineteenth-century French society, seems to rob the distinction of much significance. Pereire, the Rothschilds, and all the biggest names in Parisian financial circles appear on the lists of *abonnés* as well. Many of these bankers invested their capital with the directors, and took an active interest in the affairs of the Opéra.

Contemporary writers acknowledged and deplored dilution of the aristocratic quality of the *abonnement* over time. The librettist and critic Gaston Jollivet complained in 1913: "How many patrician and *haut bourgeois* families have failed to renew their subscriptions or to transfer them to their sons, or their daughters, or their sons-in-law...!"[7] Writers who remembered Second Empire Opéra society tended to stress the decline in social standards under the Republic, while younger men were impressed by the tenacity of the old guard, whose influence seemed to predominate even after the turn of the century. In the late 'eighties, *La Vie Parisienne* contrasted the current habitués of the coulisses — who set the tone for the rest of the subscribers, and had the best opportunities to catch the director's ear — with those of an earlier era. Formerly, the writer argued, the backstage areas "belonged to that privileged core of men of the best society who lived in Paris rain or shine, and who had a monopoly, or near monopoly, on chic and notoriety." The Jockey Club had so dominated backstage that it treated the area as a sort of fief, with the rights of *haute* and *basse* justice. Above all there had been no unknown faces, no interloping provincials, no one of dubious elegance. But by 1889, he lamented, the coulisses were full of

> Tout-Paris and even part of the provinces. Up-and-coming politicians, retired merchants, rich speculators, *la petite juiverie* in force, artists, journalists, men of the world, musicians, friends of the management, clients, *commanditaires*, and proteges of the government. And in the middle of this *alla-podrida*, of this motley, abricadabrant mob, there were a few old subscribers of the old school, lost in the crush.[8]

On the other hand, Paul Morand, a librettist's son, found the same old circles dominating the coulisses as late as 1900, and stressed the importance of social rank as a criterion for membership. In his view, the dancers would take as lovers only members of the Jockey Club or the Cercle Agricole, who were royalist dukes or Bonapartist princes, "men with white beards and bad breath who haven't missed an evening of *abonnement* since 1875."[9] Analysis of the subscriber lists tends to bear out Morand's perception. Until almost the end of the century, they show little turnover except from one generation to another within the family. Since an *abonné* who died usually left his place to his heirs, new applicants sometimes had to wait twenty or thirty years for an opening. Cabinet ministers, Presidents of the Republic, and even the courts intervened to dispose of desirable vacant boxes. Despite steadily rising prices, subscriptions continued to be highly prized and hard to come by. It was not until the 'nineties that they began to become available with any regularity. Even then, turnover averaged no more than 3.7 percent per year between 1892 and 1908; this figure includes tickets bequeathed to sons-in-law with different surnames.[10]

The subscribers who maintained their boxes at the Opéra throughout the Belle Epoque were a remarkably homogeneous group of considerable influence. P.-B. Gheusi, the librettist, journalist and eventual Opéra-Comique director, who arrived in Paris in 1889, was struck above all by the clannishness of Opéra society. He remembered it in his memoirs as a "very exclusive salon," where authentic racing and stock exchange tips were shared behind the safety of the walls.[11] Collectively, the subscribers seem to have had a hand in every serious commercial or governmental enterprise of the Third Republic. Besides

Pereire and the Rothschild family, the *abonnés* whose names appeared in *Qui Etes-vous?* included several of the other important bankers in Paris, prominent government lawyers and judges; engineers and doctors who were Academicians; diplomats; retired military officers, including a former minister of war; a Bordeaux vintner; many deputies; and high officials of the Cour des Comptes.[12] The nucleus of faithful subscribers who appear on the lists of both 1892 and 1908, though diverse in occupation and rank, enjoyed a social cohesiveness that must have multiplied the influence that they derived from their individual positions. They belonged to many of the same clubs, besides, of course, mingling at the Opéra. The most graphic evidence of their shared outlook and community of interests is the proximity of their domiciles. Out of twenty selected at random, thirteen resided in the Faubourg St. Honoré, while another five lived just west of the Avenue Kléber, in a small enclave situated between the Faubourg and the Bois-de-Boulogne (Figure I).

A small amount of turnover among subscribers, while it generated some diversity within the *abonnement* as a whole, also accentuated the distinctive quality of the old guard. While *abonnés* and administrators came and went, the longevity of these senior subscribers, their social cohesiveness, and the power and prestige of their public positions, gave them the leadership of the *abonnés* and increasing influence within the Opéra establishment. As the economic influence of the subscribers, in comparison with that of the casual patrons, varied during the course of the pre-war Third Republic, so did the directors' assessment of their comparative importance. At the Palais Garnier, the proportion of receipts deriving from subscriptions increased from approximately 42 percent during the last years of the Halanzier regime (1875 to 1879) to a high of 64 percent under Bertrand and Gailhard in the 'nineties; the influence of the *abonnés* expanded accordingly. Even after their financial importance began to decline around the turn of the century, directors continued to be most solicitous of subscribers' tastes and preferences. "It is they who keep my theatre alive, and I don't want to drive them away," Broussan said.[13]

Scholars have not as yet attempted to define the composition of the casual clientele with any precision, relying instead on the testimony of contemporary observers who referred to the opera as a bourgeois phenomenon. Just after the turn of the century, in the authoritative

APPROXIMATE LOCATIONS OF RESIDENCES FOR A SAMPLE OF OPERA SUBSCRIBERS, 1892–1909

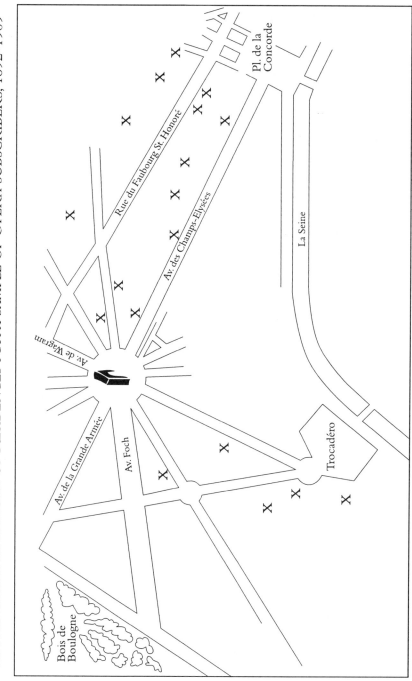

Annales du Théâtre et de la Musique, Noël and Stoullig identified "commerce and the bourgeoisie" as the "clientele of the middle places of the Opéra."[14] But at about the same time, the composer and critic Bruneau reported that there were no bourgeois at all at the Opéra on subscription nights, when non-subscription seats were available through the box office or ticket agencies.[15] Even if these accounts agreed, the imprecision of the term "bourgeois" would make them difficult to interpret. The ticket price structure provides the best clues to the true status of the occasional patrons.

According to the official *cahiers des charges* of the Opéra, prices for individual performances ranged from a minimum of two francs for a few blind seats in the "paradis" up to a maximum of nineteen francs. Even two or three francs was thought to be impossible for the working class; five francs may have been within reach of students and professors. As a result of systematic scalping, however, tickets were never available at their nominal value. During the early years of the Third Republic, management sold the cheaper seats directly to ticket agencies, where three-franc tickets regularly sold for seven, and five-franc tickets cost ten. Even after the government began to oppose this practice, it failed to counter the various stratagems by which the agencies contrived to maintain their monopoly.[16] As a result, the Opéra was prohibitively expensive not only for the working class, but also for the *petite bourgeoisie* and even the lower ranks of professionals. After the mid-'nineties, when the higher ranks of the commercial and professional classes began to join the nobility and *haute bourgeoisie* in seats reserved for subscribers, the rest of the Opéra clientele must have consisted primarily of the middle ranks of the bourgeoisie: successful merchants, senior administrators, ranking professionals, and well-to-do *rentiers*. Except for extraordinary attractions, the least expensive seats of the Opéra were difficult to fill.[17]

Contemporary descriptions of opera audiences stressed the importance of visitors to Paris. Since permanent residents attended only the great premieres and performances by particularly renowned artists, the general public of the Opéra was "composed strictly of *abonnés*, foreigners, and provincials."[18] Visitors who could afford to make one or more trips each year, or who came regularly on business, "constitute[d] an important clientele for the theatres," not least because their predominance enabled directors to limit the number of new productions and reduce the variety of the repertoire, thereby improving their profit margin.[19] During exposition years, tourists from the provinces flooded the capital, but this bonanza for the opera was accompanied by a corresponding drop in receipts in succeeding seasons.[20] While provincials tended to prefer the family-oriented Opéra-Comique, the Opéra attracted wealthy foreigners, especially Russians, who resided in Paris for long periods or passed through on springtime trips to the Côte d'Azur. The presence of large numbers of provincials and foreigners in Paris was a direct result of expansion in the French and international railway systems during the eighteen-sixties. The introduction of a direct St. Petersburg-Nice line just before the turn of the century caused a noteworthy decline in Opéra revenue. "It is a profound modification of habits," the director Gailhard lamented, "and from the economic point of view, upsets the budget of the Parisian theatres, and of the opera theatres above all."[21]

In order to generate a profitable repertoire, Opéra directors had to anticipate the tastes and opinions of this clientele of aristocratic and *haut bourgeois abonnés* and visitors. According to Romain Rolland, the Opéra was "an ostentatious, slightly faded salon, where the public is more interested in itself than in the performance — a theatre of luxury and vanity, created for a clientele of snobs, which doesn't even have the merit of leading fashion, but which follows all fashions with servility, provided they are thirty years old."[22] Analysis of the repertoire bears out Rolland's observation about the audience's preferences. In 1906, not one of the ten most frequently produced operas had been written since the beginning of the Third Republic: *Les Huguenots, Tannhäuser, Le Prophète, Der Freischütz,* and *Guillaume Tell* had been composed during the era of the July Monarchy or before, while *Samson et Dalila, Faust, Sigurd,* and *Aida* all were written between 1848 and 1871. (This is not to say that all had their premieres during the same periods.) The list also includes Gluck's *Armide,* enjoying its first Parisian performances since the days of Louis XVI.

That directors persisted in producing the works of Rossini and Meyerbeer must have been due to the influence of the subscribers, because inferior daily receipts indicated that these operas no longer appealed to casual patrons of the Salle Garnier. In 1905, *Les Huguenots* ranked eleventh in average receipts among fifteen operas in the repertoire;[23] the next year it nonetheless appeared more often than all but one of the others. *Le Prophète* ranked thirteenth in receipts but fifth in frequency of production. Likewise, although Rossini's *Guillaume Tell* earned below-average receipts in 1905, the director Broussan increased the number of performances of this old favorite the following year. Critics of Broussan's regime pointed out that catering to subscribers who no longer enjoyed their former pecuniary importance was disastrous to the financial health of the Opéra in the long run.[24] It was fortunate that some of their favorites, such as *Faust* and *Samson et Dalila*, continued to generate substantial receipts.

The subscribers would never notice, claimed one cynical critic, if some astute director put on *Faust* every night.[25] Indeed, the familiarity of the classics was among their chief virtues, since the audience could spare only minimal attention for the performance, presented in surroundings where concentration on the music was nearly impossible.[26] But the old favorites, especially the historical operas of Rossini and Meyerbeer, also served the social and political interests of the notables among the subscribers. They did so by illustrating the "great man" approach to history — the idea that individuals of transcendent genius determined the course of historical events. Such an interpretation of history appealed to aspiring great men among the aristocrats and *haute bourgeoisie* of the Opéra audience, whose family chronicles told of decisive influence in national and international affairs. It recalled to them a time when the government of the country was entrusted to them for better or worse, and confirmed them in their conviction that they were responsible to no one, that they needed only to consult notions of personal honor in order to determine political rights and wrongs, and that the common people would endorse their actions out of a sense of patriotic duty.[27] The previous chapter described a few of the new operas produced during the mid-'eighties — *Sapho, Henri VIII,* and *Patrie!* — as demonstrating some awareness of the political aspirations of ordinary people. But even in these comparatively egalitarian librettos, the most obvious message is that well-born people arrange public affairs according to their personal interests. *Henri VIII,* for example, limits the parliamentary role of the common people to faithful support for the legitimate king, then marginalizes them as a mere amusing spectacle in the divertissement, a "fête populaire."

The "great man" theme is most clearly illustrated by Massenet's *Le Cid* (O-1885) which, frankly reiterating traditional aristocratic ideology, typified mainstream Palais Garnier opera during the 'eighties. In *Le Cid*, plot and characterizations stayed close to the Corneille original, which extols the virtues of an old regime nobility willing to subordinate itself to absolute royal power. Pride and honor, with their inevitable corollary of revenge, are primary motivating qualities of the hero and heroine. The opera puts particular emphasis on valor, in part the product of heredity, and on loyalty to crown and church, the acknowledged foundations of the social system. The common people love their king, enjoy his largesse, and follow him to a war that has no justification beyond his personal will. They are morally inferior to the nobility, however, because they are more attached to material goods: physical strength and physical love, wine, gold, fêtes, beautiful women, and treasure (IIIF:i). Because they don't believe in heaven or hell, they are either overconfident or defeatist in battle; half of them flee from the field when things start to go badly. The heroic Cid, in contrast, putting complete faith in the Creator, is rewarded with the appearance of Saint Jacques, accompanied by celestial voices promising victory.

If Gallet's, d'Ennery's, and Edouard Blau's libretto of *Le Cid* represented traditional Opéra ideology in its exaltation of aristocratic leadership, it also pointed the way to the future of the repertoire in its intermixture of material and supernatural phenomena, and in the legendary proportions of its hero, whose transcendent nobility is sanctioned by God and the common people as well. In *Le Cid* we see in embryo the Wagnerian genre which swiftly displaced the ubiquitous historical operas at the Opéra, and then continued to dominate the repertoire up until the Great War. Aside from *Le Cid* and one or two other Massenet operas, the only new works embraced by Opéra audiences during the nineties and after the turn of the century were those of Wagner, which filled the hall and enjoyed the particular approval of the *abonnés* as well. In 1905, *Lohengrin*, *Tristan und Isolde*, and *Die Walkyrie* ranked fourth, fifth, and sixth in receipts per performance, and the Paris Opéra was the first house to produce *Parzifal* after the Bayreuth monopoly expired. Between 1891 and 1900, Wagnerian music-dramas accounted for 45 percent of productions of new works at the Opéra. According to Louis Laloy, well-attended productions of Wagner's operas were all that kept the institution solvent after the turn of the century.[28] In my estimation, more than 80 percent of productions of new French operas during the 'eighties also expressed important

Wagnerian elements.

The Belle Epoque notables' enthusiasm for the genre represented a stunning reversal in the fortunes of Wagner, whose works had been banned from Paris since the notorious debacle of 1861, when *Tannhäuser* was hounded off the Opéra stage by the aristocratic Jockey Club. The prejudice against his work extended also to the works of the *Wagnéristes*, French composers and librettists influenced by Wagner's example and by his theoretical pronouncements. In the late 'seventies, the impresario Halanzier rejected Reyer's *Wagnériste* opera *Sigurd* (O-1885) (with a libretto by Camille Du Locle) as soon as he heard the names of the characters. When the composer read the poem to Halanzier's successor, Vaucorbeil, he was told that "a subject like that was unacceptable in Paris."[29] *Sigurd* had to wait sixteen years, until 1885, for a Paris premiere, long after it had established itself abroad. Once it penetrated the repertoire, Gailhard had to subsidize the opera for a hundred performances, until receipts eventually justified its continued presence, because the *abonnés* "adored" it. The state theatres did not produce the works of Wagner himself until the last decade of the nineteenth century. Concert performances of his music helped prepare the way for his operas' eventual return to favor. In 1891, after careful consultation with influential subscribers of the Opéra, with the earliest French friends of Wagner, and with the Department of Fine Arts, the directors Gailhard and Ritt finally presented a tremendously successful production of *Lohengrin*.[30] Subsequently, the operas of Wagner and the *Wagnéristes* quickly conquered the repertoire of the Palais Garnier.

In 1861, opposition to *Tannhäuser* had come from a combination of opera conservatives who objected to Wagner's innovative aesthetics — especially his omission of the traditional ballet — and opponents of Louis-Napoléon's regime, which had made the production a political issue by its conspicuous patronage of a German composer.[31] The same two types of objection — aesthetic and chauvinist — persisted in keeping Wagner and the *Wagnéristes* off the stage for the next three decades. It might appear that the innovative aesthetics of Wagner delayed the acceptance of his operas by reactionary elites to whom the ideological content had become increasingly appropriate. The long-standing objections to Wagner's "music of the future," which gave the composer the capacity to convey his ideas more effectively, were indeed related to the content of the message it imparted. But the audience's attitude towards Wagnerian aesthetics was determined by their response to the ideological content of *Wagnérisme*; a change in this response was a necessary prerequisite to Wagner's readmission to the repertoire after the long hiatus.

Wagner had broken with the traditions of the French opera by omitting the ballet and by emphasizing continuous melody in place of set pieces such as duets, arias, and choruses. He also introduced the innovation of turning the house lights down during performances at the Opéra of Paris. *Wagnériste* disciples adopted specific techniques such as the *leitmotiv*, experimented with Wagnerian harmonies and orchestation, set their own librettos to music, and increasingly sought mythic rather than historical themes. This cluster of characteristics was recognized by Wagner's detractors, as well as his supporters, as having broad implications for the social function of opera and the arts: "A change in music in the opera would lead to a breakdown of the established social order," one critic of Wagnerism proclaimed.[32] Wagner's stubborn insistence on making his librettos intelligible to the audience, and on having the audience pay attention to the stage instead of each other, infuriated Opéra audiences all the more because they objected to the distinctive message associated with Wagnerism. Once they began to embrace it, in the early 'nineties, clearer articulation of the ideas became a virtue. His message may be summed up as an assault on degenerate bourgeois society. It was communicated to the opera public not only from the stage, but also through clear and systematic theoretical works with titles such as *Art and Revolution*, and through the *Revue Wagnérienne*.[33]

The absence of any significant change in the social composition of the Opéra audience in the late 'eighties and early 'nineties precludes attribution of the triumph of Wagner and *Wagnérisme* in Belle Epoque Paris to the tastes of parvenu elements. The alternative — that a shift in the old notables' position within French society altered their response to the political and social content of Wagner's librettos — makes more sense in any case. The rediscovery of Wagner occurred under a regime that threatened to dismantle the remnants of the outmoded social and political system sacred to the memory of the Opéra subscribers.

We need not take seriously Theodor Adorno's idea that Wagner's operas legitimized the existing power structure: "The *Ring*," he claimed, "transforms into transcendent destiny the hegemony of society over the opposition and the functioning of the latter in the service of the bourgeoisie."[34] On the contrary, the operas that dominated the Opéra repertoire in *fin-de-siècle* France recreated an archaic social order that preceded the hegemony of the bourgeoisie. Wagnerism succeeded in Paris the second time around because the values implicit in the operas were by that time appropriate to residual elites threatened with the final eclipse of their political power under the bourgeois republic. On stage, Wagnerian operas denounced everything the Republic stood for; backstage, the coulisses of the Palais Garnier became a center of reactionary opposition to it.[35]

In the operas, as in the view of the declining aristocracy, the restoration of decaying traditional values required completely new leadership. The audience admired the noble character of Lohengrin, who sailed in to straighten out the erring, divided and self-destructive state, and they identified their own interests with his mission. The intrigues of the opera's female villain represented frustrating Third Republic politics as usual, anathema to a class with no hope of controlling the existing political structure. Wagner's protagonists, if they took part in politics at all, did so as heroic outsiders, champions of transcendent principles, uncorrupted by ties to existing political or social structures. Lohengrin, hero of the first Wagnerian opera to be accepted in France, was the archetype of this character. He personified the Napoleonic myth of the divinely ordained outsider who was also acclaimed by the loyal populace, while his impeccable nobility reassured those who continued to dream of the restoration of the anti- and ante-parliamentary monarchy. A similar character plays a central role in *Die Meistersinger*, which first appeared in Paris in 1897, in *Siegfried* (1902), and in *Parzifal* (1914).

This archetypal hero dominates many French *Wagnériste* works as well, such as Massenet's *Le Mage* (O-1891), with a libretto by Jean Richepin. Set in Baktria around 2500 B.C., it is the story of Zarastra, a military hero falsely convicted of treachery to the royal family by corrupt and self-serving priests of the traditional religion. Appealing to Mazda, god of truth, he bids adieu to "the deceitful world; those who doubt his loyalty; sacreligious, lying priests and the gods they serve" (II-B:iii). After a face-to-face confrontation with Mazda on the Holy Mountain, in which the "law of justice" is revealed to him, he imparts it in turn to his disciples, who carry it off to dispense it to their suffering brothers (III:ii). The populace acclaim him as a magus, a role more exalted than kingship, which he disdains (III:i,iv). The opera ends with the obligatory apotheosis, featuring complete destruction of the temple of the superseded gods, with Mazda opening a path through the flames for Zarastra and his beloved.

It is the scale of the crisis, the sense of impending doom, which distinguishes Wagnerian and *Wagnériste* operas from, for instance, *Le Cid*. Whereas the Cid deploys his formidable military and spiritual prowess to assure victory in a war inaugurated by a whim of his ruler (II:iii), the Wagnerian hero's task and accomplishment is world-historical: "Regeneration by Universal Love, taught to the heros by the ruin of egoistic love and the disappearance of the social order that was its *raison d'être*," as Paul Dukas put it.[36] In other words, the hero acts independently of the morally discredited existing power structure. Civilization itself is under siege, if not already doomed; it cannot merely be patched up; it must be reborn. Given the political situation, the opportunities that historical operas had always provided for legitimizing claims to power were no longer relevant to the Opéra audience. When history abandoned them, they turned to transcendental themes in the legendary contexts of *Wagnérisme*, where the social order was not fixed or static, but where changes conformed to the eternal design.

Suitable legends of desperate times, like those in the *Ring* and *Parzifal*, could be drawn from a wide variety of settings. In Saint-Saëns' *Samson et Dalila* (O-1892), as in the Third Republic, Philistines were in power. Suddenly feeling the voice of God in his heart, the hero proposes to the enslaved Jews: "Brothers, let us break our chains and raise up the altar again" (I:i). Salammbô, in Reyer's opera of the same name (O-1892), laments the former martial spirit of Carthage, currently invested by barbarians. Berlioz' long deferred *La Prise de Troie* (O-1899), though obviously not a *Wagnériste* opera, had similarly to wait for a Paris premiere until the audience mentality was sufficiently receptive to the desperate warnings of Cassandra. In Saint-Saëns' *Les Barbares* (1901), set in the first century B.C., 300,000 Germans with no law, no heart, and no God have invaded the district around Orange. *Esclarmonde* (OC-1889), *Thamara* (O-1891), *Frédégonde* (O-1895), *La Cloche du Rhin* (O-1898), *Fervaal* (OC-1898), and after the turn of the century, *Le Fils de l'Etoile* (O-1904), *Prométhée* (O-1907), *La Fille du Soleil* (O-1910), and *Roma* (O-1912) presented comparable themes in divers settings. These *Wagnériste* operas all appeared first at the Palais Garnier, with the exception of *Esclarmonde*, which had its premiere at the Opéra-Comique during the Boulangist reaction of the late 1880s, and *Fervaal*, which switched from Opéra-Comique to Opéra when it was revived in 1912, the only opera to do so during this period.

The latter, written and composed by Vincent d'Indy, himself a descendant of crusaders, was the quintessential *Wagnériste* opera. The prologue begins with a band of common people — half peasants, half bandits — squabbling jealously over precedence as they attack the Celtic hero Fervaal. The theme of incompetent, self-serving, plebian leadership recurs in the first act (I:iii), when a former soldier (Boulanger?) appears to be about to take command; he too gets distracted by mean-spirited bickering while the moment for action passes. In dramatic contrast, the Celts gather in solemn martial council, pervaded by religious ceremonial,[37] to acclaim as chief the one preordained by God (II:ii). On the appearance of Fervaal, the assembled warriors intuitively recognize him as the sole hope of his country. Hitherto consecrated to a solitary, wandering life, he is the last of a race descended from gods, which had been dispersed during the difficult times of recent centuries. Hordes of attacking Saracens provide him with an immediate opportunity to demonstrate his leadership; overcoming the impulse of the beleaguered warriors to scatter to their individual lands, he mobilizes them for the common defense (II:ii). As their political position disintegrated during the *fin-de-siècle*, the audience of the Opéra identified increasingly closely with the implicit messages of works such as *Fervaal*. *Wagnérisme* came to strike a responsive chord with aristocratic audiences, and librettists as well, thirty years late, because they had begun to identify with the heroic outsider as a symbol of opposition to the corrupt, vacillating — in short, bourgeois — Third Republic.

If Wagner's obdurate insistence on aesthetic innovation eventually redounded to his credit among those who responded favorably to his message, what of his close identification with German nationalism, the other fundamental obstacle to his presence at the Opéra between 1861 and 1891? In 1871, Wagner compounded the crime of his German origins with *Die Kapitulation*, an offensive, insulting theatrical piece that made fun of France's recent military humiliation at the hands of Prussia. In response, Saint-Saëns, who previously had acknowledged the influence of Wagner on his own work, repudiated the debt and called for a ban on French performances of the German composer's work. As late as 1889 an attempt to produce *Lohengrin* at the Eden Theatre caused rioting in the streets, and two years later this volatile issue brought, according to some accounts, 40,000 to 100,000 people out in the streets. On the latter occasion, *Lohengrin's* Opéra premiere led to substantial destruction of property, the mobilization of several brigades of armed and mounted gendarmerie, and well over a thousand arrests.[38]

The residual nobility, however, because in many respects it had more in common with the nobility of the rest of Europe than with the bourgeoisie of its own country, was relatively immune to this standard French criticism of Wagner. In fact, the press of the traditional monarchist and clerical right was solid in its support for performing *Lohengrin* in Paris. Not only did these dispossessed elites share Wagner's disdain for bourgeois values and government, but "the hearts of the Wagner lovers are as internationalist as their ears," as the chauvinist, new-right newspaper *l'Autorité* put it.[39] The lower-middle-class proto-fascism of this paper was typical of the anti-Wagnerian newspapers that sponsored and promoted the riots of 1889 and 1891. In the streets, cries of "Down with Wagner!" mixed with "Down with the government!" and "Down with the republic!" Frequent singing of the "Marseillaise" outside the opera house was punctuated by shouts of "Long live the army!" and even "Long live Russia!" in honor of France's new anti-German ally. The chauvinist press naturally tried to portray the rioters as representative of a broadly based spectrum of society,[40] but more reliable papers, buttressed with arrest records, reported that they consisted almost exclusively of petit-bourgeois independent artisans and small shopkeepers. Squeezed by competition from large scale manufacturing concerns, and also by the advent of the department store (first introduced in Paris in the eighteen-nineties), these groups found it increasingly difficult to avoid the slippery descent into the proletariat, whom they feared and despised. They became the social core of the new right, which in the twentieth century took Jacobinism to the extreme of fascism. Only one right-wing paper responded favorably to *Lohengrin*; *Le Petit Parisien* approved of the eponymous hero's character because he "idealizes force in the service of virtue."[41]

Whether the government took the initiative in ordering the production of *Lohengrin* at the Opéra is a matter of dispute. Noël and

Stoullig reported that the ministry was reluctant and apprehensive, but opponents of Wagner, who tended to be critical of the government as well, tied their enemies together: "On the order of the minister, whose grain they eat, all the journalists of the government supported Wagner, excused his injuries to us, and exalted his musical genius, even though nineteen out of twenty of them don't know a single note of his operas."[42] Some republican reviewers of *Lohengrin* managed to find material in it worthy of partisan praise: The mainstream paper *La République Française* quoted a letter from Wagner to Liszt describing the villainous Ortrude as a *"reactionnaire,"* and identifying her with "the immensely foolish passion of noble pride."[43] If, however, as the bulk of the evidence suggests, *Lohengrin* represented an attack on the fundamental values of the Third Republic, the difficult question would seem to be why the government would have tolerated, much less supported, its production at the Opéra? Why not subject the recalcitrant aristocratic audience to a salutary dose of revolutionary ideology instead?

One explanation is that, as an element in the "cultural capital" of their social superiors, Wagnerian opera exercised a considerable attraction on the bourgeois politicians of the 'nineties; this effect will be examined below, in Chapter VII. There were also palpable political benefits, both domestic and international, to be derived at this time from abandoning the repertoire to the subscribers, even to the extent of tolerating anti-republican *Wagnérisme*. The advent of Wagner at the Opéra coincided precisely with Léon Bourgeois' desperate need to shore up legislative support for the principle of state-subsidized opera, and with his much broader strategy of the "opening to the right" as well. In the eyes of their bourgeois rivals, the *abonnés* represented a social class whose economic and cultural influence remained formidable in their political decline, and whose residual political weight retained considerable significance in the unstable alliances of Third Republic parliamentary politics. After 1889, as Brenda Nelms points out, the republican leadership felt able to take the support of the left for granted and set about to "cultivate conservative acceptance, or at least tolerance, of the republican regime."[44] As part of this strategy of the opening to the right — a strategy associated with Léon Bourgeois — the opportunist republicans of the eighteen-nineties adopted a circumspect approach to the chief amusement of the traditional right.

Clearly this precluded the propagation, at the Opéra, of the revolutionary ideas expressed in *opéra-comiques* such as *La Jacquerie* and *La Vivandière*. The Opportunists took their goal of winning over the anti-republican aristocracy to greater extremes by tolerating reactionary *Wagnérisme*.

Reinforcing this strategy were the unacceptable financial and political costs to the government of manipulating the repertoire in the teeth of opposition from the mass of *abonnés*. Any attempt to impose republican operas on the Opéra would have been self-defeating as well as futile; given the weight of the subscribers' importance to the opera budget, alienation of the traditional Opéra clientele would have caused insurmountable financial difficulties for the institution. As the director reminded his minister, "If the Opéra ceases to be the model of distinction in luxury…the greatest perils menace the institution."[45] Among other repercussions for the state, if the *abonnés* had decided to abandon the Palais Garnier, would have been an intolerable decline in the Opéra's international reputation. The government and its political allies were already quite properly embarrassed that Paris suffered from being the only capital where Wagner was not performed; even the French provinces had staged *Lohengrin* successfully. This sort of cultural prestige was of serious concern to the Third Republic, still suspect in the eyes of a reactionary international community sensitive to the threat of social revolution inherent, for them, in the concept of a republic.

From the French perspective, the theatre had an important international role to play:

> The strength of a nation depends not only on armor and cannons, but also on her moral and intellectual power. Above all it is through the theatre that this manifests itself abroad. It is by this that foreigners judge us.[46]

In addition, as the jurist Paul Sorin went on to explain in an influential treatise titled "Du Role de l'Etat en matière de l'Art Scénique," the "moral reputation of a nation is an element in its economic power." State theatre subsidies contributed to economic strength because, Sorin claimed, someone who spent the evening at the Comédie-Française or the Opéra would be better disposed to take seriously the character and industry of France than someone who visited a music hall.[47]

As a sign of the republic's adherence to the norms of cosmopolitan

Old Regime respectability, nothing could have been more powerful than the state opera's cultivation of the oeuvre of Wagner, described by Arno Mayer as "a reflection, prophecy and tool of the persistence of the old order not only in Germany but in Europe as a whole."[48] Such signs were monitored not only in foreign capitals, but also by aristocratic visitors to Paris, among whom, as we have seen, Russians were particularly prominent. Wagner's operas were among the most important icons of Belle Epoque culture in Russia, where they appealed especially to those among the intelligentsia who "feared the influence of bourgeois liberalism."[49] Gratification of the Wagnerian proclivities of Russian aristocrats passing through Paris on their way to Nice, if not a deliberate goal of the government, was at least a welcome side effect of republican tolerance for the French aristocrats' taste for reactionary opera.

That the government was prepared to mobilize the Opéra to gain allies for its political agendas is demonstrated by a series of special gala performances introduced to advertise and consolidate the new alliance with Imperial Russia in 1891. For domestic political purposes, the Opéra-Comique was more useful: After the visit of a Russian naval squadron to France in 1893, Carré, director of the Opéra-Comique, felt constrained by "the political requirements of the hour (*devant les nécessités de l'heure et de la politique*)" to produce *Le Flibustier* (OC-1894), an opera with a French theme by César Cui, one of the "Five" official leaders of Russian music, even though he knew the work would be a failure.[50] It was not coincidental, therefore, that the state should have abandoned the Opéra repertoire to reactionary *Wagnérisme* in 1891, just as it contracted the fragile, indispensible Russian alliance. Indeed, the relationship of the premiere of *Lohengrin* to the recently negotiated Entente was a significant issue for the mainstream press. Supporters of the performance claimed that alliance with Russia boosted France's international stature to a point that now permitted her to be magnanimous toward Wagner. Her newly won international prestige was threatened by the riots, according to this argument, because they appeared in other countries as a puerile, even hysterical reaction to a purely artistic question. After the government ensured *Lohengrin's* continuation in the repertoire by firmly suppressing the demonstrators, the Parisian paper *l'Estafette* quoted a Russian newspaper as saying: "After the admirable conduct of the French government in the

Lohengrin affair…France and Russia can contemplate the future with calm, without fear of being surprised by any eventuality."[51]

The policy of appeasing the nobility, domestic and international, with Wagnerian and *Wagnériste* opera lasted until the appointment of Jacques Rouché as director of the Opéra in 1913. A mass departure of subscribers triggered by the incompetent management of the previous directors Broussan and Messager appeared to the radical-socialist ministry then in power as an opportunity to re-establish government influence over the content of the repertoire. Meanwhile, the community of international aristocratic interests, of which Wagner was such an important symbol, had suffered irretrievably from the increasing antagonism of both French and Russians toward Germany. *Parzifal* made its long-anticipated foreign debut in Paris in 1914, but Rouché's public repudiation of the Palais Garnier's Wagnerian orientation marked an important change in direction for the Opéra. The outbreak of the war prevents us from knowing where he might have steered the Opéra repertoire; however, the only other opera that he introduced before the war, Bachelet's *Scemo* (O-1914), was from the *faits divers* mold popular with the bourgeois habitués of the Opéra-Comique since the turn of the century.

Abonnés always dominated the Opéra much more than the Opéra-Comique, which only introduced its first subscription series in 1885. This immediately attracted a clientele almost as illustrious as the Opéra *abonnement*, and its success led to the introduction of a second day of subscriptions the following year. At the Opéra-Comique, subscribers tended to behave as they did at the Opéra; for them the performance was "only a pretext for meeting each other and examining sumptuous toilettes and sparkling attire."[52] But in a typical year, *abonnés* provided only Fr.450,000 out of total receipts of Fr.2,500,000, or somewhat less than 20 percent of the total Opéra-Comique revenue. Perhaps because they constituted a much smaller proportion of the Salle Favart audience, this richest and most fashionable set did not set the tone; in contrast to the Opéra, most of the audience came primarily to appreciate the show.[53] Because Opéra-Comique directors depended more heavily on the patronage of occasional customers, Opéra-Comique subscribers never acquired the influence over the repertoire enjoyed by their counterparts at the Opéra. Unlike the Opéra, where the range of prices was substantially higher and the general tone more oppressively elegant, seats on the upper levels of the Opéra-Comique were "crammed with regulars."[54] In order to survive in the Opéra-Comique repertoire, operas "required the consecration of the humble public of the upper galleries, of this disinterested public which alone determines success and frequently changes it into triumph."[55]

The most obvious difference between the two audiences was the presence of women and children at the Opéra-Comique. The Opéra systematically restricted the presence of women, who only gradually won the right to occupy the stalls of the balconies and the back of the orchestra. The director Halanzier began to admit them to the orchestra on Saturdays and Sundays over the objections of those who considered that "this measure . . . makes the Opéra a secondary theatre."[56] While boxes and a few individual seats in the amphitheatre were available to both sexes by subscription, the first ten rows of the orchestra continued to be accessible only to men. In contrast, the directors of the Opéra-Comique described their house as "the family theatre par excellence, where even the most scrupulous can confidently escort their wives and children."[57] Indeed, children predominated at Sunday and holiday matinees.

The Opéra-Comique was also one of the traditional venues for matrimonial negotiations, with debutantes on hand for inspection: "And in the midst of this public, where the timid young virgin, surrounded by her family, is to interview, penned up with her parents in the box, the one whom they propose for her husband, . . . the elderly guardians of the antiquated matrimonial traditions" mischievously point out how the action on stage corresponds to what is taking place in front of them. They "hum the tune, wagging their heads in time, [and] wait for the happy moment that will unite two hearts made to understand one another; and then between the two young people passes a soft glance of contentment, and between the parents a nod of agreement."[58] The Odéon theatre took over this role when directors of the Opéra-Comique began to introduce works such as *Manon* (OC-1884), *Esclarmonde* (OC-1889), and especially *Louise* (OC-1900), with plots that subverted traditional ideas of marriage by romanticizing pre-marital sex.[59]

Journalists interested in the victims of a devastating Opéra-Comique fire in May 1887 provided descriptions of individual patrons from the range of types that made up the bulk of the audience.[60] The building was about three-quarters full for a performance of *Mignon*, one of the most popular works of the repertoire. The subscribers in the orchestra managed to escape easily, but several dozen ticket-holders from the upper levels, where the worst of the damage was concentrated, suffered injuries or perished. The newspaper reports confirm contemporary observers' impressionistic descriptions of the Opéra-Comique audiences. A large proportion of the casualties were women,[61] and most were visitors to Paris. Several family groups were in attendance, including a *rentier* from Tours with his wife and nineteen-year-old daughter come to Paris to choose wedding presents. The provincials were all *rentiers* or landowners of one kind or another. George de Miré, a captain of dragoons accompanying his mother and father and his aunt, Mme. de Saage de Saint-Germain from Mons in Belgium, protested afterwards that they had not been satisfied with their second balcony box, but had been unable to get anything better. Other foreigners included a twenty-eight-year-old Norwegian woman who had been in Paris for several years studying French and piano; an Austrian banker and his wife traveling for pleasure, who had that very morning cashed a cheque for Fr.200,000; another banker from Berlin; and no fewer than seven English ladies, five of them unmarried, including one governess.

The Parisian casualties ranged from a seventy-four-year-old *rentier*, who attended either the Opéra-Comique or the Comédie-Française almost every night, to a twenty-year-old living with his parents. A female teacher had taken seats in the second balcony with her crippled mother. Other occupations represented included notary's clerk, student at the Ecole Polytechnique, *restaurateur*, *patissière*, merchant in engravings, and in flowers. The *Gazette des Tribunaux* gave extended coverage to a deceased couple of forty-five and twenty-nine who had taken seats in the second balcony:

> …model workers, of the sort who by their industry and their good conduct frequently raise themselves to the ranks of management and the bourgeoisie. Employed as confidential clerks in a factory that produced pharmaceutical glassware…they had already acquired an interest in the firm, where they lived and boarded in some degree as family of the unmarried owner, who, as one of his letters testified, intended soon to make them his partners, and later his heirs.[62]

These workers, whose presence was so remarkable, apparently define a lower social limit of the relatively heterogeneous clientele of the Opéra-Comique, who would nearly all have felt out of place at the Palais Garnier.

Paltry state subsidies and relatively unimportant subscription receipts forced management to rely on a clientele of genuine music-lovers and patrons of the other operatic arts from upper-class and bohemian circles to supplement this bourgeois and provincial audience. As a result, the Opéra-Comique repertoire was much more innovative than that of the Opéra. This audience encouraged management, especially Albert Carré, to participate actively in current musical developments. Specializing in the *faits divers*, which was virtually unknown at the Palais Garnier, Carré produced all the current works of interest. By the turn of the century, as a result, the Opéra-Comique had completely usurped the leadership of Parisian opera, which its rival had formerly enjoyed. During the period before the war, even German critics went so far as to call the Opéra-Comique "the foremost European opera house," and "the first opera theatre of the world."[63]

If the affinity of the aristocratic Opéra audience for Wagner and the *Wagnéristes* was based on the ideological content of the librettos, with the bourgeois government and press supporting it primarily from pragmatic political considerations, the lack of enthusiasm for the genre among the bourgeois audience of the Opéra-Comique should come as no surprise. After 1882 the Opéra-Comique was entirely free to present operas that did not include spoken dialogue, though directors did need special permission to produce works imported from abroad in translation. Wagnerian operas might have had some difficulty penetrating its repertoire for aesthetic reasons; effective performances of these works benefited from the greater resources and grander scale of the Palais Garnier. The importance of this effect can easily be exaggerated, however. At least one opera from the Wagnerian corpus — *Le Vaisseau Fantôme* [*The Flying Dutchman*] — established itself at the Opéra-Comique, and the archetypical *Wagnériste* opera, *Fervaal*, had likewise been accepted and produced there before switching to the Opéra halfway through its run. The Opéra-Comique planned to perform *Lohengrin* and began rehearsing it in 1886, before changing its mind; after the war, in the 1922-23 season, it produced *Tristan*. Directors of the two houses also competed for the rights to operas by avowed *Wagnéristes* such as Bruneau.[64] If the bourgeoisie had demanded more

Wagner during the 'nineties, librettists could readily have adapted it to the traditions and capabilities of the Opéra-Comique.

The international renown of the second opera house of Paris, achieved despite a state subsidy that remained "derisory" in comparison with that of the Opéra,[65] was based instead on a completely different style known as "*faits divers*" opera. Named with reference to the genre of newspaper article devoted to violent crimes of passion and freak accidents, the *faits divers* featured, in contrast to the mythical noble heroes of *Wagnérisme*, lower-class characters in lower-class settings. This style of Opéra-comique reproduced the ideology of the sovereign bourgeoisie rather than that of the residual aristocracy. Its success depended on a combination of avant-garde aesthetics and a conservative ideology appropriate to the needs of the established bourgeoisie conscious of lower-class threats to its newly won hegemony.

Faits divers opera can be identified with "*verismo*," but must be carefully distinguished from operatic "*vérisme*." Though both operatic genres owed their origins to literary Naturalism, they developed in very different directions. Central to the issue, and to the confusion, is the work of Emile Zola, French Naturalism's most prominent exponent. Zola's willingness to tackle sordid, provocative themes dealing with relationships between members of subordinate classes forced his readers to confront unpleasant social realities. Because Naturalism threatened the interests of those who benefited from the status quo, it aroused bitter enmity within the conservative establishment. One prominent critic remarked that the muckraker Zola had entered the Augean stables — to make a contribution.[66]

So-called *vériste* opera is closely associated with the name of Zola; indeed, it arrived at the Opéra-Comique in a series of librettos written or edited by him. But by the time he began writing for the opera late in his career, Zola's aesthetics had changed profoundly, to the point where he must be considered to have abandoned Naturalism. The extensive use of symbolism and poetry in Zola's *vériste* librettos — written for the *Wagnériste* composer Alfred Bruneau — produced a lyrical quality in them that was absent in his earlier work. They represented the avant-garde for the Opéra-Comique audience, because of the association with Zola's name and reputation, but the lower-class characters in his operas acted very differently from those of his Naturalist novels. Highly idealized in comparison with the protagonists of *La Terre* or *Germinal*, they were much more charming and somewhat less shocking. Zola's librettos shared these characteristics with other *vériste* works performed at the Opéra-Comique, such as those of Gustave Charpentier and Puccini.[67]

Zola's composer Bruneau, in an important book on the subject, distinguishes the aesthetics of this lyrical *vérisme* from that of brutal, shocking, Naturalist *verismo*, progenitor of the *faits divers*.[68] He identifies the former as typically French, and the latter as characteristically Italian, but this national distinction is misleading both because Puccini's substantial oeuvre belongs with *vérisme*, and because numerous French operas — those in the predominant *faits divers* style — display the characteristics of the supposedly Italian *verismo*. More significant is the different ideological stance of the two genres. We should not be misled by the *véristes* ("realists") own valuation of their work into concluding that there was anything realistic about their portrayals of lower-class existence. But the *véristes* at least addressed social issues in their works, even if their conclusions turned out to be more romantic than revolutionary. The ideological content of the *faits divers*, though its themes were Naturalist and its effects aesthetically innovative, distanced itself even further from the threat represented by Naturalism.

Writers who embraced the *faits divers* shared the benefits and drawbacks of Zola's reputation for socially engaged muckraking; they facilitated adoption of the *faits divers* by bourgeois audiences by helping them to maintain the illusion that they were patronizing a socially progressive movement, (incidentally misleading later historians and critics as well). But by the turn of the century the *faits divers* librettists had abandoned Naturalism's original radical political implications, and grafted a fundamentally conservative message onto the aesthetic stock of the movement. These librettists cultivated a myth of the common people that deflected all serious consideration of social issues by objectifying the lower classes as the "other." In *faits divers* opera, society is static and unchanging; lower-class characters neither solve their problems through social action, nor escape them through social mobility. They are victims of a horrible fate which they bring upon themselves. Their only recourse is to react with more passion and violence to the passion and violence endemic in their social environment. It sweeps through these operas like some ineluctable natural disaster, often symbolized on stage by an avalanche or flood.

According to the *faits divers* librettos, the unending crimes and miseries that constitute the life of the lower classes originate not in social or institutional structures, but in undisciplined emotion. Laparra's *La Habanera* (OC-1908), for instance, begins with thirty-one prisoners in a local jail; one is there for larceny, and the other thirty for crimes of love. The ensuing action, in which the pathological jealousy of the protagonist leads him to stab his brother to death on the latter's wedding day, conveys the idea that the ungovernable passions and lack of restraint of the lower classes are responsible for their domestic tragedies. The opera is suffused with a climate of brooding menace which manifests itself in bloody sunsets, sudden windstorms, and other occult phenomena, reinforcing the notion that lower-class existence is fundamentally irrational.

Likewise, in Isidore de Lara's *Sanga* (OC-1908), the contrast with *vérisme* is plain. *Sanga* has all the elements of a drama of social injustice: in the first act, a cruel and avaricious landlord forecloses on a tenant who cannot pay the rent; he also evicts a female harvest laborer secretly engaged to his son. But the audience is prevented from drawing any subversive conclusions, or even from sympathizing with the downtrodden and oppressed, by the repellent personal characteristics with which the librettists invest the poor victims. The dispossessed tenant turns out to be an obvious good-for-nothing, the patron's son is shamefully weak, and the working girl becomes spiteful and vindictive after her disappointment. She invokes the avalanche curse on all of them as she leaves, and the opera reaches its climax in a flood of self-destructive passion. In the end, the patron goes mad, cursing God and the land as he throws his money into the rising water. The heroine attempts to rescue her lover by boat, but he prefers to drown himself, so she jumps in as well.

It is not the social situation that is responsible for this wild and extravagant behavior, but the characters and personalities of the individuals involved. Like the avalanche and the flood, the self-destructive tendencies of the working-class characters are implacable, inevitable, and natural. In *Le Pays* (OC-1913), a Breton fisherman who has abandoned his pregnant wife blindly stumbles into a thawing, sucking swamp in Iceland. Wolf-Ferrari's *Les Joyaux de la Madonne* (OC-1913) features a young woman whose sexual passion is aroused by wearing jewels stolen from the cortege of the Madonna; she drowns herself in the Bay of Naples.[69] Again, as in other *faits divers* operas, the focus is on the criminality, the immorality, and the irrationality of the lower classes rather than on the social and material circumstances of the characters' existence. Most horrible of all the genre is Sylvio Lazzari's *La Lépreuse* (OC-1912), the story of a Breton peasant girl who chooses not to reveal to her lover that she has leprosy. Her mother spends her life deliberately infecting young children with the disease that has made her own life miserable. The whole last act consists of a dismal official and religious ceremony that separates the newlyweds from society and joins them to the colony of dying lepers.

Denying the legitimacy of lower-class grievances by portraying the misery of the poor as a natural and objective phenomenon — as the just and inevitable consequence of their irrational patterns of ethical behavior — would have enabled the Belle Epoque bourgeoisie to dissociate itself from the social question and the need to arrive at solutions. But if the attitudes towards the social question implicit in the *faits divers* Opéra-Comique librettos are to be imputed to the *fin-de-siècle* French bourgeoisie, a substantial change in bourgeois mentality must have occurred. How do we account for the sudden obsolescence of the politically engaged, relatively egalitarian representations of class relationships characteristic of the historical librettos of the eighteen-eighties and eighteen-nineties? The creation and promotion of the discipline of functional sociology in French academic life during exactly the same period represents a precisely analogous shift in ideological paradigms, and suggests a key to the answer. Just as historical opera librettos that celebrated the rise of republican and democratic values gave way to the static *faits divers* style, Auguste Comte's evolutionary sociology, which postulated the perfectibility of mankind and human institutions, succumbed to the invasion of academic circles by Emile Durkheim's functional approach to social issues.

As Rosalind Williams suggests, the implication of Durkheim's view of social problems such as violence, suicide, and so on, is that they occur in societies that insufficiently restrain individual passions.[70] His fascination with the prevalence of suicide and criminality as endemic elements of lower class society exactly mirrored the preoccupations of the *faits divers* librettists. Alvin Gouldner's explanation for the success of functional sociology applies equally well to the emergence of the *faits divers*: It results from a change in the relative social position of the bourgeoisie vis-à-vis other social classes. According to Gouldner: "Functional sociology, with its ahistorical character and its emphasis upon the *ongoing* consequences of existent social arrangements, reflects the loss of historical imagination that corresponds to the mature entrenchment of the middle class, which no longer fears the past [by which he means "the middle class was secure from the restoration of old elites"] and neither imagines nor desires a future radically different from the present."[71] Gouldner suggests that the middle classes could adopt the functional approach only when they "did not look upon the past as a threat and did not believe that the future required anything radically different." Until the menace of the old elites' residual power had been effectively eliminated, the middle classes retained an interest in continued social change, promoted in the academy by Comte's positivism and in the opera by historical librettos. But "when the institutional requirements of commercial industrialism were fully established," further social change could only weaken the hegemony of the bourgeoisie; from that point on, the chief threat was from ambitious subordinate classes rather than from residual elites.[72]

Traditionally (although it had been eroding since 1848), an alliance between bourgeoisie and lower classes had been the foundation of the republican struggle against monarchist *notables* entrenched in French politics. During the early years of the Third Republic, the allied bourgeoisie and peasantry had been

> fighting to assert their liberal-democratic ideal against a traditional governing class whose power depended on the maintenance of a more heirarchical and authoritarian political structure.... But the alliance of bourgeoisie and peasantry soon found itself defending its essentially negative conception of the role of the state against new classes — the industrial proletariat and part of the urban lower middle class....[73]

After the turn of the century, the working class developed an increasingly militant class consciousness based on trade-union activity; this forced a reconciliation between the traditional right and the bourgeois republicans. Their mutual fear of socialism and their aversion to the new right led to the "opening to the Right" described above and to the Ralliement of Roman Catholics behind the republic, both manifestations of this reconciliation. The humanitarian appeal of the socialist left gave particular impetus to the rise of Solidarism, promoted (by Emile Durkheim among others) as a sort of organic republican substitute for liberal individualism. The timing of this change in Third Republic politics coincides with the ideological shift toward functional sociology and *faits divers* opera.

By presenting a static and unchanging picture of society after the turn of the century, both the sociologists and the librettists adapted to the evolving interests of the bourgeoisie who employed them. The works of both groups catered to the governing classes' objective interest in lower-class violence and criminal activity and reflected their utter indifference to its consequences. Indeed, the characteristic reluctance of the *faits divers* operas to address social issues constructively had its counterpart in the legislative inactivity of all pre-war Third Republic governments, even the radical ones. Gambetta denied that there was a "social question," and Clemenceau ordered his troops to fire on striking French workingmen. Though the republican bourgeoisie had been eager, until the Ancien Régime was definitively displaced, to co-opt the lower classes through electoral alliances, it refused to acknowledge their legitimate grievances, or to contemplate changes in the basic economic or social structure of France.

1 Quoted in Adolphe Brisson, *Portraits intîmes*, Série III (Paris, 1897), 40f. On the centennial exposition, Brenda Nelms, *The Third Republic and the Centennial of 1789* (N.Y.: Garland, 1987), Modern European History Series, 158.

2 "Gailhard to Emile Zola, 16 December 1901," in folder "Violaine, poème d'Emile Zola (Correspondance)," *A.N.* AJ XIII (1098-99).

3 *Annales*, 13:134.

4 For the history of the fashionable night, see Laloy, "L'Opéra," 27. Cp. Gaston Jollivet, *Souvenirs d'un Parisien* (Paris, 1928), 251; Labruyère, "Physiologie Parisienne," *Le Figaro* (12/7/1885). The most complete description of the system of subscriptions obtaining at the Opéra is Elisabeth Bernard, "L'Evolution du Public d'Opéra de 1860 à 1880," *Régards sur L'Opéra* (Paris: PUF, 1976), 37.

5 For the Prince de Sagan's remarkable position in French society, see Jules Bertaut, *L'Opinion et les Moeurs* (Paris, 1931), 186f. It was he, following the debacles of 1870-71, whom the management of the Comédie-Française asked to select from the applicants for subscriptions those who would guarantee the social success of the revived institution. He was also responsible for reviving the Opéra-Comique subscription series. See Gaston Calmette, "Les Samedis de l'Opéra-Comique," *Le Figaro* (12/3/1885). For a complete list of Opéra subscribers for the 1892-1893 season, A. LaFare, *Opéra et Comédie-Française: Carnet des Abonnés* (Paris, n.d.). I counted 105 princes, dukes, counts and barons among 573 subscribers in 1892, approximately 18 percent of the total. Laloy provides a useful short list in "L'Opéra," 26. For comparable statistics from the 1830s, cf. Gerhard, *Die Verstädterung der Oper*, 32.

6 Bernard, "L'Evolution du Public d'Opéra," 38f.

7 *L'Autorité* (11/3/1913).

8 "Les Coulisses de l'Opéra," *La Vie Parisienne* (4/13/1889). "Autrefois" presumably refers to the period prior to 1879; see Bertaut, *L'Opinion et les Moeurs*, 120f.

9 Paul Morand, *1900* (Paris, 1931), 197f.

10 These figures are derived from comparison of subscriber lists from 1892 and 1908. For cabinet interference in the assignment of boxes, see the article "Constans le Goujat," *L'Intransigeant* (2/19/91) [available in *A.N.* F

XVII (2661)]. On the demand for subscriptions, Bernard, "L'Evolution du Public," 37. Cf. "Revue des Théâtres Lyriques," *Revue et Gazette Musicale de Paris*, 42e année no.3 (1/17/1875), 21.

11 Gheusi, *Cinquante Ans*, 3:73f.

12 A complete list of *abonnés* for the year 1908 is available in *A.N.* AJ XIII (1193); *Qui Etes-Vous? 1908-9* (Paris, 1909).

13 Quoted by George Berry in a Chambre des Députés speech: Chambre des Députés, 1e séance, 1/26/1910, *Journal Officiel*, 344, (available also as B.O. P.A. 1/26/1910). In 1910, when Broussan started to require customers of the middle seats to pay the surtax on their tickets known as the "Droit des Pauvres," he exempted the *abonnés*. For a comparison of receipts derived from subscriptions and from the box office by various directors, see "Moyennes comparatives des Recettes et des Dépenses par Direction et par représentation," *A.N.* AJ XIII (1202). The proportion derived from subscriptions dropped gradually from the mid-nineties until 1908-09, when large numbers of *abonnés* abandoned their subscriptions. See the untitled report of the Director to his *commanditaires* for the year 1911, *A.N.* AJ XIII (1187), and a question in the Chambre des Députés, reported in the *Journal Officiel* 4/2/1909 no.91, [also available in *A.N.* AJ XIII (1194)], referring to the drop in subscriptions that year. For comparisons with the July Monarchy and Second Empire, Gerhard, *Die Verstädterung der Oper*, 34f.

14 *Annales*, 29:16n. For modern estimates of class composition: Link, *Literarische Perspektiven*; Heinz Becker, "Die Historische Bedeutung der Grand Opéra," in W. Salmen, ed., *Beitrage zur Geschichte der Musikanschauung im 19. Jahrhundert* (Regensburg: Bosse, 1965); Jeuland-Meynaud, "Légitimité de la Librettologie," 68f. Adorno's analyses of opera texts and music in the chapter entitled "Bürgerliche Oper," in *Klangfiguren* are much more carefully articulated than his analysis of the society he relates them to. For a more sophisticated analysis of the "bourgeois" quality of nineteenth-century opera audiences in general, see C.-H. Mahling, "Zur Frage der 'Bürgerlichkeit' der bürgerlichen Musikkultur im 19. Jahrhundert," *Musica* 31 (1977), 15. Gerhard, *Die Verstädterung der Oper*, 4, talks about the "*Verbürgerlichung*" of the opera from as early as the seventeenth century, but in the text of his work, he refers frequently to the influence of the aristocratic clientele on the content of the repertoire.

15 Bruneau, *Musiques de Russie*, 117f.

16 On the question of scalping, see "Ministry of the Interior to Ministry of Public Instruction, 6/28/1899"; "Opéra Directors to Minister of Public Instruction, undated"; "Minister of Public Instruction to Opéra Directors,

7/7/1899," *A.N.* AJ XIII (1006). On the difficulty of obtaining inexpensive tickets through the box office, see "Jules Thiriaux to M. Simonnot, Administration Général du Théâtre National de l'Opéra, 8/23/1906," dossier "Location: Lettre de Réclamation 1906," B.O. Opéra Archives 20e siècle 449. Cf. "Chef du Bureau des Théâtres to Director of Opéra," dossier "Location: Incidents 1876," B.O. Archives Opéra 19e siècle 477. For the ticket price structure, see, for example, the *cahiers des charges* reproduced in de Pezzer, "L'Opéra devant la loi," Article 22, 131f. On its implications for various classes of potential patrons, see the Chambre des Députés debate, 1/26/1910, 1e séance, reproduced in *Journal Officiel*: 344-356, passim (available also as B.O. P.A. 1/26/1910). Cf. "L'Opéra Démocratique," La France (1/5/1892) [available also in *A.N.* F XVII (2662)]; Romain Rolland, *Paris als Musikstadt*, trans. Max Graf (Berlin, 1904), 55; Gerhard, *Die Verstädterung der Oper*, 34.

17 "Ritt et Gailhard to M. le Directeur du *Matin*, 12/14/1888," B.O. Fonds Rouché, Pièce 119, 300ff.

18 "Paradoxe sur l'Opéra," *Dépêche de Toulouse* (11/5/1913). Cf. "L'Hebdomadaire," *Le Petit Républicain-Rouen* (11/8/1913).

19 Jumelles, "Le Théâtre Meurt," *Le Voltaire* (3/20/1901) [also available in *A.N.* F XXI (1339)]. For the implications for variety in the repertoire, V. Joncières' "Préface," *Annales*, 6:vii.

20 For a detailed analysis of the provincial visitors' habits, Commission des Théâtres, "Rapport de la Sous-Commission, Question de l'Opéra," B.O. P.A. 1871-1879. Cf. Jumelles, "Le Théâtre Meurt."

21 Interviewed by Jules Clarétie in "Paris l'Hiver," *Le Journal* (10/5/1900) [also available in *A.N.* F XXI (1339)]. Cf. Maurice Descotes, *Le Public de Théâtre et son Histoire* (Paris: PUF, 1964), 310ff. For a comparison of the visitors to the Opéra and Opéra-Comique, Frédéric Henriet, *Monographie du Spectateur au Théâtre* (Paris, 1892), 84.

22 Rolland, *Musiciens d'aujourd'hui*, 225.

23 Not counting operas that were presented fewer than three times. Beginning in 1903, receipts from each Opéra and Opéra-Comique performance were listed monthly in *La Revue Musicale*.

24 For criticism of Broussan, see for example, G. de Pawlowski, "M. Jacques Rouché est nommé de l'Académie Nationale," *Comoedia* (10/31/1913). It is only fair to mention that he was criticized also by those who believed that his financial difficulties stemmed from paying too little attention to the wishes of the *abonnement*.

25 "Paradoxe sur l'Opéra."

26 See below, Ch.VI, p.157.

27 Cf. Jean Duvigneaud, *Sociologie du Théâtre* (Paris: PUF, 1965), 35; Gerhard, *Die Verstädterung der Oper*, 274f.

28 Louis Laloy, "L'Opéra," 87. Cf. Report of the *commanditaires* of the Opéra, 1911, *A.N.* AJ XIII (1187).

29 For the best account of Reyer's difficulties in placing *Sigurd* at the Opéra, Adolphe Jullien, "Revue Musicale," *Le Français* (6/15/1885).

30 *Annales*, 17:20. For *Sigurd*, Laloy, "L'Opéra," 69; *Annales*, 13:2. *Sigurd* ranked only twelfth in average receipts during 1905, but sixth in number of performances the following year.

31 Réné Peter, *Le Théâtre et la Vie sous la Troisième République* (Paris, 1945), 188; Gerald Dale Turbow, "Art and Politics: Wagnerism in France," in David C. Large and William Weber, eds. *Wagnerism in European Culture and Politics* (Ithaca, N.Y.: Cornell University Press, 1984), 147-151, 154ff. Cf. Fulcher, *The Nation's Image*, 189-194; Ursula Eckart-Bäcker, *Frankreichs Musik zwischen Romantik und Modern: Die Zeit im Spiegel der Kritik* (Regensburg: Bosse, 1965), 122ff; Bernard, "L'Evolution du Public," 33f. According to an untitled and undated memorandum in the folder "Lettres concernant R. Wagner, 1891-1905," *A.N.* AJ XIII (1198), Opéra management was still worried several years later about an attempt to revive *Tannhäuser*.

32 Achille de Lauzière in *La Patrie*, quoted in Christian Goubault, *La Critique Musicale dans la Presse Française de 1870 à 1914* (Geneva and Paris: Slatkine, 1984), 46.

33 Richard Wagner, *Art and Revolution, Richard Wagner's Prose Works*, William Ashton Ellis, translator, 8 vols. (N.Y., 1892-99).

34 Theodor Adorno, *Essai sur Wagner*, trans., Hans Hildebrand and Alex Lindenberg (Paris, 1966), 189.

35 Morand, *1900*, 197f.

36 Paul Dukas, *Revue hebdomadaire* (3/27/1897), reprinted also in *Fervaal devant la Presse* (Paris, 1897), 13.

37 Cf. Robinson, *Opera and Ideas*, 113f.

38 "La Soirée," *Le Gaulois* (9/17/1891); "*Lohengrin* A l'Opéra," *La Patrie* (9/18/1891). The highest estimates came from journals opposed to the

performance, and which had an interest in exaggerating the size of the demonstrations. All accounts agree that over 1,000 were arrested. For Saint-Saëns' reaction to *Die Kapitulation*, "Introduction," *Harmonie et Mélodie* (Paris, n.d.).

39 Paul de Cassagnac, "Assez d'Allemand!" *L'Autorité* (9/18/1891). Journals of the old, aristocratic right that supported *Lohengrin* included *Le Soleil*, *L'Echo de Paris*, *Le Gaulois*, *Le Figaro*. Cf. Goubault, *La Critique Musicale*, 36. On the international outlook of the *abonnés*, cf. Gerhard, *Die Verstädterung der Oper*, 346.

40 Joseph de Godlewski, "Paris 17 Septembre," *Gazette de France* (9/19/1891); "Lohengrin à l'Opéra," *La Patrie* (9/18/1891); "Les Assomeurs du roi de Prusse," *L'Intransigeant* (9/19/1891).

41 P.G., "Lohengrin à l'Opéra," *Le Petit Parisien* (9/18/1891).

42 Henri Rochefort, "Le Vrai Malade," *L'Intransigeant* (9/15/1891); *Annales*, 17:20. In *La Critique Musicale*, 235, Goubault says *Lohengrin* was produced "sous l'influence du Gouvernement." Cf. "Théâtres et Concerts," in the well-respected *Journal des Débats* (9/9/91).

43 Alphonse Duvernoy, "Revue Musicale," *La République Française* (9/21/1891).

44 Nelms, *The Centennial of 1789*, 173.

45 "Director of the Opéra to Minister of Public Instruction, 2/5/1886," *A.N.* AJ XIII (1194).

46 Paul Sorin, "Du Role de l'Etat en matière d'Art Scénique," Thèse pour le Doctorat, Faculté de Droit de l'Université de Paris, 1902, 19. Cf. 99ff.

47 *Ibid.*, 20.

48 Mayer, *The Persistence of the Old Regime*, 212.

49 Bernice Glatzer Rosenthal, "Wagner and Wagnerian Ideas in Russia," Large and Weber, eds. *Wagnerism*, 217. Rosenthal considers that Wagner, along with Nietzsche, was the most important influence on the formation of Russian "Silver Age" high culture. The ongoing connection between Russian Wagnerism and the Paris Opéra shows up most clearly in Diaghilev's Ballets Russes, which made a sensational debut there in 1909: "Already captivated by Wagner, Paris hailed the Russian spectacles as a triumph of the *Gesamtkunstwerk* ideal," *Ibid.*, 210.

50 Carré, *Souvenirs*, 174f.

51 "Le 'Lohengrin' et la Russie," *L'Estafette* (9/25/1891).

52 *Annales* 17:134. Cf. Gaston Calmette, "Les Samedis de l'Opéra-Comique." For the introduction of the subscription series at the Opéra-Comique, *Ibid.* Cf. Albert Soubies and Charles Malherbe, *Histoire de L'Opéra-Comique*, 2:396. A complete list of Opéra-Comique subscribers for the year 1885 can be found in *Le Figaro* (12/3/1885).

53 Henri Moreno, "Semaine Théâtrale," *Le Ménestrel*, 42e année no.16 (3/19/1876), 123. For Opéra-Comique finances, see "Opéra-Comique" in E. Magnen and E. Fouquet, *Le Théâtre et ses Lois* (Paris, n.d.), 266.

54 Gheusi, *Cinquante Ans*, 4:315. Cheapest seats at the Opéra-Comique were 75 centimes.

55 *Annales*, 34:131.

56 *L'Opéra et M. Halanzier: Extraits du Journal "La Presse"* (Paris, 1877), 21. Even then, in 1880 an Assemblée report concluded that "the number of inexpensive places is very limited, and the majority of these are not available to women or children." "Rapport à la Chambre des Députés par Lockroy, membre de la Commission du budget, 1880," Chapter LI, 89, available in *A.N.* AJ XIII (1202).

57 "Exposé de la Situation du théâtre de l'Opéra-Comique présenté à MM. les Membres de l'Assemblée nationale par la direction du théâtre," dossier "Documents financiers," B.O. Opéra-Comique Archives 19e siècle 42, 7.

58 "Les Théâtres," *Le Rappel* (3/6/1875).

59 Pierre Giffard, *La Vie au Théâtre* (Paris, n.d.), 96. Cf. *Annales*, 26:83; Benjamin and Buguet, *Coulisses*, 158. Cp. Chambre des Députés, 2e séance de 2/14/1906, Comte Rendu in Extenso, *Journal Officiel*, 750 (available in B.O. Opéra Dossier P.A. 1900-1927, "P.A. 2/14/1906").

60 Information in the following paragraphs has been compiled from newspaper articles collected in the dossier "Incendie de l'Opéra-Comique," B.O. Opéra-Comique Presse 1887. The most complete description of the victims appeared in *Le Cri du Peuple* (5/29/1887).

61 The proportion of women among the casualties (approximately five women:three men) may have exceeded the proportion of women in the audience as a whole if cumbersome clothing hampered their attempts to escape.

62 "Tribunal Correctionel de Paris," in *Gazette des Tribunaux* (11/28-29/1887), 1145 (available also in dossier "Incendie de l'Opéra-Comique," B.O. Opéra-Comique Presse 1887).

63 Reported in Stephan Stompor, "Ein Opernhaus und seine Gattung," *Musikbühne* (1974), 141. Cf. Rolland, *Paris als Musikstadt*, 19.

64 Bruneau, *A l'Ombre*, 105, 109; Guieu, "Le Théâtre Lyrique d'Emile Zola," 59. For legal restrictions on the repertoires, "Nouvelles Diverses: Paris et Départements," *Le Ménestrel*, 48e année no.15 (3/12/1882), 115. On *Lohengrin* at the Opéra-Comique, Richard Servières, *Richard Wagner jugé en France* (Paris, 1887), 292. Management bowed to pressure against performing it from composers, music editors, and critics, according to Servières. On *Tristan*, Pierre Andrieu, *Souvenirs des frères Isola* (Paris, 1943), 164.

65 Carré, *Souvenirs*, 316.

66 Quoted in Jollivet, *Souvenirs*, 29.

67 See below, Ch.VII, p.204f.

68 Bruneau, *Musiques de Russie*, 271.

69 Wolf-Ferrari's opera does not technically qualify as a French opera under my definition, because it was composed to an Italian text, but its world premiere took place in French translation at the Opéra-Comique.

70 Rosalind A. Williams, *Dream Worlds: Mass Consumption in Late Nineteenth-Century France* (Berkeley: University of California Press, 1982), 327.

71 Alvin W. Gouldner, *The Coming Crisis in Western Sociology* (N.Y.,: Basic Books, 1970), 107.

72 *Ibid.*, 107.

73 R.D. Anderson, *France 1870-1914: Politics and Society* (London: Routledge & Kegan Paul, 1977), 38, 41.

74 Debra L. Silverman, *Art Nouveau in Fin-de-Siècle France: Politics, Psychology and Style* (Berkeley: University of California Press, 1989) 46, 48f.

CHAPTER V

THE OPERA
AS PUBLIC INSTITUTION

Analysis of the content of the two state opera houses' repertoires in conjunction with the social composition of their audiences shows that audience response, as interpreted and anticipated by the directors, must have played a decisive role in determining the ideology of the librettos. But while opera librettos reproduced ideological premises that might be imputed to the patrons who kept the institutions prosperous, the mechanisms controlling this congruence are by no means obvious. It seems implausible that librettos should have been selected for production according to conscious decisions based on the ideological requirements of any particular class (though they were sometimes rejected on those grounds). Even if bourgeois opera patrons had the will and capacity to manipulate the content of the librettos, it is difficult to imagine them concluding that their interests would be served by, for instance, portraying peasants in a favorable light on the stage of the Opéra-Comique. What then does it mean to suggest that *Kassya* and *La Jacquerie* served as symbolic affirmation at the opera of an electoral alliance between bourgeois and peasant capitalists?

What Pierre Bourdieu calls "the quasi-miraculous correspondence prevailing at every moment between the products offered by a field of production and the field of socially produced tastes"[1] may in this case be attributed simply to the product of free market forces. Because of the difficulty of accurately anticipating audience reactions to new works, directors continually presented a range of options to their clientele. As a result, within limits defined over time by controversies over works such as *Carmen*, *Messidor*, and *Louise*, opera retained a considerable capacity for adapting to long-term shifts in social attitudes. Opera patrons supported by their presence those operas that made them feel comfortable by reinforcing their prejudices; they need not have been aware of the process, nor of the implicit ideological content of their favorite works. Plenty of evidence suggests that in fact they were not; this issue will be addressed in Chapter VII. Within the context of the free, responsive market, audiences were vulnerable to the influence of critics, *commanditaires*, and politicians, whose social function, self-interest, and political awareness left them in a position to mold audience opinion. This chapter and the next examine the critical influence of the various audience fractions whose impact on the formation of the opera repertoire was out of proportion to their numbers.

In light of the evidence presented in Chapter III, the concept of an open market in opera ideology must especially be reconciled with opera's capacity for responding to the interests of the government. Portrayals of class relations in the opera repertoire, especially at the Opéra-Comique, do seem to have changed in accordance with the balance of political power, notably in the reorientation of opera ideology from aristocratic to democratic sentiments after 1880, and in the articulation of carefully defined political positions in operatic representations of the French Revolution. There is no clear and convincing documentary evidence, however, either in the apparently complete archives of the Ministry of Public Instruction, which contain an abundance of material relevant to the opera,[2] or in the memoirs of state officials, or those of the impresarios, that the pre-war Third Republic ever deliberately took advantage of its formidable capacity for direct interference in the opera repertoire for partisan political purposes. In the absence of documented examples of direct government supervision of the administration of the opera, which would account most simply for the close correspondence between the political content of the librettos and the interests of the government, we may postulate frequent informal meetings between impresarios and representatives of the government, in which the official viewpoint could be communicated. We would expect, in that case, to encounter many comments on such activity in the parliamentary rhetoric of the political opposition, and in the partisan press as well; these are almost entirely absent.

When the government was required by circumstance to choose operas for state occasions — gala official productions or free Bastille

Day performances — it displayed no apparent concern for the ideological implications of its choices. The same is true of official attempts to promote French opera by requiring directors to produce new domestic works. Operas that came to the stage as the result of this initiative featured some of the least intelligible librettos in all of Belle Epoque opera. Reviews of operas in the government press never included analysis of their ideological implications, even when those implications could have been construed as favorable to the agenda of the state and its partisans. Censorship of opera, like that of all theatrical works, naturally occurred on ideological grounds among others, but it was increasingly discreet and unobtrusive, relying heavily on self-censorship on the part of directors and librettists. Though the state had the capacity to influence opera's content indirectly through grants of subsidies and sinecures to librettists, there is no evidence, until the very end of the era under discussion, that political or ideological considerations influenced the disbursement of these funds either. The official policies of the Republic effectively encouraged writers, including those who wrote librettos, to stay in the unexceptionable, indefinable mainstream. The same holds true for appointments of opera directors.

Unobtrusiveness was the chief characteristic of the state's control over the repertoire. The government was so consistently invisible in its supervision of opera's content that there is legitimate room for doubt that it was even aware of the influence that it appeared, on the basis of the results noted in previous chapters, so effectively to wield. In fact, the state had its cake and ate a lot of it too. It managed to accomplish the greater part of its political agenda while preserving the illusion that social and political commentary was extraneous, even irrelevant, to the opera. This paradox accounts for the profound ambivalence toward the pedagogic potential of the opera that characterizes both Third Republic government rhetoric and administration of the opera. The paradox can be resolved by more careful articulation of a system which, through the institution of the Tout-Paris of the opera, enabled politicians to influence opera audience opinion while at the same time they were co-opted into the value system of the social elites.

While previous chapters emphasized the responsiveness of the opera ideology to the interests of the government, they also recorded frequent anomalies in this pattern. The government's acquiescence in the propagation of antipathetic doctrines had sometimes to be explained away with reference to short-term political advantages. The evidence in this chapter suggests that such equanimity, even nonchalance, on the part of the government was an aspect of a more general phenomenon requiring explanation: the strikingly muted response, across the whole opera establishment, transcending political and social differences, to operas that might have been expected to arouse partisan reactions. I conclude that the opera contributed to the formation of ideological consensus among the socially and politically diverse elements comprising the audience, including republican politicians among the most significant. As long as the discrepancy between the ideological orientation of the audience and the goals of the political parties in power remained within reasonable limits, the government apparently stood to benefit more as a discreet and effective participant in a cultural hegemony process than as an independent, contentious wielder of partisan propaganda.

Among the tangible benefits that the state derived from its investment in opera were facilities for the entertainment of foreign dignitaries and the celebration of diplomatic triumphs. At the Opéra, the President of the Republic received the Shah of Persia, the Kings of Spain and Portugal, and the King and Queen of Denmark. The government's use of this venue to cultivate and advertise its Russian alliance, which had rescued France from diplomatic isolation and which formed the cornerstone of her pre-war diplomacy, has already been described above. In 1893, a gala Opéra performance celebrated the visit of a Russian squadron to France. The next year, the government ordered a free show at the Opéra in honor of the Russian emperor's coronation; on that occasion the audience joined the principals in singing the Russian national hymn and the "Marseillaise." A similar spectacle marked the triumphant return of President Félix Faure from an official visit to St. Petersburg, and so on.[3]

On occasions when one of the opera houses functioned as the site of an official government fête, the Ministry of Public Instruction selected from the current repertoire the particular show to be performed. There is, however, no discernible pattern to the choice of operas presented. In 1875, the ministry ordered *Les Huguenots* to gratify the expressed desire of the visiting Grand Duchess Catherine of Russia. Royalty often saw *Samson et Dalila*, the most successful grand opera of the Belle Epoque. Surprisingly, there was not even any emphasis on works by French composers; the visiting sheiks of Algeria heard *Aida*, perhaps because of its African setting. The Russian fêtes featured *Rigoletto* and Mozart's *Don Juan*, the latter because it was "one of the most brilliant spectacles" in the repertoire at the time.[4] The government clearly preferred to dazzle foreign dignitaries with the superiority of French performance practice instead of impressing them with any specifically French (much less republican) point of view. Such choices helped to legitimize the republic in the eyes of the monarchical states by persuading their representatives that France, despite her eccentric political organization, continued to embrace the high culture of the international European elites.

Official decisions concerning the shows to be presented to the populace at free Bastille Day performances were the occasion for considerable debate in the press and within the government, according to the critic (and librettist) Albert Wolff. He commented that the minister required an opera "to be at the same time moral, instructive, national, and humanistic, to raise the intellectual level of the population, to propagate great sentiments so that the humble spectator leaves with an ample provision of ideas for a whole year."[5] Wolff's irony exposes the hollowness of government rhetoric that defended state administration of the opera with grandiose claims for its effect on popular morality when, in practice, the state confined its active intervention on behalf of the populace to one show per year. It is impossible to conclude from analysis of the official selections that the government paid any attention at all to the political or social content of these free shows, except perhaps to guarantee that they included the whole range of possible alternatives. The choices of the government merely illustrate how thoroughly republican officials implemented their public posture of impartiality. The classics of the French school of the late sixties — Thomas' *Mignon* and *Hamlet*, and Gounod's *Roméo et Juliette* — predominated. But foreign works, including *Aida*, *Rigoletto*, and even *Lohengrin* often graced the national fêtes as well. Operas chosen during their first year of production ranged from Bruneau's and Zola's controversial *Messidor* [6] to the esoteric revival of Rameau's *Hippolyte et Aricie.* An old-fashioned costume epic —Vidal's *La Burgonde* (O-1898) — followed the year after Lazzari's *faits divers* opera *La Lépreuse.* Instead of implementing republican rhetoric or propagating the political principles of the ministry, the choice of operas for the July 14 performances sounded the gamut of options offered by the repertoire.

Other activities of the state with regard to the opera, including the subsidies and sinecures provided to needy writers, and the appointments of opera directors, also suggest that the goal of the state was not to promote any partisan point of view, but rather to reinforce the free market in opera librettos. When it came to influencing the content, ideological and otherwise, of the repertoire, by these indirect or clandestine means, the state again abdicated in favor of audience opinion.

Altogether, at least twenty librettists active during this period held government jobs,[7] not even including those who were paid for honorary positions with nominal duties, such as the nine "Officers of Public Instruction." None of the twenty made more than a modest salary — Henri De Bornier, for instance, collected only Fr.600 per year from his government library position — but any regular income was a welcome supplement to the problematical rewards of a literary career in its early stages. Some of the librettists with government jobs, such as the hospital administrator Louis Gallet, were dedicated and capable administrators. As part of the government bureaucracy, his administrative posts had a certain amount of slack time built in. But he held a series of positions of obvious authority requiring technical expertise — from hospital director to "chief of the division of hospitals and asylums" — which were not mere government sinecures. P.-B. Gheusi rose to the position of secretary-general of the Ministry of the Colonies during the Third Republic, while Ludovic Halévy gave his conscientious attention, some of the time at least, to a variety of Imperial government posts, including bureau chief in the same ministry.[8]

But most employees who demonstrated a talent for literature never aspired to advance above the lowest ranks of the administrative hierarchy, where tolerant supervisors required little real work from them. As members of the "intermittent bureaucracy," they were permitted, even encouraged, to devote their work time to literary pursuits. One of Ludovic Halévy's biographers described the Second Empire this way:

> It was the happy epoch when the most diverse and original talents surged from every bureaucrat, when in the words of Henri d'Alméras, "An intelligent liberality that surprised or shocked no one permitted intermittent bureaucrats to wait without too much impatience for the public, the theatre directors and the editors to become aware of the merits of their work."[9]

Edmond Gondinet began as an itinerant provincial tax assessor in the same office as his brother and nephew. One of his colleagues wrote: "Both of us children of *fonctionnaires*, we had entered the administration to obey our families, and we both wanted to leave as soon as literature could guarantee us our daily bread."[10] Shortly after Gondinet transferred to the main office of the Imperial Ministry of Finance at age thirty-three, he began to establish himself as a playwright. From that point on, he installed a hammock in his office and never did any administrative work at all. His supervisor, an enthusiast for the theatre who benefited from the author's complimentary tickets, allowed him to arrive at noon. They spent the afternoon discussing politics and art or entertaining actresses who came to call. Armand Silvestre had an even easier time. Like Gondinet, he had been a genuine *fonctionnaire* earlier in his career. After literary success overtook him, he was promoted to assistant director of the office of the library and archives in the Ministry of Finance, where he was required to show up once a month, on payday.[11]

State-administered libraries, archives, and museums were favored repositories for authors who lacked the aptitude or background for any other branch of administration, but whom the government, or more accurately, individuals of influence connected with the government, wished to patronize. "Their supervisors never got angry," wrote the librettist Robert de Flers; "they were men of spirit and sense and they

knew perfectly well that one couldn't spend all his time filing
documents or annotating reports and that it was necessary, from time to
time, to do something serious."[12] François Coppée found time to
publish several volumes of poetry while shuffling paper at the Imperial
Ministry of War, where his father was a low-level employee. In 1869,
the prodigious success of Sarah Bernhardt in one of Coppée's plays
brought him to the attention of Princess Mathilde, chief imperial
patroness of the arts, who found him a sinecure at the library of the
Senate. On another occasion, she sought employment for Catulle
Mendès, who was, however, immediately fired by a minister who did
not share her opinion of his work. As an alternative she provided the
author with an outright pension.[13] The most important vehicle for
patronage of writers was the Ministry of Public Instruction. After
fleeing to Paris from his provincial seminary, Alexandre Bisson almost
starved before he thought to write to the Emperor Louis-Napoléon,
who appointed him supernumerary in the Bureau of Fine Arts. Having
a desk and ink but no apparent function, he spent his time writing
plays. For a few months, ending with the fall of the Empire, Gaston
Jollivet had the good fortune to serve as administrative assistant to a
friend who had been appointed secretary-general under the Minister of
Fine Arts. With nothing to do but screen visitors all day, both male and
female, mostly actors, actresses, painters and so on, who wanted
something from his superior, he enjoyed what he later called the
happiest days of his youth.[14]

Imperial patronage of the arts reaped its reward in loyalty to the
Bonapartist regime, loyalty which in some cases even survived the
debacle of 1870. While other librettists who expressed anti-republican
sentiments of one sort or another during the seventies eventually
became resigned to the republic, the Bonapartists among them often
retained a sentimental attachment to the regime that had looked
after their interests so well. Jollivet, who had happily served in the
Ministry of Fine Arts in 1870, described his lifelong allegiance in the
following terms:

> Bonapartist with the Prince Imperial, I remained a Bonapartist when
> he was no longer there, but my Bonapartism, more or less aimless,
> almost retrospective, was nothing more than a chimera in mourning;
> my heart stayed faithful, out of pride, perhaps, and partly because I
> never saw anything, in the melee of political passions, worth the
> sacrifice of my dream.[15]

François Coppée likewise regretted the Empire for the sake of Princess Mathilde, to whom he owed his government job as well as his introduction to society.[16]

Whether conditions changed much for these writers following the demise of the Empire is not clear. Most of the librettists' jobs survived the change of regime: Coppée stayed on at the Senate library until 1873; the Vicomte de Bornier, hired as supernumerary at the Arsenal library in 1860, continued to work there until 1880. Silvestre's administrative career at the Ministry of Finance ended only in 1886, after which he was appointed Inspector of Fine Arts. The Grévy administration moved to eliminate a few sinecures in the early eighties, including a library job held by Charles Monselet. But Edmond Haraucourt began one at the Ministry of Commerce in 1883. Appointed supernumerary there, just at the time his literary career began to take off, while his friend Waldeck-Rousseau was Minister of the Interior, Haraucourt typically arrived after lunch and immediately hung out a "Do Not Disturb" sign. His duties — editing dispatches from consuls abroad for the ministry journal — left him time to put out several volumes of verse.[17]

Writing after the turn of the century, P.-B. Gheusi characterized the era of the eighties as the good old days of literary patronage, when writers had been rewarded solely for their literary achievements. In his own period, by contrast, the government took into account their party affiliations:

> It was still the time when the Republic gave *litterateurs* without means positions with a regular monthly stipend.... Literature was, at that time, honored and rewarded according to merit....

> Now everything is changed. Nobody, in these days, is *inspecteur* or *gardien supérieur* of Fine Arts unless he has been a militant radical-socialist for twenty years or a subscriber to *La Lanterne* for a quarter of a century.[18]

Such political activity smacks more of the patronage that rewards and secures party loyalty than of any systematic attempt to influence the ideological content of the beneficiaries' works. Of course, the well-founded hope that government employment would survive transitory, short-lived regimes dictated discretion even to those whose party was currently in the ascendant. By widespread direct government patronage of librettists of a variety of political persuasions, the state heightened writers' sensitivity to the disadvantages of expressing political opinions of any kind in their works. Like the Académies of Louis XIV, Second Empire and Third Republic subsidies promoted the arts at the same time that they helped to control their content. But these government subsidies for the librettists were not designed to generate a series of Bonapartist or radical-socialist librettos so much as to keep librettists' bodies and souls together long enough for them to learn to cater effectively to audience taste. As long as subsidized librettists had material reasons for avoiding open attacks on the government in power, it did not need to promote its interests more actively by paying writers to favor its policies.

It is in fact impossible to demonstrate that the librettists who accepted government jobs, including the radical-socialists, wrote librettos that differed in any significant way from the others. Since the government had no intention of politicizing the opera, that presumably constituted a sufficient return on the investment. Government money might have helped assimilate writers from diverse social and political backgrounds to the outlook of the dominant elites, but the evidence is too thin to permit any confident assessment of this effect. Information about librettists' opinions on political issues is spotty. Among forty-seven librettists for whom such information is available (about 45 percent of the total), thirty held opinions that might be characterized as left of center, compared with twelve to the right of center, with the remainder somewhere in the middle. But the data undoubtedly underrepresent the strength of the political center through the tendency of the historical record to preserve the most noteworthy, visible, differentiating characteristics of its subjects. And what was leftist in the 1850s was not necessarily leftist in the 1890s.

All the librettists whose opinions of the events of 1848-1851 are known were republicans of one sort or another, including some, such as the candidate for Opéra director Charles de La Rounat, with very advanced opinions. In the years after 1871, on the other hand, when the form of the new regime was still an open question, half the librettists expressed anti-republican sentiments. With the exception of the surprisingly committed Bonapartists mentioned above, many of these became "*républicains de résignation*," as the Orléanist librettist Ludovic Halévy put it, during the 'eighties. Later, just before the turn of the century, the Dreyfus affair again polarized their opinions. Some of the most prominent anti-Dreyfusard intellectuals wrote librettos, including Jules Lemaître and François Coppée, founders of the Ligue de la Patrie Française, in which Vincent d'Indy also played an important role. The Dreyfusard librettists outnumbered the anti-Dreyfusards about two to one, and included Emile Zola in their number. Mme. Armand de Caillavet brought up her son Gaston in the salon that served as social and political center for the most important Dreyfusard intellectuals. In the first years of the twentieth century half a dozen librettists, such as the young symbolist poets Henri de Regnier and Ferdinand Hérold, had some claim to be called socialists or anarchists.

This is interesting evidence for the general political milieu of the librettists, but the connections between those of their views that are well-documented and the ideological content of their individual librettos are ambiguous at best. The Bonapartism of Coppée shows up in his libretto for *Maître Ambros*, but Albert Wolff, noted for "exceeding tolerance and great liberalism in political and religious questions,"[19] was co-author of the reactionary *Egmont*. The authors of some of the most interesting revolutionary texts of the eighteen-nineties left no independent record of their political convictions. As the Epilogue illustrates, to the extent that the librettists consciously used the opera as a forum for the propagation of their personal political opinions, it was disgust with politics in general that they chose to dramatize. We may speculate that the spectacle of the government suborning journalists, opera directors, and even poets, contributed to this pervasive disaffection with the Third Republic.

Directors might be dismissed who aroused the personal animosity of some powerful minister, but they usually managed to win reappointment when their terms expired unless they burdened the government with requests for increased subsidies. State funds and prestige were invested in the opera; the government could not afford the risks of a quixotic or narrowly partisan approach to the appointment process. Instead, the candidates' ability to manage money competently — above all by responding to the tastes of those who supplied it — was the most important factor in their selection. It was obvious that investors, by withholding the necessary independent capital; subscribers, by threatening to withdraw en masse; casual customers, by staying home; and the Société des Auteurs, by denying access to their products, all could ruin directors financially, and therefore that no government could maintain a director against their wishes for long. Simply by ensuring that the directors' primary goal was to make money, the government effectively limited their options to the range of works acceptable to these various groups.

The decision of Jules Ferry, discussed in the previous chapter, to replace the Opéra director Halanzier with Vaucorbeil rather than with the republican de La Rounat, was the first of many such decisions distinguished by a conscientious disregard for political or ideological considerations. Vaucorbeil's regime was not a success; according to Louis Gallet's charitable explanation, the director was so devoted to Art that he proved to be entirely unconscious of the fiscal exigencies of the enterprise. In fact, his obstinate refusal to put on any of the lower-priced "popular" performances required by his *cahiers des charges* suggests that he understood the financial situation perfectly well. To ease the burden of Vaucorbeil's artistic endeavors, the Ferry regime readily acquiesced in this neglect of his democratic responsibilities. It was not enough, however; continued financial reverses led to Vaucorbeil's early demise after only five years in office.[20] A brief experiment with direct state management was a fiasco: During a two-week stint as provisional Opéra director, the chef du bureau des théâtres managed to lose Fr.30,000. Subsequent Third Republic ministries followed Ferry's lead in choosing directors without regard for any conspicuous republican background or beliefs. In an attempt to solve the different kinds of problems posed by the Halanzier and Vaucorbeil regimes, the government decided to appoint co-directors: a baritone to supervise the artistic side, with a businessman partner to control the money. The combination of Gailhard and Ritt worked well enough to encourage later governments to repeat the technique, associating the composer Messager with Broussan, a former director at Lyon, and the critic and librettist Gheusi with the Isola brothers, Algerians of modest social origins but considerable and varied experience as theatrical entrepreneurs.[21]

In sharp contrast to the librettists, whose memoirs bristle with partisan sentiment, the career impresarios were extremely reticent about expressing any political opinions that they might have had. P.-B. Gheusi, the only impresario to address such questions in print, many years after he had retired, merely emphasized his ability to stay on good terms with all sides. When he first arrived in Paris, he regularly contributed literary articles to the reactionary newspaper *Le Gaulois*. This allowed the monarchists, who, he says, took literature seriously, to consider him one of themselves. His family traditions and friendships, on the other hand, placed him firmly in the camp of the militant republicans. Of his personal convictions, the strongest were hatred of parliamentarism and of the unprincipled pursuit of money — standard whipping boys of the Third Republic right and left, respectively. [22] Gheusi's memoirs apart, the emphasis on personal and professional reminiscence in the impresarios' literary remains was so exclusive as to suggest that expressing opinions on social and political issues might seriously have hindered their careers.

No ideological bias is discernible in the preferences of any of the directors, either in new works chosen for production, in the selection of works from the standard repertoire, or in the frequency with which they staged them. This approach may be attributed in part to the socializing effect of the profit motive during the early stages of their careers. Directors were promoted not according to their artistic sensibilities, much less their political beliefs, but by demonstrated capacity for making financial successes of theatrical enterprises. Most directors rose to the pinnacle of the profession after successful apprenticeships at provincial theatres; the chief requirement for continued advancement within the field was that they maximize receipts while minimizing expenditures. Halanzier had progressed triumphantly through Rouen, Marseille, Bordeaux, Strasbourg and Lyon, and Eugène Bertrand had performed in and directed theatres in the United States and Lille before arriving in Paris. Carré started as a prompter and copier in Neufchâtel as a teenager during the war before turning briefly to acting. Later, Halanzier and Ritt subsidized him to the tune of Fr.250,000 for a venture as director of the theatre of Nancy, where he turned a profit of Fr.40,000 in eight months. Bertrand, director of the Vaudeville, arranged for Carré to succeed him there in 1890, when he moved up to the Opéra.[23] Thus the directors constituted an exclusive and narrow guild, whose members often co-opted their successors. Those who wanted to get ahead learned to sacrifice their personal tastes to audience preferences.

In discussions surrounding the appointments, including those in the press, references to the candidates' political or social views are almost completely absent, while the candidates' capacity for effective financial management emerges as the crucially important criterion in their selection. Only in the case of Jacques Rouché's appointment to direct the Opéra in 1913 was there a hint of partisan politics. Rouché was a *polytechnicien*, experienced in both government and business, who had married perfume money. As director of the innovative Théâtre-des-Arts he successfully revived operas by Rameau, Lully, Couperin, and Monteverdi, and published a book about theatre décor. At the time of his candidacy, Rouché was director of the radical-socialist *Grand Revue*, which he had made into one of the most important avant-garde publications of the era "from the literary and artistic point of view, as well as from the political."[24] Louis Barthou, who made the appointment, was minister of public instruction and premier of one of the few moderate republican ministries in an era dominated by radical-socialists. Because his government depended on radical-socialist support for its political survival, some journalists speculated that Rouché might have been chosen as part of a political deal for the short-term advantage of the ministry.[25]

Certainly no one attributed strong or even substantive political opinions to Rouché. In public pronouncements of his intentions for the Opéra, Rouché confined himself to tapping the rising tide of pre-war chauvinism. He emphasized the restoration of French art, "invaded by the art of Munich," and pledged to "give to our artists their rightful place and their prestige, and dedicate the Opéra to French musicians, singers and decorators."[26] The political implications of this anti-Wagnerian attitude have been explored above, but there is reason to believe that Rouché was more concerned with protecting French singers than composers.[27] If pressure from radical-socialists did influence the appointment, it was probably more a matter of patronage than ideology; as we have seen, they were notorious for looking after their own at the Department of Fine Arts.

Rouché's charge was to arrest the precipitous decline of the Opéra, manifested in deteriorating standards of production and persistent insolvency resulting from mass defections among subscribers and a revolt of the *commanditaires*. It is not clear whether the inferior productions were the cause or the consequence of the financial difficulties, but more of the blame fell on Broussan, the incumbent financial director, than on Messager, the artistic director. According to the government, Rouché's chief qualification was his great wealth: "M. Rouché can, by his own means, assure that this weighty enterprise will prosper financially and administratively," declared Barthou when he announced the appointment.[28]

The state's efforts to promote the composition and performance of operas by French composers during the 1890s evince the same refusal to manipulate the social and political content of the repertoire that is apparent in the selection of government galas and 14 July fêtes described above. The effect of the state's initiative in this area was to reinforce the critics' campaign to minimize the impact of any ideas that might creep into the opera. In an era when, thanks to the influence of Wagner, librettists and composers became increasingly aware of opera's capacity to communicate ideas, new French operas introduced under pressure from the state had as their salient characteristic an old-fashioned emphasis on extravagant effects.

The explicit requirement imposed by the government on Opéra directors was that they produce works by new French composers totalling twelve acts — that is, three or four full-length operas — during each seven-year concession. The *cahiers des charges* never specified the particular works to be presented, however. Without government encouragement, it is unlikely that such works would have appeared at all, because operas by untested French composers were expected to fail, in which case they represented a considerable financial burden for directors. The importance of minimizing expenditure led to a general prejudice on the part of directors against new works, which entailed extra costs for costumes and decors and for rehearsal time as well. A new Opéra production often cost more than Fr.200,000, and the majority of them were failures that lost about Fr.4,000 per performance. Unlike old war-horses in the public domain, newer operas also required payment of 6 to 12 percent of their gross receipts as authors' royalties. The Société des Auteurs eliminated this inducement by requiring directors to contribute an equivalent amount from public-domain performances to its pension fund, and later by successfully lobbying for a change in the copyright law to secure royalties for authors' heirs in perpetuity. The financial pressure on directors to limit the introduction of new works nevertheless remained considerable. Left to themselves, opera impresarios introduced new works so seldom that the state had to insist on a yearly minimum number of new operas.[29]

The government's attempt to combat the Wagnerian invasion by promoting the French operatic industry produced a string of failures which are now of interest only to the historian, having been justly ignored by opera lovers and musicologists. The opera historian Paul Pelissier listed a series of works — Lefebvre's *Djelma* (O-1894), Augusta Holmès' *La Montagne Noir* (O-1895), Rousseau's *La Cloche du Rhin* (O-1897), Vidal's *La Burgonde* (O-1898), Joncières' *Lancelot* (O-1900) and Huë's *Le Roi de Paris* (O-1901) — introduced specially to satisfy these requirements of the *cahiers des charges*, all of which folded before their fourteenth performances.[30] At least a couple of the composers who benefited from the government policy were known to have political ties to the regime. Augusta Holmès, for instance, had been commissioned to produce for the centenary of the Revolution a symphonic "Ode Triumphale" which celebrated the triumph of the ideals of the Revolution and the Third Republic.[31] But even these composers' operatic works contain no themes or messages that could be interpreted as serving the interests of the government that exerted itself on their behalf.

Many of these operas have *Wagnériste* elements, as one might expect from novice composers and librettists attempting to penetrate the repertoire of the Opéra during the 'nineties, but they are distinguished from other *Wagnériste* operas by the superabundance of local color that suffuses them. The new French operas on Pelissier's list combined the most exotic settings with the most complicated, incoherent and ridiculous librettos in all Belle Epoque opera. The composers and librettists attempted in each case to saturate every detail with the most spectacular dramatic effects, regardless of their relevance to the action.

As a result, the characters are one-dimensional yet wildly inconsistent; their actions revolve around the most improbable misunderstandings and incomprehensible oversights. A brief recapitulation of any of these operas is bound to minimize their fundamental confusion, thereby misrepresenting what is in essence an accumulation of incongruous details. I have attempted, nonetheless, a brief summary of the action of Vidal's *La Burgonde*, doubly interesting since it was also selected by the government as one of the operas to be performed free for the populace on Bastille Day.

The opera is set in the time of Attila the Hun. He has taken as hostage scions of the ruling families of Burgundy, Worms, and Aquitaine, and in the course of the first act the audience learns that the two male princes are both in love with the young Burgundian princess Ilda. Attila is attracted to her as well, but she resists his savage attempts to install her as queen over his other wives and concubines. Abetted by the incumbent queen, the brave, heroic Gauthier of Aquitaine determines to get Attila drunk at an upcoming fête, flee with Ilda, and raise a rebellion against the conquering hordes from the East. The second act takes place at the fête of the sword of the Huns, the symbol of their culture and its link with their ancient roots and homeland; the sword has never been and must never be bloodied. Gauthier's plan succeeds, but his treacherous rival, Hagen of Worms, who has just been released from captivity, returns in disguise to alert Attila. He contracts to bring back the fugitives in exchange for the wife of his choice.

The third act provides a lyrical interlude when the fleeing lovers miss the last boat of refugees crossing the river to Aquitaine. While Gauthier builds a raft, using construction techniques remembered from his childhood, Ilda pauses, before they embark on their responsibilities, to remark how happy they are alone together in exile, forgotten by the world. When the last act opens, Hagen returns the captives to Attila and claims Ilda for his wife, but the king decides to keep her for himself. She desperately offers her body in exchange for Gauthier's release, but Attila merely makes her queen by force. This gives her custody of the sacred sword. Meanwhile, Hagen has experienced an inexplicable moral revulsion against his own behavior; he resolves to sacrifice himself for the two lovers. He releases Gauthier, while Ilda kills Attila with the sacred sword. Since the Huns refuse to fight against it, the two lovers manage to escape before the curtain.

Some of the audience may have interpreted this story of a proto-Frenchman rescuing a Burgundian from the savage Hun in a *revanchiste* spirit, but none of the reviews of the opera that I sampled, from papers with a variety of political outlooks, so much as alluded to this possibility. If they missed the patriotic potential, it is even more far-fetched to imagine opera-lovers, including the working-class patrons of the gratis Bastille Day performance, leaving a performance of *La Burgonde*, or any of the operas on Pelissier's list, with a heightened sense of the advantages and responsibilities of republican government. This was apparently not the intention of the government.

Extravagant theatrical effects, as the state was well aware, interfered with the coherent development of characters and situations capable of illustrating a point of view with social or moral implications. As the director of the Opéra pointed out to the minister of public instruction: "The Lyric Drama contains always, and first of all, a moral and a lesson; but the music covers the instructive part of the work with the charm and the beauty that belong to it, and that interesting part escapes the comprehension of most people."[32] As difficult as it was, under normal circumstances, to draw coherent conclusions from the action on the operatic stage, the surfeit of artistic effects in the government-sponsored operas multiplied the obstacles. If any deliberate strategy on the part of the government can be inferred, it must have been more concerned with suppressing the possibility of any social or political interpretation of opera than with reproducing its own ideology for the edification of the opera clientele.

Surprisingly, the activities of the censorship office raise similar questions about the intentions of the government. Censorship was an area in which the state was expected to offer overt, sometimes even public evaluations of the social and political content of theatrical works, a responsibility that it took seriously. According to the republican playwright and librettist Emile Augier, the vigor with which the state pursued censorship was a sign that it recognized that the theatre was the most influential means of instruction in morality.[33] Indeed, many writers and politicians believed that the intervention of government censors seriously inhibited the development of the French theatre. In an 1897 Assemblée debate, a former director of fine arts said: "If we don't have the social works that we ought to" — he mentioned Hauptmann and Ibsen as models — "the blame lies largely with the censorship."[34] Emile Zola adduced an example in "Nos Auteurs Dramatiques":

> His deputy is nothing but the deputy permitted by the censorship.... If an author deviates from this facile and inoffensive outline, he is immediately stopped, and his character is reduced to the desired dimensions. I mean to say that he is forbidden to probe the politician too deeply, to make a real person out of him.[35]

The conservative writer Maurice Barrès likewise thought the prospects for French social theatre were dim because of repressive censorship, which "constantly prevents any development of the two characters on which modern civilization is based — the Priest and the King."[36]

The Third Republic reinstated censorship for all theatres in 1874, after a brief hiatus initiated by the Government of National Defense, along the lines established by the Second Empire; not only the structure of the censorship office remained the same, but the personnel as well. The censors' notoriously erratic judgment and lack of artistic sensibility frequently aroused the antagonism of writers and performers. Only two types of people ever became censors, the librettist Robert de Flers claimed. The first was the son of a well-known father who had tried everything and succeeded at nothing, or perhaps never even tried anything, but whose father had to find him some kind of job. The other was the bureaucratic functionary who had worked hard all his life and then opted for something with a little amusement to it, who rushed home to tell his mistress all the jokes that he heard before anyone else. "Art, literature, esprit, good taste are vain chimeras that he never bothered about — impressive words, but hollow," wrote Flers.[37]

Censors acted under the authority and according to the direction of the director of fine arts. All theatre scripts had to be submitted in advance to the ministry. Productions rejected for performance in Paris were prohibited everywhere in France, and prefects from the provinces could ban additional works on their own initiative, according to local conditions. Thus *Les Huguenots*, the second most frequently performed work at the Paris Opéra during the pre-war Third Republic, could not appear in Nîmes, where references to the Wars of Religion still provoked riots at the end of the nineteenth century.[38] Since operas were subject to very close supervision by the state, and too expensive to take risks with, anything likely to attract the censors' attention would normally have been eliminated at an earlier stage of production. But documentary evidence taken from censors' responses to other types of dramatic production may with caution be used to infer official attitudes towards the opera as well.

For a few years after the Paris Commune, reactionary Third Republic governments banned plays explicitly on the grounds of their social content. In March 1878, for instance, the director of fine arts noted with regard to a play called *Le Pacte de Famine*, which ends with the storming of the Bastille:

> These tableaux of famine, of common people stirred up against financiers, of rich people as horrible villains, are they not profoundly provocative to the unfortunate classes? Do they not present dangerous parallels to the minds of suffering people even though they take place a hundred years ago? Is there not in this play a stimulus to violence?[39]

Similar considerations operated in the case of *L'Ouvrier* — "a very bad play. Nothing but the antagonism between rich and poor" — and of *Le Chiffonier de Paris* by the Communard Félix Pyat. In 1875 the government even banned a piece of music titled "Ouverture des Girondins." When republicans took control of the theatre administration, they reacted against the politically repressive censorship of the monarchists; very few plays were banned on explicitly doctrinal grounds after 1879. Most of those that were rejected attacked the state itself, by portraying its police as brutal or its legislators as venal. Such a censorship policy could offend no one with access to political influence. A consensus of the dominant elites would certainly have supported the censors' suppression of the play *Yanetta*, for instance, which portrayed judges as motivated by ambition and servile to critical journalists, and *gendarmes* assaulting a female suspect in the presence of a judge.[40]

Under Jules Ferry and his successors, the republic usually banned politically dubious works ostensibly on the grounds that they were threats to public safety — liable to cause civil disorder in the streets and theatre — rather than specifically for their unacceptable content.

Several important theatre riots provoked by plays to which the government had no ideological objection gave plausibility to its rationale. Even operas caused riots: Besides the case of *Les Huguenots*, mentioned above, *Lohengrin* prompted violent anti-German protests outside the Eden Theatre in Paris during the Schnäbele Affair, and again at its Opéra premiere in 1891.[41] In the latter case, as we have seen, the government intervened to suppress the riots and safeguard the performance. Invoking the specter of public disturbance enabled the government to control the social content of the theatre without directly acknowledging it. Of course the transparency of the device became apparent when the government tried to apply it to works sponsored by politically powerful groups. When police suppressed *Thermidor*, Victorien Sardou's controversial, right-wing interpretation of the French Revolution, which threatened to cause riots outside the theatre, the decision itself caused a riot — in the Chamber of Deputies.

Through the 1890s, a good deal of censorship activity was accomplished verbally by censors in interviews with authors. The government further lowered the profile of its ideological control by depending heavily on self-censorship for the enforcement of its norms. If the censorship office very seldom suppressed theatrical works on political grounds, the threat of official intervention nonetheless kept playwrights and librettists highly sensitive to the state's implicit standards. For obvious reasons, the effects of self-censorship are difficult to illustrate, as Emile Zola explained in his brochure "La République et la Littérature":

> A well-meaning man said to me, "Cite for me the works of talent that the censorship has prevented from playing." I replied to him, "I cannot tell you the titles of the masterpieces of which the censorship has deprived us, precisely because these masterpieces have not been written." That is the whole issue. If the censorship does not play a very active role, it has the inhibiting effect of a scarecrow; it paralyzes the evolution of dramatic art. Everyone knows the plays he shouldn't write, those which couldn't be performed, and no one writes them.[42]

The government reinforced the operation of self-censorship by requiring that official inspections of theatrical works take place at rehearsals "with the décors, the costumes, the accessories, complete lighting of the stage, in such a way, in other words, that none of the effects of the performance will be hidden."[43] In order to avoid the enormous waste of time, effort, and money of staging a show that might be rejected just before it was ready to open, directors and writers had to anticipate the disapproval of the censors. From motives of financial self-preservation, directors chose or altered works with the censors in mind, and authors wrote the same way. Supporters of preventive censorship during the Third Republic, including even some opera librettists who had had poems, songs, or plays rejected by the censor, as well as (unanimously) the executive committee of the Société des Auteurs et Compositeurs Dramatiques, considered it preferable to the alternative, which was police surveillance of works already before the public. Either huge sums of money would be wasted on impossible shows, supporters of censorship thought, or theatre directors would have to exercise a vastly more restrictive self-censorship.[44] After 1906, when the legislature effectively abolished theatrical censorship by dropping its allocation from the budget, the police did close down productions from time to time.

The elimination of formal censorship had little impact on the state theatres, which had always been subject to very close supervision by the government: "If a work causes trouble, the Administration can suspend or even prohibit its performance, or order that modifications be made," stated one of the provisions of the Opéra-Comique *cahiers des charges* of 1911.[45] The ministry rarely allowed works under production to reach the point where censors had to intervene, however. As a result, operatic censorship is more revealing for what it permitted than for what it banned. The variety of sexual activities displayed on the stages of the Opéra and the Opéra-Comique is particularly striking. Audiences were exposed to adultery and incest, prostitution, strip tease, *ménages-à-trois*, and lesbianism (but no male homosexuality, even in *Cinq-Mars* or the other Henri III librettos), and even women smoking cigarettes.

The government was less than aggressive in investigating and censoring prurient librettos even when forced by public pressure to do so. In 1901, for example, the notorious Senator Bérenger of the Central Society for Protest Against License in the Streets informed the minister of public instruction that "the Opéra has been performing for a few days a new opera, *Astarté*, of which the extreme license in the choice of subjects as well as in the audacity of the costumes and of the dancing has been the subject of every conversation." The minister responded with an ultimatum to the Opéra director Gailhard: If he did not immediately modify everything that might "wound the legitimate susceptibility of the spectators," the minister would be obliged to forbid its performance. He reminded Gailhard: "Please don't lose sight of the fact that you direct the Académie Nationale de la Musique, and that, at least in what concerns taste and decency, the works that you perform should be beyond reproach." The next day, Gailhard answered that he had modified the "staging, changed or suppressed the dialogue indicated by the minister, and arranged for the publication of a new libretto that conformed to the new words."[46] But P.-B. Gheusi, a close friend of the director, and himself a director of the Opéra-Comique in later years, described the censorship of *Astarté* as trivial and farcical. The leading soprano, Mme. Heglon, provided the following example for the press: "Yesterday the censor struck out the word 'intoxication' from my role and replaced it with 'tenderness.' It's puerile."[47] The minister, Gheusi said, merely played along with this farce.

Government officials recognized that sexual spectacle could serve as an attractive and politically useful alternative to social theatre. Napoleon III, following the advice of his uncle, instructed his censors to take an indulgent approach to theatre that evinced an equivocal sexual morality, — *La Dame aux Camélias* was its symbol — so that the public would be less likely to interest itself in government affairs.[48] The intimate connection between local color and the obfuscation of the moral lesson was also evident to writers committed to treating objectionable themes; they learned that they could avoid having their works suppressed by muffling the messages in historical or exotic settings. In the case of a dramatic work originally titled *L'Adultère Passif*, a priest suggests to a young woman that she will not be guilty of adultery if she submits entirely passively to the sexual advances of her husband's creditor. After the censorship office rejected the play, presumably to defend the reputation of the priesthood, the author tried repeatedly to win official approval by modifying the setting in which the drama occurred. He first transported the action to the era of Louis XV, hoping that the Old Regime church made a less sensitive target, but the play was rejected in this form also. Only by changing the title to *Le Trahison*, the locale to India, and the abbé to a Hindu priest, did he eventually get it past the censor. The principle was clear to both author and censor: The thicker the layers of local color, the less subversive the social criticism.[49]

In promoting sex as an alternative to the clear and unambiguous expression of social and political ideas, Third Republic censorship policy was exactly comparable in effect to the state's efforts to foster the production of new French operas suffused with spectacle. The apparent preference for local color over social commentary, like the other official initiatives discussed in this chapter, reinforces the idea that the state deliberately eschewed the use of the opera as an instrument for the propagation of specifically republican values. The short-term political benefits of this policy have already been explained: Republicans could establish the respectability of the republican form of government by reassuring the conservative opposition of the fundamental discretion of the regime. The long-term benefits were much more significant: Disguising the active influence of politicians over opera's content enabled the opera to maintain its reputation as a harmless, ideologically neutral amusement, permitting it to function more effectively as a vehicle of cultural hegemony.

NOTES TO CHAPTER V

1 Bourdieu, *Distinction*, 231. He elaborates on this idea in the following terms: "...any change in tastes resulting from a transformation of the conditions of existence and of the corresponding dispositions will tend to induce, directly or indirectly, a transformation in the field of production, by favoring the success, within the struggle constituting the field, of the producers best able to produce the needs corresponding to the new disposition." On the difficulties directors encountered in predicting audience reaction during this period, Descotes, *Le Public de Théâtre*, 3.

2 *A.N.* Series AJ XIII, F XVII and F XXI.

3 For descriptions of the gala performances, *Annales*, 15:10; 22:24; 23:28, 37f.

4 *Ibid.*, 23:28.

5 Albert Wolff, *La Gloriole* (Paris, 1888), 261. Opéra directors consulted with the Director of Fine Arts before submitting a suggestion to the Fêtes Nationales committee of the Parisian municipal council. See "Director of the Opéra Ritt to the Director of Fine Arts, 6/23/1891," B.O. Fonds Rouché, Pièce 119, 462.

6 By 1897, when *Messidor* appeared, the number of free performances had been increased. This particular opera did not appear on July 14, but at one of the other free performances. See *Annales* 23:16.

7 Of those whose works had premieres at the Opéra or Opéra-Comique between 1875 and 1914.

8 Roujon, *Artistes et Amis des Arts*, 244. Cf. Hansen, *Ludovic Halévy*, 157ff.

9 H. Nicolle, "Ludovic Halévy: Le Centénaire de la naissance d'un grand écrivain," in B.O. Dossier d'artiste/Ludovic Halévy. For the original of the quote, Henri d'Alméras, *Avant la gloire: Leurs débuts* (Paris, 1902) première série, 127.

10 André Theuriet, *Souvenirs des Vertes Saisons*, 2nd. ed. (Paris, 1904), 210.

11 Paul Léon, *Du Palais Royal au Palais Bourbon* (Paris: A. Michel, 1947), 124; Theuriet, *Souvenirs*, 211ff.

12 Robert de Flers, "Meilhac et Halévy: Leur Vie et Leur Carrière," *Conférence*, 18ième année no.19 (9/15/1924), 291.

13 d'Alméras, *Avant la gloire*, 90.

14 Jollivet, *Souvenirs*, 64f.

15 *Ibid.*, 264.

16 Coppée, *Souvenirs d'un Parisien* (Paris, 1910), 105.

17 Edmond Haraucourt, *Mémoires Des Jours et Des Gens* (Paris: Flammarion, 1946), 163.

18 Gheusi, *Cinquante Ans*, 3:161f. Cp. Priscilla B. Clark, "Stratégies d'Auteur au XIXe siècle," *Romantisme* 17–18 (1977), 96.

19 G. Toudouze, *Albert Wolff, histoire d'un Chroniquer* (Paris, 1883), 44.

20 For a brief biography of Vaucorbeil, see "Grand Opéra," B.O. Opéra Archives 19e siècle (183), Fonds Le Coupé No. 831, 365. Cf. Laloy, "L'Opéra," 51; Gallet, "Quatre Directeurs," 216–219, passim. For Ferry's actions with regard to the lower-priced performances, see "Observations presentées par M. Gailhard devant la Commission Supérieure des Théâtres," *A.N.* AJ XIII (1194), 20. Cf. Proust, *L'Art sous la République*, 91f., 96ff.

21 Carré, *Souvenirs*, 403. For the experiences of the unfortunate chef du bureau, *Ibid.*, 205ff.

22 Gheusi, *Cinquante Ans*, 4:358f. Though an anti-Boulangist and a Dreyfusard, he was in later life attracted to a sort of corporate socialism that sounds like fascism; he ended up as a Pétainist. *Ibid.*, 3:10, 4:405.

23 For Paravey and Carvalho, Carré, *Souvenirs*, 147, 204. The career of Bertrand is outlined in Benjamin and Buguet, *Coulisses*, 160. Brief biographies of Vaucorbeil, Gailhard, Ritt, Bertrand, Messager, Broussan, and Rouché are available in Gourret, *Ces Hommes*, 148–157.

24 J.L. Croze, "La Guerre en Musique," *L'Eclair* (10/31/1913).

25 *Le Cri de Paris* (11/9/1913); Spectator, "Derrière la Toile," *Eclair de Montpellier* (11/8/1913), (available also in B.O. Dossier d'artiste/Jacques Rouché).

26 Quoted in "La Direction de l'Opéra," *Les Nouvelles* (10/30/1913).

27 "Bloc-Notes Parisien," *Le Gaulois* (10/31/1913). This was certainly the primary concern of the radical-socialists. See *La Lanterne* (10/31/1913) (available in B.O. Dossier d'artists/Jacques Rouché).

28 Interviewed in *Gil Blas* (10/31/1913), available also in B.O. Dossier d'artiste/Jacques Rouché, where a large number of press clippings relative to the appointment of Rouché have been assembled. Of particular interest

are three articles referred to above: "La Direction de l'Opéra"; Croze, "La Guerre en Musique"; "Bloc-Notes Parisien."

29 "Théâtre National de l'Opéra-Comique, Cahier des Charges 1911," in "P.A. 1/24 mai 1911," B.O. P.A. 1900-1927. To be precise, the requirement was defined in terms of a minimum number of new acts that could be divided among new operas of different lengths. For the costs of new operas, see Pelissier, *Histoire administrative*, 189f. On the question of authors' royalties, Peytel, "Jurisprudence," 3885; Eugène Ortolan, "Rapport à l'Assemblée Générale de la Société des Compositeurs de Musique," 1/26/1867, *A.N.* AJ XIII (499), 6.

30 Pelissier, *Histoire Administrative*, 189f.

31 Brenda Nelms, *The Third Republic and the Centennial of 1789* (N.Y.: Garland, 1987) Modern European History Series, 182.

32 "Director of Opéra to Minister of Public Instruction, July 1893," *A.N.* AJ XIII (1194). Cf. Richard Wagner, *Opéra et Drame*, Translated by J.G. Prod'homme, *Oeuvres en Prose*, Vol.IV. (Paris, n.d.), 174.

33 Emile Augier, "Préface" to *Lionnes Pauvres*, reprinted in Chambre des Députés, Commission relative à l'abolition de la censure, Séance du 5/27/1891, Journal Officiel (Janvier, 1892), 2545 [also available in *A.N.* F XXI (1337)].

34 Chambre des Députés, Séance de 12/3/1897, *Journal Officiel*, 2682 [also available in *A.N.* F XXI (1337)]. Cf. "Rapport par M. Turquet, Sous-Secrétaire" (1879) in *A.N.* F XXI (1041): "as Beaumarchais said, as long as one doesn't refer to authority or religion, or politics, or morality, or to people in high places, or the fashionable set, or anyone who amounts to anything, one can say anything freely, subject to the inspection of two or three censors."

35 Emile Zola, *Nos Auteurs Dramatiques*, *Oeuvres Complètes*, 43:246.

36 Interviewed by Emile de Saint-Aubin in "Le Théâtre Social," Le Soleil (2/14/1901) [also available in *A.N.* F XXI (1339)]. Cf. Alphonse Séché and Jules Bertaut, *L'Evolution du Théâtre Contemporain* (Paris, 1908), 60.

37 Robert de Flers, *Revue d'Art Dramatique* (March, 1900), 196f. [also available in *A.N.* F XXI (1337)]. For the hiatus in the early seventies, Dupré et Ollendorff, *Traité*, 2:336. Krakovitch says that censorship was never more severe than during the 1871-1874 interim, when Paris was under military government: Odile Krakovitch, *Hugo Censuré: La liberté au théâtre au XIXe siècle* (Paris: Calmann-Levy, 1985), 249. For the continuity between Second Empire and "monarchist" republic, *Ibid.*, 247. Cf. Nolte,

"Government and Theatre," 357. For application procedures and a brief account of censors' credentials, *Ibid.* 359-64.

38 Chambre des Députés, Séance du 1/24/1891, *Journal Officiel*, 150.

39 Director of Fine Arts, "Note sur *Le Pacte de Famine*, drame en cinq actes, 3/19/1878," *A.N.* F XXI (1332). The correspondence between the Minister of Public Instruction and the prefects of various departments in this dossier and in *A.N.* F XXI (997) is an excellent source for the official justification for censorship of various works before 1879.

40 "Roujon to Minister, 2/16/1900," in *A.N.* F XXI (1336). See also the press clippings assembled in the same dossier.

41 Newspaper clippings describing the circumstances of the Eden Theatre riots have been collected in *A.N.* F XVII (2662). For internal memoranda relating to censorship guidelines, see Minister of Public Instruction and Fine Arts, "Memorandum, 6/1/1891," *A.N.* F XXI (1330); "Memorandum: Ministère de l'Instruction Publique et des Beaux-Arts/Département des Beaux-Arts," *A.N.* F XXI (1337).

42 Emile Zola, *La République et La Littérature* (Paris, 1879), 34f. Cf. Antonin Proust, (formerly Gambetta's Minister of Fine Arts), Chambre des Députés, Séance de 5/27/1891, Annexe No.2, Enquête de 1891, Commission relative à l'abolition de la censure et à la liberté des théâtres, 2543; Krakovitch, *Hugo Censuré*, 248.

43 "Sous-Secrétaire d'Etat des Beaux-Arts à M. le Directeur du Théâtre, 2/16/1879" in folder "Circulaires aux Directeurs de Théâtres, 1840-1875," *A.N.* F XXI (1330).

44 For the official position of the Société, see *La Liberté* (5/29/1891) and other relevant press clippings collected in *A.N.* F XXI (1336) and (1337). Cf. "Chambre des Députés, Séance de 12/3/1897," *Journal Officiel*, 2679, 2682 [also available in *A.N.* F XXI (1337)]. The same dossiers contain press clippings relevant to the opinions of various playwrights and librettists. Cf. Sudik, "The French Administration of Fine Arts," 80; Marvin Carlson, *The French Stage in the Nineteenth Century* (Metuchin, N.J.: Scarecrow Press, 1972), 177. For the 1891 proposal to abolish the censorship, "Chambre des Députés No.1167, Annexe au procès-verbal de la séance du 1/31/1891," *Journal Officiel* [also available in *A.N.* F XXI (1330)].

45 "Théâtre Nationale de l'Opéra-Comique, Cahier des Charges 1911," Article 66.

46 "Bérenger to Ministre de l'Instruction Publique, 2/29/1901," "Ministre to

Gailhard, 2/28/1901," "Gailhard to Ministre, 3/1/1901," *A.N.* F XXI (1336).

47 Interviewed by André Gaucher, "La Question *d'Astarté*," *La Liberté* (3/7/1901) (also available in B.O. Dossier d'artiste/Louis Grammont); Gheusi, *Cinquante Ans*, 2:120ff.

48 Krakovitch, *Hugo Censuré*, 227.

49 "Correspondance; Préfet d'Indre et Loire, 1888: 'L'Adultère Passif,'" in *A.N.* F XXI (1337). Cf. Herbert Lindenberger, *Historical Drama: The Relation of Literature and Reality* (Chicago: University of Chicago Press, 1975), 105f.

CHAPTER VI

FORMING PUBLIC OPINION:
CRITICS AND TOUT-PARIS

Because, in contrast to modern U. S. American newspapers, with their claim of objectivity, the French press adopted a frankly political or ideological approach to journalism, we might expect reviews of operas to draw out and comment on the ideological implications of the various operas discussed in Chapters III and IV. It should be possible to infer the response to the various operas discussed above of different social and political groups associated with the various newspapers. Instead, opera critics, seduced by the luxury of the opera, and intent on perpetuating their privileges through loyalty to the interests of the opera establishment, pre-empted their editors' attempts to use opera to further their political agendas. They did so most notably by developing an aesthetic of opera that undermined the authority of ideas. The reviewers contributed to the role of the opera as an instrument of cultural hegemony by diverting attention from the significant impact that opera had on the political and social values of its clientele, and by extending this clientele to include readers of opera reviews who rarely or never attended performances. Only as participants in the exclusive Tout-Paris of the opera, the true font of public opinion during this period, could the most powerful individual professional critics enter an arena for action that compensated them for the squandered prestige of their fraternity.

A distinguishing feature of the French press — one that was even more marked at the end of the nineteenth century than it is today, when everyone is quite aware of it — makes it quite possible to identify particular newspapers as representing a monarchist position, for instance, or a conservative republican, a radical republican or a socialist position. There were in addition numerous single-political-issue newspapers, of which the most important were clerical or anti-clerical. The comprehensive *Histoire Générale de la Presse Française* edited by Claude Bellanger has systematically categorized the dozens of papers that proliferated during the period of the pre-war Third Republic. Bellanger writes that "the opposition between conservative and republican was, at the beginning of the Third Republic, sufficiently sharp that each paper clearly defined its program and may therefore be easily located in one of these political categories."[1] The authors also make very shrewd educated guesses, based on the style, cost, circulation data, and political orientation of the various newspapers, as well as on documentary and anecdotal evidence, of the social composition of their clientele. With the help of Bellanger's indispensable guide, it should be possible to use opera reviews in newspapers with different readerships and different political orientations to identify the attitudes of various political and social groups toward the opera in general, toward specific operas, and even toward specific issues concerning the different constituent art forms within the opera.

Among the very few journals — all of them out of the political mainstream — that ignored the opera completely were the newspapers of the far left, whose readership never attended the opera and whose editors were offended both personally and politically by the conspicuous luxury displayed there. The Marxist *Le Cri du Peuple* confined its coverage to repeating the cry for an end to government subsidies for an art form that was inaccessible to its own working class subscribers.[2] On the reactionary, monarchist right, *La Croix* and *l'Univers* might have been expected to take an interest in the traditional amusement of the kings of France if they had not also been ultra-Catholic to the point of dismissing the opera as immoral. The typical mainstream newspaper, from the anti-republican but nonclerical right to the socialist but non-revolutionary left, gave a remarkable amount of space to the opera. Even the relatively inexpensive journals, intended for people of moderate means who could not possibly afford to attend, devoted extensive resources to it.

Coverage of a new opera would typically begin with the dress-rehearsal; this first review outlined the plot and called the attention of the readers to highlights of the music that they might listen for when they attended — or that they might discuss intelligently whether they attended or not. The day following the opening of a new work, there would be an account of the premiere by the "soiriste." He would concentrate on descriptions of the audience: who had been there, what clothes they had worn, how enthusiastic they had been. He might also comment on visual aspects of the production such as costumes and *décors*, and sometimes on the performances of the lead singers and dancers. A few days later, usually on the following Monday, would appear a full-scale review by the music critic, who addressed any aspect of the opera that attracted his attention. In some cases the drama critic might also provide a separate review. When *Le Journal* sponsored Bruneau's *L'Attaque du Moulin* financially, the paper provided, in addition to the coverage described above, a lead article by Emile Zola, on whose book the libretto was based, on the subject of the new lyric drama, and an eight-page illustrated supplement with sketches of the various scenes. Following the premiere, *Le Journal* published for its readers the guest list and menu of its fête in honor of the authors.[3]

Among the fifteen operas for which I surveyed the reviews systematically — in ten or more newspapers — there were numerous instances in which the political orientation of the paper corresponded to the reviewer's response to what was happening on stage. Some newspapers had specific axes to grind, in their opera reviews as in everything else they published. The egregious anti-semitism of *l'Echo de Paris*, for instance, showed up in its critique of the libretto for *Le Cid*: "This epoch will see the triumph of industrialism and Jewry in all the arts.... Corneille is crucified by d'Ennery and the two adapters."[4] Similarly, the monarchist *Gazette de France* vented its clerical, anti-populist spleen on the opera *Henri VIII*, saying of the lead character: "Henri VIII appeals to the people — like a simple Bonaparte — and causes the *canaille* of London to invade the hall of Parliament — a proceeding worthy of a heretic of the sixteenth century, or a republican of the present day."[5]

In a number of suggestive cases, the opera reviews split along political lines in their judgments of entire operas or of individual episodes within them. All the reviewers commented on the stirring chorus of noble conspirators in the Renaissance costume drama *Cinq-Mars* (mentioned above in Chapter III), who sing: "Let us save the king, the nobility and France. Let us deliver the throne and the altar." But whereas the reviewer from the monarchist journal *Le Soleil* commented, "This is truly elevated and elevating," the reviewer for *La*

République Française, the paper of the radical Gambettistes, suggested that "it is almost irritating that the music found accents of genius for lyrics that sound so hollow." *Le Rappel*, further to the left, referred to "these verses of another era."[6] This ultra-radical paper also carried the only favorable review (among the range of those that I read) of the libretto of Delibes' *Kassya*, in which the hero leads a violent peasant revolt against a rapacious local lord. More significant, perhaps, is the extent to which the leftist papers dwelled, in describing this plot, on the iniquities of the evil count, while those on the right devoted the bulk of their coverage to the love affair.[7] In the case of the opera *Sapho*, about a revolutionary conspiracy against an evil tyrant, which had run afoul of Napoleon III's censorship thirty years previously, only the radical paper *La Justice*, and again *Le Rappel*, reviewed the opera favorably.[8] Eight other papers, ranging from moderately republican to far right, were ambivalent or much more critical.

On the whole, however, precise correspondence between the content of the reviews and the politics of the journals is the exception rather than the rule. Despite these examples to the contrary, the social and political orientation of the newspaper is not a reliable guide to the reviewer's response to operas that should have been politically controversial. How could the critic from the radical, anticlerical *La République Française* call the religious episodes in *Le Cid* the most "elevated in the new work," and review this reactionary opera favorably? "First, the prayer of Rodrigue is of a beautiful character," he writes, "then the voices from heaven, which little by little insinuate themselves in the general sonority to accompany and sustain the pious appeals of the young chevalier, give to this mystical tableau a penetrating poetry which moves and profoundly touches the sincere listener."[9] Generally speaking, within limits defined by the most volatile works of the repertoire, such as *Carmen*, opera reviews did not serve as a focus for the political and social agendas of the various groups that edited newspapers.

Such discrepancies cannot be attributed to independent reviewers' writing in cavalier disregard of their employers' opinions. The monarchist journal, *Le Gaulois*, conspicuously hired reviewers without regard for their politics and allowed them free expression, but the paper was unique in this regard. Editors of other newspapers naturally attempted to insist that their own outlook clearly and consistently pervade the pages of their papers, and they employed a variety of strategies for enforcing such conformity. A general perception that theatre critics required no particular expertise or training meant that there was no lack of ambitious young litterateurs willing to replace recalcitrant writers. Even in the worst possible case, of a particularly prominent critic with a personal following among the readers, editors were perfectly capable of disclaiming his opinions and providing a separate review representing their own outlook.[10] In the long run, however, they were helpless before the reviewers' predisposition to conformity.

Not merely is there little correlation between the political orientation of the various journals and the ideological content of their opera reviews, but reviewers from across the political spectrum were remarkably uniform in their attitudes toward problematical operas. There was, to be sure, a discernible difference in approach in the organs of those groups that had no real prospect of participation in mainstream politics, such as *Le Rappel*. Parties or movements that rejected the conventional rules of political behavior caused considerable embarrassment to the opera establishment, as the proto-fascist new right demonstrated in the affair of *Lohengrin*'s premiere in 1891. Otherwise, the uniformity of opinion that pervaded the reviews of all the newspapers from fairly far left to traditional right is striking. I conclude that opera's social and political function was to help integrate political factions that were potential candidates for a share of power into a common culture and outlook.

The strength of the impetus towards conformity is illustrated by the case of the reviewer who apparently neglected to work the foyers and coulisses of the Opéra during the intermissions and after the premiere of *Henri VIII*, so as to get a clear impression of the consensus of opinion. Realizing the next day that he was the only one among his colleagues to have reviewed the opera favorably, he found himself under the necessity of hedging his original review a week later by explaining away some of the rhetoric, reinterpreting some of the rest, and providing a list of successful operas that were not appreciated at first.[11] Cozy, club-like relationships among the well-known reviewers helped to submerge political differences that might otherwise have divided them. One critic of the critics describes them as a corporation, complete with an official banquet.[12] Reviewers were to be seen walking arm in arm in the corridors, in the foyer for the audience or that for the actors during the entr'actes.

In selecting new candidates for the position of critic, the range of their acquaintance was much more important than their critical capacity. Co-opted into the Tout-Paris of the opera, the most elegant club in Paris, with its ambience of conspicuous luxury and its formidable perquisites, newcomers willing to play the game were invited to subscribe to an approach to opera criticism that transcended the factional political differences of the papers they worked for. They wore the same clothes, dined at the same hour, and shared similar systems of beliefs: that high culture was more valid than popular culture, that bourgeois men acted rationally while women and lower-class men were dominated by their passions, that lower-class women were at the disposal of bourgeois men, and above all, that ideas had no place in the theatre. Reviewers would be judged by their peers according to the extent that they incorporated such values into their reviews.

Dismissing the importance of ideas in the theatre helped the best critics to maintain their positions in the fraternity without sacrificing their integrity and self-respect. It was said of Francisque Sarcey, the grand old man of the theatre whose prejudices every author who aspired to popular success had to take into account, that he preferred that "theatre should not be a means of education, but a means of promoting digestion in an overstuffed audience by stimulating the erotic and sentimental juices."[13] Resistance to the intrusion of ideas was especially strong in the case of the musical theatre. Beginning under the Second Empire, and continuing for most of the pre-war Third Republic, the ultimate criterion for judging an opera was the pleasure it provided. The classic protest against the adulteration of opera with ideas appeared in the *Revue des Deux Mondes* in 1859 under the byline of Scudo, who, in his day, "reigned over Parisian musical opinion":

> It is a sure sign of decadence to pretend to extract from arts like music or painting supposedly profound effects which it is not in their nature to produce.... Without the form, which should above all please my senses, it is in vain that you invite me to reflect or meditate at length.... Let us beware of this hollow German symbolism.... I do not go to the theatre to take a course in metaphysics, nor to meditate on the government of empires or the mysteries of Providence; I go there seeking a delicate pleasure.[14]

The consequences were clear to an outsider such as P.-J. Proudhon, the most prominent French socialist of his era: "At the theatre of the Opéra...the words and drama are disdained, and only the instruments and voices are listened to."[15] Clearly the dominant mode in criticism described by Scudo and Proudhon represents a shift in emphasis away from the kind described by Fulcher as characteristic of the July Monarchy, when critics focused their commentary on the implicit political content of the operatic arts. This shift may be attributed to the wholesale reorientation of French journalism accomplished by Louis-Napoléon's repressive regime, which through the activities of its censorship office, supplemented by physical intimidation of journalists, virtually eliminated public references to politics from the press. Once politics had been banished as a subject for discussion, the success or failure of journalistic ventures came to depend on discursive columns of commentary on the passing social and literary scenes, in which substance was prudently subordinated to elegant prose, creative imagination, and the essential *esprit*.

What had been merely dangerous under the Second Empire became unfashionable under the republic. After the liberalization of the Empire, and especially after the triumph of republicanism during the late seventies, when the public again began selecting newspapers on the basis of political content rather than literary quality, theatre criticism continued to be the preserve of the resolutely apolitical. Until the 1890s, when the advent of *Wagnérisme* encouraged the French public to take opera — and especially the ideas conveyed by the words — more seriously, arbiters of taste conformed to an approach to opera criticism that subordinated its social and political content to strictly aesthetic concerns. The implications were profound. Eschewing overt partisan political persuasion permitted critics to present as ideologically neutral, as common sense, ideas that actually had the interests of particular groups embedded in them, those that favored the status quo and the distribution of power incorporated in it. Hence the perception illustrated by the author of "La Critique musicale" that "in the long run, the critics only wrote for those who thought like they did."[16] As theoreticians of opera, they could, and did, define the acceptable range of discourse to exclude any discussion of the relationship of art to controversial social issues.

When therefore, during the Belle Epoque, public or even internal controversies erupted over operas with volatile social or political themes, the apparent focus of the debate was on aesthetics: on Galli-Marié's acting in *Carmen*, on the realistic clothes and tavern of the gypsies, on the "naturalism" of Bizet's music, on the settings and costuming for *Louise* and *L'Attaque du Moulin*. Henry Roujon, director of fine arts, declared "unacceptable the long dirty boots, the large corduroy trousers, the filthy cap, and the rough open shirt of the revolutionary, Mathias,"[17] in Zola's *Messidor*. His reaction reinforces the notion that such aesthetic controversies had important ideological subtexts. The integral relationship between the political and the aesthetic manifests itself most dramatically in the press reaction to *Carmen*, the most controversial of Third Republic operas. In that case, the political orientation of their newspapers was the crucial factor in determining the critics' response to the aesthetic qualities of the opera. Criticism of Carmen's values is mixed up with horror at Galli-Marié's interpretation of the role, but the theme common to all the complaints is a profound uneasiness at the realism inherent in Bizet's innovative approach to the genre of the *opéra-comique*.

Le Figaro, the most influential of all the newspapers in opera circles because of its subscription list, "the golden book of the aristocracy, of the wealthiest bourgeoisie, of great commerce, of the highest industry, of the army, of the most elegant of the foreign colony," and still, at this time, Legitimist in its political outlook, calls the heroine of the opera "absolutely foul and odiously repulsive," and reports that the audience didn't like it.[18] This *Carmen*, says *Le Siècle*, is a case more likely to provoke the solicitude of a physician than to interest the honest spectators who come to the Opéra-Comique in company with their wives and daughters. The critics from *L'Ordre*, official organ of the Bonapartists, and *Le Pays*, the clerical, militarist, anti-republican organ of "progressive" Bonapartism, take a similar approach, criticizing Galli-Marié's interpretation of the leading role, emphasizing the break with the traditions of the Opéra-Comique, and gloating over the opera's inevitable failure. While claiming to wish *Carmen* well, *Le Pays* gives it no chance of success. Having found some praiseworthy elements in the opera, the critic for the conservative, Bonapartist daily, *Le Gaulois*, also comments on the disappointment of the audience, who out of sympathy for the authors of the piece had wanted nothing better than to like it. He writes that Mme. Galli-Marié seemed to take pleasure in emphasizing the scabrous side of her "dangerous" role. "It would be difficult to go farther down the road of casual affairs without provoking the intervention of the police," he concludes.[19]

The threat represented by Galli-Marié/Carmen is a recurring theme among reviewers from the right who are critical of the realism of the role. The reviewer from the monarchist Paris-Journal, after roundly denouncing Bizet and his school, lashes into Galli-Marié, who "found the means to trivialize and render the role of Carmen more odious and more abject than Merimée imagined. She treated it with the brutally realistic methods of M. Courbet…"[20] Simon Boubée, though otherwise utterly misguided in everything he says about the work, does manage to express the fears of the rightist critics most succinctly. Writing in the Orléanist Gazette de France, he condemns Galli-Marié particularly for making Carmen "canaille." For Boubeé, Carmen struck a little too close to home:"Mme Galli-Marié seems to think she is in one of the faubourgs of Paris."[21] Jules Guillemot, in the center-right Le Soleil, locates the action even more precisely:"While Escamillo is triumphing in a bullfight, the scene which I just described is taking place in the Rue Oberkampf!… I mean in the plaza de toros."[22]

What previous analysts of the press reaction to Carmen's premiere have missed, in attempting to account for the antagonism of the reviewers, is the accuracy of Bizet's references to the real world of the working-class districts of Paris.[23] It would not have been uncommon, in the newspaper world of the 1870s, for opera reviewers to have doubled as police court reporters, in which capacity they would have seen numerous women like Carmen either as victims or perpetrators of so-called crimes of passion. Because their trials were often causes célèbres, well attended by bourgeois aficionados of the law courts, the type of Carmen, suddenly appearing on the stage of the Opéra-Comique, would have been not only threatening, but all too familiar as well. Joëlle Guillais has studied such trials systematically for the decade of the 1870s, precisely the one in which Bizet's Carmen appeared. The results of her research, described in La Chair de l'Autre, confirm the prevalence, among working-class women involved in such judicial proceedings, of a type that might easily be taken as a model for Bizet's character:

> …Apparent in the dossiers of the archives [are] their positive, distinctive traits, namely their emotional and sexual freedom, and

above all a formidable instinct for survival which expressed itself every so often with a certain warmth and a certain exuberance.

Aside from the fact that the majority of them belong to the lower classes and that they work, the strongest common denominator among these women of the people, of these indefatigable working women, is situated in their will to dispose of themselves.... Each one demonstrated individually her power and her needs in her daily resistance to masculine power by struggling with determination to remain free to dispose of her body and her time.[24]

Guillais distinguishes these working-class women from those of the middle class, who were much more seriously constrained in the ways they could dispose of their time and their emotions, in part because they were completely subject to their husbands' financial management. Even more limiting for middle-class women was the sense that the street "did not belong to them." It was full of "forbidden zones," including public places such as cafés and cabarets, where, by contrast, working-class women could become regular patrons on the same terms as men. Guillais notes the resistance of the working women to attempts by working-class men to impose on them the bourgeois ideal of the angel in the house: "...Free to circulate through the town by day as by night, women wanted to occupy and arrange their work time and their leisure time according to their own will, without being constrained in their movements by a too curious companion."[25] Just as *Carmen* was condemned by the critics of the right and by the rest of the Tout-Paris, so the subjects of Guillais' study, whether victims or criminals, were condemned by the magistrates for similar reasons:

Accustomed to looking after themselves come what may, they are more capable of defying masculine authority — with firmness if their happiness or their survival depends on it. Perceived as dangerous, as guilty because disorderly, these women who do only as they wish, "who want to be their own masters," who come and go, irritate the magistrates. Condemned and judged severely, they are made responsible for the spread of crime.[26]

The failure of *Carmen*, at least in the short run, demonstrates the influence that these critics and their allies within the Tout-Paris of the premieres had on public opinion. The power of the monarchist press was all the more impressive since it was out of proportion to the volume of its circulation; on that basis, popular, inexpensive, republican papers such as *Le Petit Journal* would have predominated. But the right included the leaders of fashion whose opinions set the tone for those who wanted to derive from the opera the social cachet that attendance afforded. On the other hand, contrary to the impression left by Mina Curtiss in a description of the *Carmen* premiere, which has been accepted as standard, the press was far from unanimous in its denunciation of the opera or of Galli-Marié's interpretation of the title role. This is not to deny that the opera was perceived as a failure, nor that the reaction of the press contributed to this result. But by no means all the critics reacted negatively. Republican papers consistently approved of *Carmen* for the same reasons that most papers of the right rejected it.

Le Petit Journal, while not exactly effusive, was generally favorable to the opera, and said that Galli-Marié was well applauded. Reyer, in the *Journal des Débats*, had scarcely a word of complaint, and seemed to think that *Carmen* might eventually be a success. Several reviewers, though ambivalent toward the opera as a whole, and especially toward the character of *Carmen*, approved of the authors' and composer's initiative in trying to overcome the limitations of the traditional *opéra-comique* form. Gambetta's paper, *La République Française*, contained serious criticisms of the piece, but complimented Meilhac and Halévy, at least, for having contributed to an aesthetic "revolution." The reviewer also had high praise for Galli-Marié, and described the applause for her as very enthusiastic. Further to the left, *Le Rappel* devoted a large part of its review to making fun of the traditional genre. The reviewer didn't think the Opéra-Comique had, as yet, attracted as much of an audience for corpses as it had for weddings, but he hoped that *Carmen* would help people to get used to them. He too had "nothing but praise to give to Galli-Marié."[27] Weber, in *Le Temps*, found the character of Carmen unsympathetic, but complimented Bizet for bringing novelty and realism to the Opéra-Comique stage. Among the most favorable of the reviewers was Charles de La Rounat, writing in *Le XIXe Siècle*. He was full of praise for the libretto, the score, and for Galli-Marié, for whom the role was a "triumph." Far from glossing over the realistic aspects of *Carmen*, he admired Galli-Marié particularly for having brought to the stage "a character of gripping realism."[28] Adolphe Jullien scolded Bizet not for the risks he had taken or the innovations he had accomplished, but for the compromises he had felt obliged to make with the integrity of the piece. He strongly supported the interpretation of the leading character:

> Galli-Marié deserves nothing but praise. Carmen is and will remain her most remarkable creation. Actress, singer, and dancer by turns, she knew how to give this strange figure of a gypsy girl an arresting cachet of truth...[29]

Confronted with a real-life Carmen, the bourgeois men who wrote opera reviews for republican journals would undoubtedly have been as predatory, or as unnerved, as those who worked for monarchist papers. The republicans' support for the opera, and for Galli-Marié's performance in particular, stemmed not from the character and values of Carmen, which they disparaged as often as not, but from the break with tradition represented by Bizet's commitment to stage realism. In the eighteen-seventies, these writers of the left were fighting a political battle in which art could play a significant role by forcing its audience to confront social reality. If dirty, violent, subversive, threatening gypsies such as Carmen were not sympathetic allies in this fight, at least the conventional, colorful, submissive, Opéra-Comique gypsies, whom Bizet and his director wanted to reconstruct or to replace, were obvious agents of the enemy.

The degree of influence that critics held over the opinions of the opera audience is difficult to assess. The distinguished composer and critic Ernst Reyer, writing in the well-respected *Journal des Débats*, claimed considerable authority for them: "With the exception of some free spirits who claim to obey only the impressions that they experience, all the others take as their rule... the opinion that the most authorized judges have traced for them."[30] Some individual critics not only molded audience opinion, but played a prominent role in the deliberations of opera management and the government. Sarcey, the scrupulous, thoroughly conservative drama critic for *Le Temps*, dominated his profession during the early part of the Belle Epoque. By virtue of impeccable integrity and exceptionally hard work, he established a wide and faithful following who trusted him as the representative of the average theatregoer. Even after his formal retirement, Sarcey's opinion could be decisive in the appointment of a director of fine arts.

Alfred Edwards, editor of *Le Matin*, had similar power, according to

Gheusi; his public threats forced the reinstatement of Gailhard as co-director of the Opéra following his dismissal by the government. On another occasion, Edwards imposed one of his mistresses on the management of the Opéra-Comique as second lead in *Guernica*, and then required the directors to eliminate two acts of the opera because she did not appear in them:

> "Wait," said one of the librettists, when Edwards got up to leave the first reading, "there are two acts more. Paul Vidal will play them for you."
>
> "Not at all," declared Edwards. "The piece is finished and it is a success."[31]

In this case, however, the powerful journalist failed to deliver the goods; the truncated *Guernica* attained the embarrassingly low total of only seven performances.

Editors who dictated the slant of their reviews sometimes did so out of personal, but more often out of financial considerations. Established papers typically discouraged "Quixotism" by critics in order not to jeopardize subscriptions. Newer operations adopted a deliberately provocative tone, as the aspiring critic Emile Bergerat noted following his interview with an editor of the fledgling *Evènement*:

> He demanded severity, because they always want severity to begin with. "...We have to cleanse the theatre," he declared to me magnificently, "chase the vendors out of the temple, reconquer the old supremacy."
>
> "... Yes, yes, make way for youth," I blurted out excitedly.
>
> "...*C'est ça!* You are just the man we need."[32]

According to Bergerat (a notorious *blagueur*), when he arrived at the offices of *l'Evènement* to begin work, the editors were all practicing fencing. Unfortunately, the evident connection between the circulation drives of such papers and the tone of their critics compromised the reviewers' integrity and reliability as much as if they had joined the club.

The critics also undercut their own authority, during the Belle Epoque, by encouraging the public to think of opera as a mere pleasant diversion. A disadvantage of the strategy that de-emphasized the intellectual content of the theatre, especially the musical theatre, was that it bred cynicism among reviewers and readers alike. Bergerat eventually established himself as a critic of some reputation but always looked down on journalism as an inferior art or no art at all; he continually begrudged the time that it took away from the poetry and drama on which an enduring reputation depended. Refractory when asked to modify his artistic creations for commercial reasons, he never had qualms about subordinating his journalistic endeavors to the same requirements. Independent, conscientious reviewers who might have resisted the seductions of the fraternity in order to engage in genuine theatre criticism gave in or got discouraged after years of waiting for an opportunity; others went to work for very small journals that quickly failed because no one read them.[33]

The professional standards of the critics were lax in the extreme. Charles Monselet, one of the best-known literary figures in Paris, stopped attending the theatre altogether following a duel with an offended playwright, but continued covering premieres for *Le Monde Illustré* for thirty more years, basing his criticisms on articles by other journalists. It was commonly understood that a portion of the fraternity was susceptible to bribery; some writers attributed the critical failure of *Carmen* to the unwillingness of the Opéra-Comique director to bribe the bribable press. Others critics engaged in obvious cabals that discredited not only the individuals involved but their colleagues as well.[34] "The critics are blasé," wrote Emile Zola in 1880; "there are very few who are really conscientious enough to get worked up over an opinion; some rely on style, others are just good old boys [*font de la camaraderie*]; still others are simply making a living."[35]

One common type was the *petit fonctionnaire* who had done well at school in rhetoric and orthography, who was bored at the office and loved the theatre, but didn't have the money to gratify his passion. As a critic he could attend as often as he liked, bring his mistress, take notes conspicuously in the middle of the orchestra, sitting next to Théophile Gauthier. When the secretaries and ticket-takers recognized him, he began to consider himself an important person; he met actors and actresses less educated than himself. When he received perfumed thank-you notes, his bosses and co-workers accused him of pretending to sleep with actresses every night and of arriving at the office late, tired out from orgies.[36] Particularly notorious for their incapacity during this era were those who reviewed music, including the opera. Critics of the critics agree that it was common for newspapers to assign literary critics to cover musical events. Calvocaressi asserts that the same journalist might be responsible for music, literature, political bulletins, and the sports news.[37] An influx of incompetent practioners into the field naturally discredited the profession. Because reviewers no longer had to demonstrate the capacity to manipulate ideas, audiences concluded that they themselves, or at least the leaders of fashion among them, could just as well determine what was pleasant and amusing. Encouraged by the critics' demystification of the opera, the audience took responsibility for its own judgments of individual works, effectively reinforcing the operation of the free market in opera ideology. As a result, while the critics in general had less and less impact on the success or failure of individual works, the Tout-Paris of the opera enjoyed unparalleled influence.

"Tout-Paris" was the name by which, through metonymic transformation, various groups attempted to establish hegemony over Parisian fashion. There was a Tout-Paris of the salons, a Tout-Paris of the great funerals, of the law courts, of the Institut, of official receptions, of sermons, of the race course, and of the Bois de Boulogne.[38] The Tout-Paris of the premieres saw its primary function as defining the acceptable limits of audience taste by monitoring the moral and aesthetic content of new productions. Both Tout-Paris and professional critics directly affected the content of the repertoire by influencing the decisions of directors sensitive to critical opinion. The Tout-Paris, in addition, enabled the subscribers quickly to deploy their economic power — based on the implicit threat of mass defections — to inhibit performances of any controversial piece and the subsequent introduction of similar uncongenial material. The power that the Tout-Paris of the opera had demonstrated so effectively at the premiere of *Carmen* in 1875, they successfully retained throughout the Belle Epoque, despite increasing public notoriety.

Analysis of the librettos' content in Chapter III strongly suggested that the government had a role in effecting the shift in Opéra-Comique ideology in 1879-80. Likewise, a completely free market in Opéra-Comique librettos could hardly have produced so precise an articulation of government interests as the French revolutionary operas of the nineties displayed. The Tout-Paris deserves special attention in this context because investigation of its activities provides some important answers to the question posed at the beginning of the previous chapter, as to how the repertoire of the Opéra-Comique, especially, could have responded so closely to the political interests of the state while the latter preserved a conscientious official neutrality. The Tout-Paris formed a crucial nexus between the audience and the government, representing each to the other. As delegates of the government to the Tout-Paris, officials and their clients helped unofficially to mold audience opinion. At the same time, the Tout-Paris co-opted members of the various governments to the outlook of the Palais Garnier establishment.

The composition of the Tout-Paris of the theatrical premieres varied from house to house, but a nucleus of regular members could be found at every opening. While Massenet estimated its size at only about one hundred people, other writers have been less exclusive. Charles Garnier, Academician and architect of the new Opéra, defined the Tout-Paris of the premieres, in which he claimed membership, as consisting of the press, both political and literary; of deputies and senators, including past, present and future ministers; of directors and actors from the various theatres; and of others more or less attached to the world of the theatre by position or personal relations. To confirm the importance of the political component, and in general the accuracy of his analysis, his list can be compared with any of a number of newspaper descriptions. *Le Figaro's* account of the premiere of *Le Cid*, for instance, names several government ministers who were in attendance, along with the president of the Chamber of Deputies, many other deputies, all of the Parisian branch of the Rothschild banking family, and numerous other notables.[39]

In its heyday, according to Garnier, members of the Tout-Paris took their ability to mold public taste seriously and considered that they were performing a public service. His claims for the prestige and authority of the institution cannot be disputed, even though, as he put it, the public occasionally disagreed with its opinions. Garnier compared the Tout-Paris to a highly articulated judicial system in which the journalists served as *rapporteurs*. The theatre critics evaluated the play and the actors; the artists studied the form and color of the costumes and decors; the architects, the lighting, acoustics, and exits and entrances of the set. The women judged the clothes of the actresses. The social butterflies were indispensable as a means of communication among the various groups: They distributed the pollen to the flowers.[40] In his elaborate description of the group's *modus operandi*, Garnier omits to assign to anyone the task of investigating the new works' social and political implications, just as he fails to assign any particular task to the senators and deputies, or to "past, present and future ministers." Garnier's omission illustrates the discretion with which they exercised their functions, confirming the pattern of informal government influence over the opera that emerges from all accounts of the politicians' activities in this sphere.

The individual politician's influence within the opera establishment depended on his capacity for manipulating patronage decisions, which was, in turn, a function of his ability to make trouble for directors. Deputies who announced their intention of participating in the Chamber's opera subsidy debate received complimentary tickets as a matter of course. Legislators who were particularly interested in the opera might aspire to the Commission consultative des théâtres, which attended pleasant private previews, ostensibly in order to advise directors about works to be considered for production. Because any ordinary deputy could arrange to delay a subsidy vote, directors quickly learned to be accommodating.[41] The ballerina with a deputy behind her was automatically promoted to first chorus:

> No one who has set foot on the boulevard during the last thirty years is unaware of the names of all the official actresses, paid out of the budget, who were the mistresses, the nieces, the daughters of ministers, of influential deputies, or of tame journalists. In Paris these liaisons are public knowledge. We have seen the careers of "subsidized actresses" and the careers of politicians undergo the same fluctuations with touching parallelism. When the deputy becomes a minister, the *artiste* passes from the Odéon to the Comédie-Française.[42]

One deputy whose *protégée* failed to win a leading role managed to launch a full-scale Chambre des Députés investigation of Albert Carré's Opéra-Comique concession. He was unable to contrive the director's dismissal or to prevent his subsequent reappointment, but the public scrutiny of Carré's administrative practices had its embarrassing moments.[43]

At the highest level of political patronage, even decisions about the appointments of directors — decisions inexplicable on ideological

grounds — may be explained on the principle of *"cherchez la femme."*
P.-B. Gheusi ascribed the dismissal of his close friend and associate
Pedro Gailhard as Opéra director to the intrigues of vindictive sopranos
close to Clemenceau, then President of the Council of Ministers. A
more circumstantial version of the same story, to the effect that Gailhard
was replaced because rivalry for the affections of the soprano Rose
Caron led him to bar her dressing room to the Tiger, may perhaps be
dismissed as gossip. Gheusi is unreliable at best; elsewhere in the same
book he provides a third account of Gailhard's demise, attributing it to
the influence of a cabinet minister's wife whose modesty had been
offended by certain scenes in *Astarté* (O-1901). The persistent theme
running through Gheusi's inconsistency is his evident belief in the
decisive importance of private political influence at the upper reaches
of opera management. This must have been a basic premise of his own
administration as director of a state opera house, as it probably was of
Gailhard's as well. Gheusi's stories also make more plausible the press
speculation that Vaucorbeil owed his appointment as Opéra director in
1879 to Jules Ferry's wife, his former student. The prevalence of abuses
of official influence under the regime of Carvalho, as well, is
corroborated by his successor Carré's description of his own struggles
to eliminate them. The biographer of his successors, the Isola brothers,
describes similar scandals during their tenure also — at other theatres.[44]

There is little direct evidence of private manipulation of the
repertoire by politicians, but cabinet members apparently were able to
indulge their wives and mistresses to the extent of arranging for
production of individual works in which they took a particular interest.
The editor Durand, for instance, mentions a minister's wife who
intervened to have a piece by Ravel performed at the Opéra-
Comique.[45] This is not to say that politicians' wives and mistresses
systematically influenced the content of the repertoire, much less its
ideology. But these examples demonstrate how control over patronage
and administrative decisions enabled the circle of ministers and
influential deputies and their clients to insinuate themselves into
leadership of the Tout-Paris of the opera.

Indeed, the composition of the Tout-Paris varied according to
changes in political fortunes, altering its response to the social and
political content of the various offerings in the repertoire. In 1880,
while Ferry was affirming his government's commitment to an

apolitical conception of the opera, a new generation of republican politicians was taking its place in the prominent official boxes and in the coulisses, of the Opéra, which had been previously been occupied by monarchists. These newly elected politicians took on a leadership role in the Tout-Paris of the state theatre premieres, becoming an unofficial vehicle for the transmission of government opinion to opera directors, librettists, critics, and other creators of operatic ideology. The wives and mistresses of republican ministers lobbied to gratify their tastes, which the "tame journalists" of the republicans helped to establish as norms for public opinion to follow. Likewise, the relaxation of censorship in the post-1880 period, though it had little direct impact on the opera, legitimized the activities of journalists and playwrights with more radical republican views, giving them access to the Tout-Paris also. The capacity of this institution for registering political change informally enabled groups of newly elected politicians to impress on opera management developments such as the transfer of power to republicans after 1880, and to bring the ideology of new librettos into line, while allowing the government to maintain an official neutrality.

The influence of the government was especially strong in the Tout-Paris of the Opéra-Comique, as the evidence of Chapter III suggests. Presidents of the republic regularly attended special dress rehearsals in company with members of the government and senior administrative officials, besides appearing at the free fête-day performances as well. The critic from *La République Française* mentions in his review of Massenet's *Esclarmonde* that "the chief of state on many occasions led the applause."[46] The president of the republic and "all the official world" attended the premiere of *Louise*, according to Albert Carré, director of the Opéra-Comique after the turn of the century. "The Opéra-Comique was the theatre of choice of M. et Mme. Loubet, as it became that of M. and Mme. Fallières, and of M. et Mme. Poincaré, not to mention M. Clemenceau, who came just as a simple spectator" wrote Carré, who claimed the title of "*amuseur en titre*" to the Third Republic.[47] As a result, during the eighties and afterwards, the Opéra-Comique not only took over some of the Opéra's ceremonial functions, but it responded closely to the political interests of the republicans in power as well.

Toward the end of the century, the Tout-Paris gradually lost its influence over the opinions of the audience, and consequently over the decisions of the directors and librettists. This was partly the result of increasingly scandalous public behavior on the part of its members. Even their champion, Garnier, admitted that many of them "look at prudery through the large end of the lorgnette," and Emile Zola concurred that "it was best not to pry into it too closely, if one was delicate, because one would come across improper things." The socialist critic Urbain Gohier described the Tout-Paris as a collection of the least virtuous people in the capital: "In the hall, everyone knows and points their fingers at the *ménages à trois*, the *ménages à quatre*; they note the *chassés-croisés* that take place between couples from one show to the next."[48] Even allowing for differences in their political outlook, the contrast is striking between Garnier's description of the group's membership in 1884, quoted above, and Gohier's, from 1901. Like Garnier, the latter included as members the journalists writing for professional reasons. But his second category consisted of "*boursiers*," whose living revolved around the stock exchange, and "*boursecotiers*," or speculators. The actors and actresses in the Tout-Paris he described as retired or looking for work. Then there were the gossip columnists for scandal sheets, the *fêtards*, or people who lived only for fêtes; the colony of renegade anti-semitic Jews; politicians trying to give themselves a Parisian veneer; and *chevaliers* "swimming in their own juice."[49] To a group whose ostensible function was to alert the public to breaches of decorum and morality, a reputation for individual and collective immorality would have been particularly damaging. In the long run, after the turn of the century, it contributed to a serious decline in their authority as arbiters of taste.

Around the same time, as explained below, Wagner's influential prose works also helped re-establish opera as an intellectual activity. After 1900, in response to the perceived need, the Ecole de Journalisme of the Ecole des Hautes Etudes Sociales inaugurated a course in musical criticism to supplement an already existing course in dramatic criticism.[50] When opera once again seemed to require trained professionals to interpret and criticize it, the Tout-Paris exposed its own limitations. Its failure to appreciate *Pélléas et Mélisande* in 1902 caused a severe crisis in its confidence and called attention to a gradual decline in its prestige. The Debussy opera not only survived a charivari from the opening night audience, but with firm support from patrons of the cheaper seats and from knowledgeable critics such as the composers d'Indy and

Dukas, it achieved the status of a recognized masterpiece. From that point on, according to the vindicated director Carré, the Tout-Paris preferred to wait for informed opinion before crying success or failure.[51] The erosion of its authority coincided with the emergence of controversial operas with potentially subversive social content, such as those of Zola, Maeterlinck, and Charpentier — testimony to the Tout-Paris' efficiency in previous years at restricting the ideology of the opera to what was acceptable, or rather invisible, to the audience.

The active participation and leadership of the government in the Tout-Paris suggests that it is misleading to place government and audience opinion in opposition. A more accurate description of the relationship would portray the Tout-Paris as contributing to the formation of interlocking elites that included parvenu republicans in an increasingly comfortable alliance with Second Empire *abonnés*. The absence of controversy over revolutionary operas such as *La Vivandière*, on the one hand, and the republicans' support for *Lohengrin* on the other, are manifestations of this arrangement. But did the politicians control the opera through the Tout-Paris, or did the Tout-Paris control the politicians through the opera? The older elites gained from the alliance the assurance that their traditional amusement would be subsidized and supported at the highest official levels, and moreover, that the government would make no deliberate attempt to politicize the opera. The republicans had to give up their traditional goal of a state opera that would forge a republican nation from its audience, but in return they gained entrée to the most exclusive salon in Paris, together with the cultural capital that this entailed; increased respect for their regime in the eyes of royal Europe; and considerable unofficial leverage over the content of at least the Opéra-Comique repertoire.

That this trade-off was acceptable to the republicans is attested by their privileging of financial over political credentials in the appointments of directors, by their foreswearing of ideological considerations in the selection of operas for official performances, and by their subsidies of librettists regardless of political persuasion. They also administered the censorship office and subsidized new French operas in such a way as to distract attention away from the implicit ideological content of the librettos. This cooperative working arrangement between republicans and *abonnés* explains the ambivalence in the republicans' attitudes towards the rhetoric of moral improvement through the opera. It explains the paradox of the obvious responsiveness of the opera establishment to opera opinion, together with the apparent reluctance of the government to participate directly in the administration of the opera for partisan political ends.

In the next chapter, the question will have to be addressed whether and to what extent this was a conscious arrangement. Were republican politicians aware of having made such a deal? Audiences almost certainly were not. The reticence that we encounter in the press with regard to the ideological content of opera librettos, across almost the whole of the political spectrum, even with regard to operas in which the political implications would seem to have been impossible to ignore, suggests that audiences remained oblivious to them. A pervasive prejudice against political or social opera on the part of the critics, in both their theoretical pronouncements and their day-to-day activity, contributed to the audiences' capacity to disregard the ideological content of the repertoire. In promoting this approach to the opera, the critics acted on behalf of the established elites while at the same time systematically influencing their outlook.

NOTES TO CHAPTER VI

1 Claude Bellanger et al., *Histoire Générale de la Presse Française*, 4 vols. (Paris: PUF, 1972), III:178.

2 See, for example, Trublot, "A Minuit," *Le Cri du Peuple* (4/4/1884).

3 Un Monsieur en habit noir, "L'Attaque du Moulin," *Le Journal* (11/24/1893).

4 Henry Bauer, "Le Cid," *L'Echo de Paris* (12/2/1885).

5 Simon Boubée, "Musique," *La Gazette de France* (3/6/1883).

6 "Les Théâtres," *Le Rappel* (4/9/1877); Jules Guillemot, "Théâtres," *Le Soleil* (4/8/1877); Jean Bertrand, "Drame et Musique," *La République Française* (4/9/1877).

7 Georges Bertal, "Les Théâtres," *Le Rappel* (3/26/1893). Compare reviews in *La Bataille* (3/27/1893) and *La Justice* (3/25/1893) on the left with those in *L'Eclair* (3/26/1893) and *La Liberté* (3/27/1893) on the right.

8 Edouard Durranc, "Courrier Dramatique," *La Justice* (4/7/1884); Julien Serment, "La Soirée d'Hier," *La Justice* (4/3/1884); "Les Théâtres," *Le Rappel* (4/4/1884).

9 Alph. Duvernoy, "Musique," *La République Française* (12/4/1885).

10 Edmond Stoullig, "Les Premières," *Le National* (9/18/1891). For the exception of *Le Gaulois*, Raymond Manévy, *La Presse de la IIIe République* (Paris: J. Foret, 1955), 85f.

11 Simon Boubée, "Musique," *La Gazette de France* (3/13/1883). Cf. Alfred Vallette, "Pélléas et Mélisande et la Critique Officielle," *Mercure de France* (July, 1893), 238.

12 Jean des Gaules, "Le Monde Comme Il Va," *Le National* (3/7/1883); Frédéric Hellouin, *Essai de critique de la critique musicale* (Paris, 1906), 135. For a thorough description of the recruitment, credentials, education, and other occupations of the music critics, Goubault, *La Critique Musicale*, 158ff. Cf. Duvigneaud, *Sociologie du Théâtre*, 47.

13 Emile Saint-Auban, *L'Idée Sociale au Théâtre* (Paris, 1901), 22.

14 Scudo, "Revue Musicale," *Revue des Deux Mondes*, 23 (10/15/1859), 1016. His idea of a good opera was Rossini's *Guillaume Tell*. For the quotation describing his power, (and a critique of his competence), Goubault, *La Critique Musicale*, 19.

15 P.-J. Proudhon, *Du Principe de l'Art et de sa Destination sociale* (Paris, 1865), 373.

16 M.-D. Calvocaressi, "La Critique Musicale: ses devoirs, sa méthode," *Courrier musicale*, XIII no. 20 (10/15/1910), 665.

17 Bruneau, *A l'Ombre*, 90. As in the case of *Carmen*, the actor successfully insisted on the more effective interpretation.

18 Bénédicte, "Opéra-Comique," *Le Figaro* (3/5/1875). For the political orientation of the paper at this time, Claude Bellanger, *Histoire Générale*, III:196f. Descriptions of the social and political orientations of the various newspapers mentioned in the text all come from Volume III of this source.

19 François Oswald, "Musique," *Le Gaulois* (3/6/1875); *Le Siècle* quoted in Halévy, "La Millième Représentation," 10; L. de la C., "Les Premières," *L'Ordre* (3/6/1875); C.D., "Théâtres," *Le Pays* (3/5/1875).

20 Frédérick, "Premières Représentations," *Paris-Journal* (3/6/1875).

21 Simon Boubée, "Revue Musicale," *Gazette de France* (3/8/1875).

22 Jules Guillemot, "Revue Dramatique," *Le Soleil* (3/9/1875).

23 For a survey of contemporary and more recent reactions to the opera, Susan McClary, *Georges Bizet: Carmen*, Cambridge Opera Handbooks (Cambridge and New York: Cambridge University Press, 1992), 111-29. Though I agree that Bizet's experience with Céleste Vénard may have been formative, it seems unnecessary and rather strained to invoke the dangers of the Paris Commune and the world of the prostitute, as McClary has done, to account for the threat projected onto Carmen by the critics of the right: *Ibid.*, 35, 38-41.

24 Joëlle Guillais, *La Chair de l'Autre: Le Crime passionel au XIXe siècle* (Paris, 1986), 167ff.

25 *Ibid.*, 175.

26 *Ibid.*, 196.

27 "Les Théâtres," *Le Rappel* (3/6/1875); Emile Abraham, "Théâtres," *Le Petit Journal* (3/6/1875); Reyer, "Revue Musicale;" "Théâtres," *La République Française* (3/8/1875).

28 Charles de la Rounat, "Causerie Dramatique," *Le XIXe Siècle* (3/16/1875); J. Weber, "Critique Musicale," *Le Temps* (3/9/1875).

29 Jullien, "Revue Musicale." Jullien wrote for *Le Français*, a journal that represented the Catholic, anti-democratic *notables* of the center right, but

he was conspicuous among the opera critics of his era for his intelligent, perceptive, knowledgeable, and independent-minded aproach to his task.

30 E. Reyer, "Revue Musicale," *Journal des Débats* (12/6/1885).

31 Gheusi, *Cinquante Ans* 3:238ff., 2:54f. For Sarcey's influence, Jollivet, *Souvenirs*, 234f.; Roujon, *Artistes et Amis des Arts*, 50-53; Adolphe Brisson, *Le Théâtre et ses Moeurs* (Paris, n.d.), 8.

32 Emile Bergerat, *Souvenirs d'un Enfant de Paris*, 4 vols. (Paris, 1911-13), 2:12f.

33 "A Monsieur Eugène Manuel," July 1872, *A.N.* F XXI (957).

34 Eymieu, "De l'Influence de la Critique," *Le Monde Musical*, III no. 60 (30 October, 1891), 5. Cf. Calvocaressi, "La Critique Musicale," 664. For Monselet, André Monselet, *Charles Monselet, sa vie, son oeuvre* (Paris, 1892), 176f.

35 Emile Zola, "Le Public des Premières," *Oeuvres Complètes*, Maurice LeBlond, ed., 50 vols. (Paris, 1927), 50:196.

36 "A Monsieur Eugène Manuel."

37 Calvocaressi, "La Critique musicale," 663; Henri Eymieu, "De l'Influence de la Critique," 5. Cf. Eckart-Bäcker, *Frankreichs Musik*, 21; Lionel Dauriac, "A Travers l'Esthétique Musicale: La Critique Musicale au Temps Présent," *S.I.M. Revue Musicale Mensuelle*, VI no.7 (1910), 470; Goubault, *La Critique Musicale*, 179.

38 Charles Garnier, "Le Tout-Paris des Premières," *Annales*, 9:ixf.

39 Un Monsieur de l'Orchestre, "Le Cid," *Le Figaro* (11/27/1885). Massenet, *My Recollections*, 82; Garnier, "Le Tout-Paris," viiiff., iii.

40 Garnier, "Le Tout-Paris," viff., xiv, iiiff.

41 Gheusi, *Cinquante Ans*, 2:57. For the composition of the Commission consultative, Dupré and Ollendorff, *Traité de l'Administration*, 1:59f. Fulcher attributes considerable influence to this body under the July Monarchy, but I found only one reference to its activities under the Third Republic: *La Chronique Musicale*, Troisième Année 9 (July–September 1876), 187.

42 "Subventions théâtrales," *l'Autorité* (7/11/1900) [available also in *A.N.* F XXI (1339)].

43 For the Carré debate, Chambre des Députés, 2e séance de 2/14/1906, *Journal Officiel*, 745-749 (also available in B.O. Opéra Dossier P.A. 1900-1927, P.A. 2/14/1906).

44 Andrieu, *Souvenirs des frères Isola*, 220. Gheusi, *Cinquante Ans*, 2:120ff., 391; Carré, *Souvenirs*, 214f. Cf. M. Georges-Michel, *Un Demi-Siècle de Gloires Théâtrales* (Paris: A. Bonne, 1950), 240f.

45 Durand, *Quelques Souvenirs*, 2:11f.

46 "Premières Représentations," *La République Française* (5/16/1889).

47 Carré, *Souvenirs*, 256, 259.

48 Urbain Gohier, "Au Théâtre," *l'Aurore* (9/13/1901) [available also in *A.N.* F XXI (1336)]; Garnier, "Le Tout-Paris," iv; Emile Zola, "Le Public des Premières," 50:194.

49 Gohier, "Au Théâtre."

50 Hellouin, *Essai de critique*, 139f., 134f.

51 Carré, *Souvenirs*, 364. Cf. Eugen Weber, *France: Fin de Siècle* (Cambridge, Mass.: Belknap Press, 1986), 153.

Chapter VII

Opera and
Cultural Hegemony

The attempt to define the sources of opera's ideological content, and the mechanisms by which it was brought to the stage, has revealed a notable reluctance on the part of the government to impose on the opera ideas that challenged the prejudices of the audience. Politicians could influence opera's content only as long as they avoided confrontations with the *abonnés* by repudiating any overt attempt to advance an official ideology. As the evidence of Chapter V showed, government leaders eschewed the available opportunities for propagating partisan political opinions through the appointment of directors and the selection of shows to be performed on state occasions. Politicians in power entered the gratifyingly exclusive salon that was the Tout-Paris of the opera at the cost of subordinating their political agenda to the delicate pleasures of sex and sentiment. But if they could propagate their opinions only as long as these failed to arouse the attention of the audience, what possible benefits could accrue?

Implicit in this formulation of the question, and indeed in all of the preceding work, is the idea that messages conveyed through the drama of the opera could serve the interests of those responsible for introducing them. Opera could accomplish this, presumably, by promoting the adoption of ideas or values that, more widely accepted, would help to maintain various classes or fractions of classes in power, or to increase their power relative to others. Among the likely candidates for this sort of influence were the prominent investors, or *commanditaires*, whose role has yet to be explored. The other side of the question then remains to be investigated: whether attendance at the opera resulted in modification of the beliefs and behavior of subordinate groups. My answer draws on cultural hegemony theory, which in turn raises the issue of whether any such domination and subordination should be conceived as a deliberate, self-conscious strategy on the part of its beneficiaries.

With the exception of Rouché, who made up his working capital entirely from his own resources, and perhaps also of Olivier Halanzier, all the directors of this period raised money from financial backers called *commanditaires*. Unless they were very wealthy themselves, the established directors' autonomy extended only to choosing between groups of investors with different motives for controlling the opera repertoire. Thus, directors who arrived at the top of their profession with independent ideas intact, or with a clear picture of their clientele's prejudices, immediately mortgaged their freedom of action. Ritt and Gailhard, co-directors of the Opéra from 1885 to 1891, each posted only Fr.100,000 of the Fr.800,000 operating capital required by the government; twenty-eight investors made up the rest. In 1908, Messager and Broussan held only two shares each in the Opéra concession, while forty *commanditaires* divided fifty-six shares among them.[1]

In years when the director turned a profit, his backers earned dividends from their investments. Because the finances of the business were chronically precarious, however, no one invested in the opera in confident anticipation of a satisfactory rate of return. On the other hand, *commanditaires* were in an excellent position to promote the production of works in which they had financial interests. The Société des Auteurs et Compositeurs prohibited directors from producing works written or composed by the investors themselves, since the potential for abuse of their influence was patent. (This did not prevent frequent performances of *Le Clown*, by the prominent *commanditaire* Isaac de Camondo, which aroused some unfavorable comment).[2] Music publishers regularly invested in the opera in order to advance the interests of composers whom they had under contract. Because one great operatic success could establish the fortunes not only of the composer and librettist but of their publisher as well, the enormous potential for profit made an otherwise risky investment worthwhile. The publisher Durand wrote that his father, the head of their firm, "moved heaven and earth" to get Saint-Saëns' *Ascanio* (O-1890) produced at the Opéra; "the number of letters written and letters exchanged on the subject was considerable."[3]

The *commanditaires'* willingness to put up the capital required to run the opera put considerable power over the selection of the operas to be performed, and over the selection of directors as well, into the hands of these businessmen. Absent from their number was the publisher Hartmann, the best known of those who specialized in the avant-garde, who championed the works of younger, more innovative composers, and supplied them with librettos. Though Hartmann frequently prevailed on directors of the Opéra and Opéra-Comique to gamble on the works of his proteges, including the young Massenet, Charpentier, and Augusta Holmès, he never accumulated sufficient capital to establish himself as a *commanditaire.*[4] The system of publisher/ *commanditaires* served primarily the interests of the wealthiest mainstream publishers.

Competition among them was fierce, and their power was enormous. The director Gailhard, along with many journalists, attributed the street riots surrounding the premiere of *Lohengrin* to the influence of one or more music editors who wanted to discourage competition from foreign rivals. A number of editors, including Heugel and Choudens, felt compelled to deny the charge formally.[5] Whenever a vacancy occurred in the directorship of the Opéra or Opéra-Comique, groups of potential *commanditaires* lobbied aggressively for their own candidates. They were also capable, when necessary, of forcing the resignation of directors who demonstrated persistent ineptitude.[6]

Toward the end of the Belle Epoque, directors unwilling to submit to the music publishers' too exigent demands began to find financial backing elsewhere. Carré, for instance, in an interview with the press immediately following his appointment to the Opéra-Comique, stressed his independence from vested interests: "Know first of all that I have with me no editor, no ticket merchant, no author. I have Fr.1,200,000 subscribed by Parisian high society.... I addressed myself only to individuals from the fashionable set."[7] These *"personnalités du monde élégant"* who constituted the groups of Belle Epoque *commanditaires* were also prominent businessmen, many of them with government connections. Backers of Ritt and Gailhard at the Opéra included Julizot, founder of the Printemps department stores and former deputy from the Nièvre; the lawyer Caron, former Président du Conseil Général de la Seine; and Sallès, Président de la Banque Suisse et Française. The composition of the group behind Messager and Broussan in 1908-09 was very similar. It included the banker and deputy Rafael Bischoffsheim, the manufacturer Sénateur Gaston Menier, the secretary of the Senate Gérard, members of the Clermont-Ferrand and de Reinach families, and Henry Deutsch de la Meurthe, the petroleum mogul. Like the publishers, these *haut bourgeois commanditaires* were in a position to lobby effectively for individual works, and to withhold essential financial support from potential directors with political opinions.

Individuals willing to undertake the substantial financial risks inherent in these investments frequently had strong tastes of their own to cultivate. The best-known supporter of both the Opéra and Opéra-Comique at the turn of the century was the Jewish banker Count Isaac de Camondo, the "prototype of the *abonné*, veritable pillar of the edifice, moral and financial prop of the management...."[8] It was his well-publicized formula that set the standard of disinterest for wealthy patrons of the opera willing to sacrifice their financial interests in the cause of art: "Sirs," he said to Messager and Broussan on behalf of the *commanditaires*, "we ask of you artistic dividends above all."[9] Camondo regularly promoted the avant-garde, saying to Albert Carré: "Support *Louise* and *Pélléas* at all costs, we are behind you."[10] He also offered to guarantee fifty performances of the next opera with a libretto by Emile Zola, when his latest effort had been hounded from the repertoire by anti-Dreyfusards who dominated the Opéra's subscriber list.[11]

The success of the maverick De Camondo suggests that a determined impresario could have imposed on the public the tastes of any *commanditaires* with sufficient means, at least occasionally and within certain limits. Under completely independent management of the lyric theatres, the influence of big money must have eclipsed entirely that of other constituent elements of the opera establishment. As it was, state subsidies and supervision ensured that directors would be subject not just to *commanditaires*, but to *abonnés*, to casual patrons who provided the bulk of the receipts, to critics and cognoscenti who helped determine audience tastes, and to groups and individuals whose political influence exceeded their financial power. The government seems to have acted as a guarantor of the free market, concerned above all to make sure that no one — librettists, directors, *commanditaires*, even politicians of the party in power — imposed a point of view on the opera in opposition to audience taste. The wealthy investors were effective only as an element in the interlocking elites that defined the acceptable limits of opera's ideological content.

If the librettos had simply reflected the outlook of these elites back to themselves, opera would still have fulfilled an important social function of the type that Arnold Hauser terms "ideological." This means, according to his well-known formulation, that it "obscures truth in order not so much to mislead others as to maintain and increase the self-confidence of those who express and benefit from such deception."[12] That is, opera would have served to consolidate and reinforce, perhaps even to define or develop, the point of view appropriate to dominant or contending groups in the social and political circumstances in which they found themselves. At the Opéra-Comique, for example, the attitude toward the lower classes expressed in the *faits divers* librettos reinforced the prejudices of the *fin-de-siècle* bourgeoisie. These librettos would have struck a responsive chord particularly among "the humble public of the upper galeries," marginal bourgeois of the type most concerned with elaborating the distinction between bourgeoisie and lower classes precisely because they were most vulnerable to derogation.[13]

But there is an important difference between Hauser's concept of the ideological and the truly hegemonic, which, as Raymond Williams defines it, "has also to be seen as the lived dominance and subordination of particular classes."[14] In order to make a case that opera had a genuinely hegemonic function in Williams' sense, the question needs to be addressed: Who would have been the object of this subordination? The working class would be an obvious candidate, except that it hardly qualifies as a victim of operatic hegemony. Reduced-price performances, ostensibly intended to introduce the lower classes to the opera for the beneficial effect on their morality that would result, never succeeded in enticing them to attend. Not only was their access to the institution very limited, but there are both theoretical and empirical reasons for believing that the lower classes would have been relatively resistant to the messages of the works presented there. If they had attended, the lower classes would have been most capable of identifying the bourgeois and aristocratic values implicit in the operas as political propaganda.

The working classes were undoubtedly enthusiastic for the opera under the right circumstances. Airs from the repertoire were sung in the streets of Paris, but only by laborers newly arrived from the provinces, where some of them had had regular access to inexpensive performances. In Rouen, the cheapest seats regularly cost only 60 centimes, and management cut these prices in half twice a month; the municipal government also appropriated one hundred tickets per week for the free use of workers and domestic servants. In Paris the response was overwhelming when the director Carré opened the balconies of the Opéra-Comique to seamstresses and other working women for a performance of *Louise* in 1901; he had 3,742 requests for 400 tickets. Thousands of patrons were turned away from free Bastille Day performances each year, as well. "One sees even the least cultivated spirits moved to frenzy every time that free performances permit those disinherited by fortune to become acquainted with the masterpieces of our great masters," wrote one advocate of popular theatre.[15]

Working-class access to the Parisian opera remained entirely exceptional, however. Each of the 447 employees of the Opéra received three complimentary tickets per year. Concierges frequented both houses, but it is rash to conclude from this, as Bernard does,[16] that common people regularly occupied the cheapest seats at the Opéra, for concierges were in a unique position to obtain unwanted tickets. During the early performances of each new work and at performers' debuts, several hundred tickets went to *claquers*, distinguished from the regular clientele by their shabby clothes. But these were *lumpenproletariat* in the pay of the bourgeoisie. In addition, it was easy for some young working-class women — the "*lorettes*," who were often daughters of *portiers* — to find escorts from high society. Like the *claquers*, they were hired to embrace the outlook of their patrons. According to Théophile Gauthier, the *lorettes* employed exclusively the vocabulary of the Jockey Club and the theatres. If they did not marry foreign princes, they returned where they came from to raise *portiers*' children.[17]

But no one could attract ordinary working people to regular performances at the Palais Garnier, no matter how inexpensive they made them. Attempts to distribute tickets gratis to Parisian factory workers failed utterly. Evening performances were out of the question to begin with, as the deputy Jules Auffray pointed out during a Chamber debate on popular opera.[18] Working people had to allow at least an hour to get home from work, eat, dress, and so on, only to face the problem of transportation from the suburbs where they lived. Performances often ended around midnight, with the prospect of another long trip to follow. If ordinary workers could overcome these obstacles, they faced the intimidating effect of the luxurious Palais Garnier and the evident preoccupation with dress — both their own and others' — characteristic of the regular clientele.

Despite the official rhetoric of the Third Republic, which proclaimed its deep commitment to "democratization" of the Opéra clientele, government efforts to expand the potential audience were half-hearted and ineffectual. In 1879 the newly installed republican ministry introduced to the *cahiers des charges* of the Opéra a provision requiring directors to provide Sunday performances at reduced prices. But ticket scalping was rife, and the refreshment concessions' failure to reduce their prices also contributed to the high cost of the entertainment.[19] In succeeding years, the government turned a blind eye when the director Vaucorbeil systematically neglected to present the reduced-price performances. His successor Bertrand enthusiastically reintroduced the program in 1892, only to suspend it the following year in order to pay for a series of galas requested by the state.

Some officials argued that it was in any case "a bad example for the common people to invite them to sit down in the velvet seats and have them admire the excessive luxury that always obtains at Opéra performances."[20] Or, in the rhetoric of the popular press, the regular patrons were sensitive to the risk of finding sausage skins under the seats after reduced-price shows. As a result, later "popular" opera plans concentrated on bringing it to the people in their own neighborhoods. This program met with some success, though scalping continued to be a serious problem. It never enjoyed much official support, however; the progressive Opéra-Comique director Carré repeatedly complained of government indifference to his initiatives in that direction.[21]

This systematic exclusion of the lower classes from attendance at the opera makes it impossible that they should have been influenced by the ideas expressed there. This is not to say that state opera made no contribution to the subordination of the lower classes. To the extent that attendance at the Opéra-Comique was perceived as a distinguishing feature of the Parisian aristocratic and *haut bourgeois* style of life, it contributed to what Pierre Bourdieu calls "the definition of the hierarchy between the fractions, or, which amounts to the same thing, the definition of the legitimate hierarchizing principle."[22] In other words, the very exclusion of the subordinate classes from the opera would have contributed to the maintenance of their subordination. But the ideas presented on stage played no role in this.

Whether the lower classes would have been susceptible to the hegemonic effect of bourgeois or aristocratic opera, if they had been able to attend, is in any case problematical. Because their access to the government and the media was limited, and they had no input into the repertoire, the lower-class opera lovers' predelictions are difficult to determine. Bourgeois critics, even those who sympathized with the idea of popular opera, generally imputed naive and reactionary tastes to the working class. Laurent Tailhade, in *La Petite République*, suggested that male workers liked romance, while working women preferred the *distingué*. His sensitivity as an observer is open to doubt, unfortunately, since he went on to quote the Goncourts' definition of the beautiful as that which your mistress and your servant find naturally repulsive. Hellouin, in his *Essai de critique de la critique musicale*, suggested that the common people "go to the same works that delight the bourgeoisie, but to the worst of them."[23]

The radical *Le Rappel*, on the other hand, claimed that ordinary people had fairly sophisticated taste, commending both Gluck and the works of the younger composers to its readers. If critics from the socialist and anarchist press accurately represented the tastes of working-class opera lovers, we may infer that these were supporters of Wagner in 1891. The best evidence suggests that lower-class taste was actually rather eclectic: The audience of the Bastille Day shows responded enthusiastically to Mozart, Weber and Gluck, and also to Bruneau's and Zola's *Messidor*, a "brilliant success" in a free performance in 1897.[24]

As members of those groups whom Antonio Gramsci identified as being immune to hegemony because they deny their "spontaneous consent" to the dominant group's social leadership,[25] the working classes would have been the least fertile ground for the dissemination of dominant ideologies. Indeed, socialists were virtually the only group in French society to recognize and call public attention to opera's social and political content. While many critics noted the equivocal morals and hypocrisy of the Tout-Paris, Urbain Gohier in the socialist paper *l'Aurore* was the only one to point out its predominant influence over the ideological content of the Parisian theatre.[26] Resentful of official support for a culture that excluded them, socialist critics and politicians were also among the most vigorous and committed opponents of state subsidies for the opera, both in the Chamber of Deputies and in the press. According to the leftist deputy René Chauvin, speaking in the Chamber of Deputies,

> The writers of today, if they want to have their plays performed, are obliged to create a special theatre, a class theatre, for the special public of the premieres and of the *abonnements*. It is this special public which constitutes the tribunal charged with judging these works, and manual workers and intellectuals are rigorously excluded; under these conditions, how can you expect our modern authors to express elevated thoughts and severe criticism of social conditions? The public that judges them is composed entirely of *satisfaits*.[27]

To correct the problem, he advocated the distribution of free tickets for the state theatres to workers, and challenged the hegemony of the Tout-Paris by demanding twice as many tickets for opening-night performances. Unfortunately for Chauvin and his constituents, "*satisfaits*" dominated the Chamber too; they defeated his proposal by a vote of 385-95, the minority consisting largely of Guesdistes.

The distance between the dominant classes' perceptions of social realities and those of the working class gave socialists such as Chauvin and Gohier insight into the ideological function of the opera and the other state theatres that was hidden from other social groups. As Bourdieu and Passeron put it: "Contrary to popular or semi-learned representations which credit publicity or propaganda and, more generally, the messages conveyed by the modern media, with the power to manipulate if not to create opinions, these symbolic actions can work only to the extent that they encounter and reinforce predispositions."[28] According to this reasoning, the middle bourgeoisie who were enamored of the opera would have been more vulnerable than the working classes to the seductions of the social and political messages conveyed there. It should not be surprising, therefore, that the Opéra's reduced-price performances, which never succeeded in attracting working-class people, should have had the unanticipated, felicitous effect of subsidizing the attendance of the middle class. Government efforts to "democratize" the Opéra through lower-priced performances in practice enabled habitués of the upper balconies to occupy from time to time places normally reserved for the elite subscribers.

After the first "popular" performance presented by the director Bertrand, he optimistically proclaimed that the audience was "not at all the same" as for the subscription nights. Some journalists commented on the presence of "employees with their families," "soldiers enamored of intelligent distractions," "*petits fonctionnaires*, teachers and tradesmen." Others, however, remarked on the high proportion of Saint-Cyriens, Polytechniciens and other students on holiday with their mamas and papas: a distinct new group for the Opéra, but one "which is infinitely closer to the 'great' than to the 'little.'"[29] By the end of the first season, it was evident that patrons of the third-, fourth-, and fifth-level boxes had regularly taken advantage of the lower prices to move down to more desirable seats; the diminution of receipts for performances immediately before and after the popular nights was indisputable.[30] Though Bertrand conceded that democratization had failed, government support for the program suddenly kindled; subsequent ministries required directors to maintain and even extend the program of reduced-price performances. In effect, the government insisted that directors subsidize opera attendance for the middle ranks of the bourgeoisie during the rest of the Belle Epoque.

Because, as Gramsci further observed, antagonistic groups such as the working class can only be dominated through repressive state apparatuses, whereas kindred and allied groups are open to "intellectual and moral leadership,"[31] subsidies for middle-class attendance make perfect sense. The middle bourgeoisie's participation in opera society, especially when they began creeping closer to the stage, made them powerfully predisposed to follow this leadership. As the middle bourgeoisie came to occupy the mental space of their social superiors as well, they learned to embrace the undemocratic ideology of the residual aristocracy, as the *haute bourgeoisie* had before them. For the middle bourgeoisie, there were two alternatives: avoiding an offense against good taste by accepting the values of their betters as ideologically neutral, or banishment from the society of the opera with loss of the distinction that it conveyed.

Michael Hays concludes from his study of theatre architecture during this period that the Opéra "was a place where the [audience] could observe itself in the process of proclaiming its social and artistic perspective for itself and others."[32] Members of the audience only saw the stage by accident, says a critic for *Le Figaro*, in passing from observation of the boxes to the left of the stage, to those on the right.[33] Corresponding to the desire of the *abonnés* to be observed, rather than to observe the stage themselves, was the voyeurism of the occasional clientele who purchased publications that identified the subscribers of each box and stall. That the Opéra *abonnés* also were more interested in the show in the audience than the one on stage is evident in descriptions of audience behavior during Palais Garnier performances. Fashionable subscribers regularly arrived between nine-thirty and ten for an eight o'clock curtain, and left before the end. Until the 'nineties, when the advent of *Wagnérisme* prompted a general revolution in concert hall manners, the raising of the curtain had no effect on ongoing conversations. House lights remained undimmed for "the great battle of elegance," new arrivals and their ushers caused continual commotion, and even musicians, dancers, and choruses contributed to the hubbub when they were not performing. Opéra boxes were intended above all as a genteel locale for visits with friends and associates; they came with a small salon or antechamber attached, to be furnished and decorated by the subscriber.[34]

The effect of all this elegance, according to Charles Garnier, architect of the Paris Opéra, was to assimilate opera aficionados into the ethos of the social elites:

> A hall is beautiful, of noble appearance, agreeably comfortable, with a sumptuous color, such as is, for example, that of the Paris Opéra; the spectators who enter into it undergo a sort of moral impression from which they cannot distance themselves completely. They feel themselves surrounded, encompassed, by a sort of elegant atmosphere that influences their thoughts, their character, even their speech and their bearing; they sense instinctively that a certain dignity is appropriate, and that to let themselves go too much would be unsuitable.[35]

During the Old Regime and July Monarchy, a similar effect had fostered the assimilation of the *haute bourgeoisie* into the nobility. By the time of the Belle Epoque they were subscribing to such reactionary models as *Le Cid* and *Lohengrin*. "Behind grandiose historical facades, the grand staircases, tiered loges, and mannered foyers were ideally suited for the rites of imitation that promoted and reflected the aristocratization of the bourgeoisie," Arno Mayer explains.[36]

According to Raymond Williams' explication of cultural hegemony, cultural forms only serve the hegemonic interests of dominant classes when "the pressures and limits of what can ultimately be seen as a specific economic, political and cultural system seem to most of us the pressures and limits of simple experience and common sense."[37] To propagate even desirable messages deliberately, or simply to acclaim their presence, would have been self-defeating, because once their existence was acknowledged they escaped into the arena of the debatable. Instead of attempting to impose on them values that were patently antagonistic to their social and political interests, their social superiors depended on the normal aspiration of subordinate social groups to display the characteristics of the dominant class. Bourgeois opera lovers from the upper balconies moved down into seats traditionally occupied by the aristocracy and *haute bourgeoisie* in order to acquire what Bourdieu calls cultural capital, one of "the different forms of capital, the possession of which defines class membership."[38] In this case, the cost of acquiring cultural capital was repudiation of the republican tradition of social theatre in favor of the dominant aesthetic, which claimed that delicate sensibilities were offended by reading into the opera any ideas whatever.

That paved the way for the republican politicians' investment in Wagner, which in turn bought them acceptance into the elite society of the Opéra *abonnés*. As they consolidated their hold on power, they realized an extra dividend: control of an apparently apolitical Opéra-Comique, which made a more effective vehicle for cultivating their long-term class interests than an obviously partisan one could have been. As long as the political messages of the French Revolution operas, for instance, attracted little attention among friends, or enemies, or servants of the regime, they could function in a hegemonic way while allowing the government to maintain a pose of official non-involvement. It therefore behooved the official state censors to accomplish their goals by indirect intimidation rather than by regular overt manifestations of their power. Similarly, as the socialist Chauvin pointed out in the Chamber of Deputies speech quoted above, the Tout-Paris operated primarily by influencing the economic calculations of playwrights and directors, so that the true extent of its control over the theatre's ideological content was disguised.

Thus Williams' work provides a theoretical explanation for the empirical evidence that critics, politicians, and other articulate elements within the audience typically denied that ideas had any place on stage and rejected attempts to introduce controversial subjects there. In explaining why contemporary audiences were largely oblivious to social and political interpretations of opera, his theory not only overcomes one of the traditional objections to their very existence, but turns it into the cornerstone of a new understanding of the social function of opera. There was nothing remotely conspiratorial, or even self-conscious, about the actions of the government or of the Tout-Paris. Its members denied and resisted the presence of ideas in the opera not in order to serve their class interests, but because they genuinely, naively preferred frivolous plots with sexy ballets. Despite its central role in determining the ideological content of the repertoire, the Tout-Paris never acknowledged its interest in the ideas presented at the theatre.[39] As Bourdieu explains it, "...the practical mastery expressed in everyday choices (which may or may not be capable of being constituted as political in terms of the dominant definition) is based not on the explicit principles of an ever vigilant, universally competent consciousness, but on the implicit schemes of thought and action of a class habitus, in other words — if one must use the simplistic formulae of political discussion — on a class unconscious rather than a class consciousness."[40]

The almost complete absence of controversy over the social or political content of the Belle Epoque opera implies genuine blindness to the ideological or hegemonic function of the institution among dominant and subdominant elites alike. Unable to recognize their own values, conveyed through the medium of the opera, as having ideological content, the audience elites genuinely believed that opera had no ideological function. As long as the opera repertoire bore messages compatible with their interests, critics, librettists, audiences, and the Tout-Paris of the opera failed to remark that it did so, because such messages seemed to them to be common sense, and therefore unremarkable. Another requirement of cultural hegemony theory — that the implications, and indeed the very existence, of opera's ideological content should have remained hidden from those who benefited from it — is met.

As the evidence in Chapter VI demonstrated, this self-deception was strongly reinforced by the prominent critics of the early Third Republic. Though the incompetence and unprofessional behavior of many of the group reduced their capacity to influence the reception of individual works, it did not undermine their authority to establish the criteria for judging them, which was the real basis of their cultural influence. During the first three decades of the Third Republic, the critics not only abdicated their traditional role of calling the attention of their clientele to the ideological implications of the theatre, they codified their abdication in a coherent philosophy of opera criticism that maintained that opera neither could nor should convey ideas, and that operas that did so were distasteful. Librettos that pleased Sarcey and Scudo seemed to them to be uncontroversial and free of ideology because these librettos faithfully reproduced the tastes and prejudices of the critics' and audiences' own class.

The hegemonic interests of dominant elites were served not only by delegitimizing overt social commentary at the opera, but by sanctioning its opposite. While republican politicians informally, without any conscious political motives, prevailed on directors to produce implicitly republican operas, the official policies of republican governments constrained the state opera to produce meaningless exotic spectacles by novice French composers. As described in Chapter V, these operas had the common failing of a superabundance of effects, which precluded any coherent interpretation of their characters' motives or points of view. Censorship policy, in privileging the sexual over the social, had the same result.

From this the corollary may be drawn, following Bourdieu, that central to the hegemonic behavior of the dominant fractions is the limitation of the field of legitimate art to that which most obviously appears to be ideologically neutral. Such a restriction not only makes any art used by subordinate groups for political purposes by definition illegitimate, it also helps to render invisible the dominant values inherent in the art. Particularly vulnerable to this effect are subordinate fractions who embrace an aesthetic ideal for the social distinction it conveys. While the drama, "which even in its most refined forms still bears a social message,"[41] conveys in simple, profoundly insidious terms the values of class fractions capable of manipulating the opera repertoire, these values come submerged in the art forms in which opera abounds.

Just as composers, librettists, and especially directors learned from the financial consequences of the *Carmen* debacle to draw back from controversy, so the republican critics recognized, as their papers drifted into the mainstream, the expediency of retreating to safer, more familiar ground. As cultural hegemony theory would predict, spokesmen for groups closest to the center of power came to value most highly, and spend most of their time discussing, those operatic arts that were least explicit in their messages. Journalists became more and more preoccupied with the external aspect of the productions. According to M.A. Deville in *La Philosophie au Théâtre* (1883): "The papers talk a lot about the theatre, but concern themselves very little with the ideas (there are no true critics anymore); they describe the costumes and the decors, the staging and the choreography, the acting, everything that is material in a show."[42] In this they behaved much like the modern French bourgeoisie, whose affinity for music, according to Bourdieu, "represents the most radical and most absolute form of the negation of the world, and especially the social world, which the bourgeois ethos tends to demand of all forms of art." The same relationship to art is manifested in the inclination of the bourgeoisie "toward a hedonistic aesthetic of ease and facility, symbolized by boulevard theatre or Impressionist painting." These tastes are attributes not of the bourgeoisie as such, but of the bourgeoisie in its capacity as "dominant fraction of the dominant class," whose social position leads inevitably to a "high degree of denial of the social world."[43] Opera was more receptive than orchestral music to the intrusion of social and political ideas, but the audiences and critics selected from its constituent arts those most conducive to denial of the social world of the Belle Epoque.

This analysis of opera's social function follows from the main lines of argument in the preceding chapters. The opera was capable of conveying social and political ideas through its dramatic action. On the whole, the directors responsible for selecting the repertoire kept from the stage operas with unsuitable or offensive messages, learning and testing the limits of the acceptable through occasional controversies. The financial structure of the opera gave considerable influence to wealthy *commanditaires*, but the state's subsidies and supervision kept their activities within bounds. Though the state had the formal capacity to manipulate the repertoire, republican rhetoric about opera's moralizing effect was intended largely for external consumption.

Despite the close correspondence of Opéra-Comique ideology to the needs of the party in power, there is little evidence of official government manipulation of the repertoire. The government's main concern was to reinforce the operation of the free market in opera ideology in order to prevent the politicization of the opera; it accomplished this by ensuring that directors were motivated primarily by profit. The ability of politicians to influence the social and political content of the opera informally and unobtrusively, especially through the Tout-Paris of the premieres, sufficiently accounts for the shift from aristocratic to democratic values around 1880, and for the specific content of the French Revolutionary operas of the eighteen-nineties. But this shift could be accomplished only because Opéra-Comique audiences, from which the working classes were excluded, were generally receptive to bourgeois ideology. At the Opéra, where the political opinions of the audience did not correspond to those of the government, the propagation of partisan political doctrines would have alienated the public, with disastrous consequences. Instead, republicans in control of the government promoted their domestic and international political interests by tolerating the introduction of Wagner and *Wagnérisme* in the eighteen-nineties.

The absence of public discussion of Belle Epoque opera's well-disguised social and political content was virtually complete, except in aberrant cases such as *Carmen*, where controversy still manifested itself only obliquely, as an argument over aesthetic issues. Pierre Bourdieu's theoretical constructs, applied to Raymond Williams' theory of cultural hegemony, effectively account for this reticence, as well as for the corresponding public preoccupation with those operatic arts that least obtrusively conveyed dominant values. One consequence is that attempts to relate the history of the opera to the social history of the Belle Epoque might benefit from systematic examination of the ideological subtext of aesthetic commentaries. A future comprehensive social history of the genre and institution might be based in part on a thorough survey of the implicit ideological content of arts — costuming, *mise-en-scène*, acting, and above all music — that did engage the attention of critics, government officials, and Tout-Paris.

Bourdieu, through systematic interpretation of public opinion polls, has gone far toward distinguishing the tastes of various sectors of contempory French society; Bellanger's work on the French press permits historical sociologists to apply the same sort of procedure to Belle Epoque society. Analysis of the tastes of critics from a variety of late-nineteenth-century newspapers, with the aim of cracking the code of opera criticism, should reveal the social and political dimensions of what the critics thought of as purely aesthetic judgments. We may hope eventually to articulate more clearly the social significance of the aesthetic content of supersaturated operas promoted by the government, of the traditional repertoire with its anachronistic social and political messages, and of operas with apparently meaningless, trivial librettos such as *Le Tribut de Zamora*, which introduced this work.

I hope such analyses may benefit from comparison with conclusions based on the more direct references to social and political values discovered in the librettos described above. It has been a goal of this work to identify these values with the ideological requirements of patrons who were apparently unaware of, and in denial of, opera's capacity to convey social and political ideas. The responsiveness of opera to the unarticulated interests of its clientele, together with the predominance of opera's other constituent arts over the words, and the efficacy of the former at disguising the messages inherent in the dramatic action, made Belle Epoque opera the hegemonic art form par excellence.

NOTES TO CHAPTER VII

1 The untitled report of the meeting of *commanditaires* of Messager and Broussan in 1908 includes their names and number of shares. Similar data for the *commanditaires* of 1894 can be found in B.O. Fonds Rouché Pièce 120, no.152. The *commanditaires* could not constitute themselves formally as joint-stock companies, a form of organization explicitly prohibited by the *cahiers des charges* of the Opéra and Opéra-Comique. See Pelissier, *Histoire Administrative*, 162.

2 Goubault, *La Critique Musicale*, 292. *Commanditaires* could and did intervene on behalf of their friends, at least under the Empire. See A.L. Malliot, *La Musique au Théâtre* (Paris, 1866), 175f.

3 Jacques Durand, *Quelques Souvenirs d'un Editeur de musique*, 2 vols. (Paris, 1924-5), 1:65, 118f. For restrictions on *commanditaires'* activities, Magnen and Fouquet, *Le Théâtre et ses Lois*, 92.

4 For Hartmann's financial difficulties, Harding, *Massenet* (London: Dent, 1970), 88, 101; for his success, G. Servières, "Les débuts de Massenet à l'Opéra," *Rivista Musicale Italiana*, Anno XXXII Fasc.1 (1925), 40n. Cf. George Favre, *L'Oeuvre de Paul Dukas* (Paris: Durand & Cie., 1969), 20; Durand, *Quelques souvenirs*, 94.

5 Valère, "Lohengrin à l'Opéra," *L'Autorité* (9/18/1891); "Un Coup de Théâtre," *Le Gaulois* (9/11/1891); "Lohengrin," *Le National* (9/22/1891).

6 Gheusi, *Cinquante Ans*, 3:238ff.; Chambre des Députés, 2e Séance du 2/14/1906, *Journal Officiel*, 745 (also available in B.O. P.A. 1900-1927). The Opéra and Opéra-Comique sometimes had *commanditaires* in common. See *Plaidoirie et Réplique de M. Poincaré, Avocat* (Paris, 1906), 18.

7 Quoted in Jules Huret, "Le Directeur de l'Opéra-Comique," *Le Figaro* (1/14/1898) (available also in B.O. Dossier d'artiste/ Albert Carré). His *commanditaires*, Carré said, also constituted the nucleus of his *abonnement*: Carré, *Souvenirs*, 222.

8 Gabriel Astruc, *Le Pavillon des Fantômes: Souvenirs* (Paris, 1929), 164.

9 Untitled report of the meeting of *commanditaires* of Messager and Broussan in 1908.

10 Astruc, *Le Pavillon des Fantômes*, 164.

11 Alfred Bruneau, *A L'Ombre*, 110.

12 Quoted in Haskell, "Capitalism and the Origins of the Humanitarian Sensibility," 348, in the context of an extended discussion of the concept of self-deception as a theoretical tool.

13 For a vivid description of this mentality from the childhood of one of the librettists, see Brisson, *Portraits intimes*, 2:340.

14 Williams, *Marxism and Literature*, 110.

15 "Proposition au Conseil Municipal de Paris pour la création immédiate et économique d'un Grand Opéra populaire et Théâtre Lyrique annexé, 12/12/1878," *A.N.* F XXI (1041). For the response to *Louise*, *Annales.*, 26:91f. Later in the Belle Epoque the number of free shows increased to four, equivalent to a total of approximately 9000 free tickets per year in the case of the Opéra. This was plenty, Gailhard thought: "Ministre des Beaux-Arts to Director of the Opéra, 4/8/1903," and response, in *A.N.* AJ XIII (1006). Cf. Chambre des Députés, Séance du 12/3/1897, *Journal Officiel*, 2689, [available in *A.N.* F XXI (1337)]. The Opéra-Comique alone turned away 1000 people on 14 July 1902, according to Noël and Stoullig, *Annales*, 28:123. The Minister Léon Bourgeois referred to provincial workers familiar with operatic airs in a speech reported in *Le Temps* (9/14/1891) [available also in *A.N.* F XVII (2662)]. For Rouen, Henri Geispitz, *Histoire du Théâtre-des-Arts de Rouen, 1882-1913* (Rouen, 1913), 294f.

16 There were two *concierges* among the Opéra-Comique fire victims. Another *concierge* sitting with her daughter in the fifth balcony of the Opéra died in a freak accident when a lighting counterweight fell on her. Bernard, "L'Evolution du Public," 40. Cf. *Annales*, 22:21.

17 Gauthier, *Souvenirs de Théâtre*, 187-191. For the *claquers* see Bernard, "L'Evolution du Public," 37. This institution was in decline by the beginning of the Third Republic, and had minimal impact on public opinion.

18 Jules Auffray, Chambre des Députés, 2e séance de 2/14/1906, *Journal Officiel*, 751, (available also in B.O. P.A. 1/26/1910). Cf. "L'Opéra Démocratique"; Bernard, "L'Evolution du Public," 44ff.; Gerhard, *Die Verstädterung der Oper*, 36.

19 "La Matinée d'hier à l'Opéra," *Le Jour* (1/5/1892) [available in *A.N.* F XVII (2662)]. On an attempt to distribute free Opéra tickets to workers, see "Director of the Opéra to Minister of Public Instruction, July 1893," *A.N.* AJ XIII (1194). The "Rapport au Conseil Municipal de Paris, relatif à l'organization de représentations populaires à prix réduit, 1884," [available in *A.N.* AJ XIII (1194)] is very revealing on negotiations for the introduction of a reduced-price opera series.

20 "Observations présentées par M. Gailhard devant la Commission Supérieure des Théâtres," *A.N.* AJ XIII (1194), 22. For Vaucorbeil's failure

to present the required performances, *Ibid.*, 20. Cf. *Annales*, 6:38n. For Bertrand's experience, "Bertrand and Gailhard to Ministre de l'Instruction Publique, 10/1/1893," B.O. Fonds Rouché, Pièce 120, 98f; "Ministre des Beaux-Arts to Messieurs les Directeurs de l'Opéra, 10/4/1893," *A.N.* AJ XIII (1006). The galas were in honor of the visit of the Russian fleet to Toulon, admittedly a popular cause.

21 Carré, *Souvenirs*, 228, 302. Paul-Boncour suggests that suburban theatres suffering from the competition were at the root of the opposition: *Art et démocratie*, 200. A good account of various proposals for popular theatres is Ch.-M. Couyba, *Les Beaux-Arts et la Nation* (Paris, 1908), 201ff. One of Carré's attempts is reported in *Annales*, 30:105f. Cp. Bernheim, *Trente Ans de Théâtre*, 1:296-318, 3:16f. The reference to sausage skins occurs in Pédrille, "La Journée d'Hier à l'Opéra," *Le Petit Journal* (1/4/1892) [available also in *A.N.* F XVII (2662)].

22 Bourdieu, *Distinction*, 316.

23 Hellouin, *Essai de critique*, 217; Laurent Tailhade, "Le Théatre Gratuit," *La Petite République* (1/11/1901) [available also in *A.N.* F XXI (1339)].

24 *Annales*, 23:16; "Rapport Présenté par M. Viollet le Duc…au Conseil Municipal de Paris, 1878," *A.N.* F XXI (1041), 8. Cf. "Proposition au Conseil Municipal pour la création d'un Grand Opéra populaire"; Paul-Boncour, *Art et démocratie*, 192. For the opinion of *Le Rappel*, Frédéric Montargues, "L'Opéra Populaire," *Le Rappel* (4/9/1883).

25 Antonio Gramsci, *Prison Notebooks*, 12.

26 Gohier, "Au Théâtre."

27 Chambre des Députés, Séance du 12/3/1897, *Journal Officiel*, 2689 [available also in *A.N.* F XXI (1337)]; Hellouin, *Essai de critique*, 213f.

28 Pierre Bourdieu and Jean-Claude Passeron, *Reproduction: In Education, Society and Culture*, Richard Nice, trans., SAGE Studies in Social and Educational Change (London: SAGE Publications, 1977), 25.

29 See the newspaper articles collected in *A.N.* F XVII (2662), including especially "La Matinée d'hier à l'Opéra"; Conbert, "Le Peuple à l'Opéra," *Paris* (1/5/1892); Pédrille, "La Journée d'Hier"; Gaston Calmette, "Les Matinées de l'Opéra," *Le Figaro* (1/4/1892); Bertrand interviewed in "L'Opéra Populaire," *Paris* (1/5/1892). Cf. Paul-Boncour, *Art et démocratie*, 193; Henry Roujon, *En Marge du Temps* (Paris, 1908), 96.

30 For an analysis of the failure of the reduced-price performances, see "Director of the Opéra to Minister of Public Instruction, July 1893," *A.N.*

AJ XIII (1194).The same phenomenon occurred at the Opéra-Comique: Chambre des Députés, "Rapport de la Commission du Budget, 1881," Chapter XIII, 87, available in *A.N.* AJ XIII (1202). Cf. "Ministre des Beaux-Arts to Director of the Opéra, 3/18/1903," *A.N.* AJ XIII (1006). Cf. also the budget report quoted in *Annales*, 29:16n.

31 Gramsci, *Prison Notebooks*, 57.

32 Michael Hays, *The Public and Performance: Essays in the History of French and German Theater, 1871-1900* (Ann Arbor: UMI Press, 1974), 5. I have substituted the term "audience" where Hays uses "bourgeoisie" so as not to confuse readers persuaded by the argument in Chapter IV of this work that the aristocratic element in the Opéra audience set the tone for the behavior of the audience as a whole.

33 Labruyère, "Physiologie Parisienne."

34 Bernard, "L'Evolution du Public," 37. For the influence of the cult of Wagner on the manners of the audience, Eckart-Bäcker, *Frankreichs Musik*, 143. Cf. Bruneau, *Musiques de Russie*, 124ff. Cp. Bernard, "L'Evolution du Public," 41. For the behavior of the audience, Parisis, *La Vie Parisienne* (Paris, 1887), 262; Gaston Jollivet, *L'Art de Vivre* (Paris, 1887), 74; H. Moreno, "Semaine Théâtrale," *Le Ménestrel*, 42 année no.16 (3/19/1876),123 and no.17 (3/26/1876),130f; Calmette, "Les Samedis de l'Opéra-Comique," 33.

35 Charles Garnier, *Le Théâtre* (Paris, 1871), 16.

36 Mayer, *The Persistence of the Old Regime*, 210.

37 Williams, *Marxism and Literature*, 110.

38 Bourdieu, *Distinction*, 315.

39 Garnier, their spokesman, wrote that the members were "concerned for the future of France," but this generally meant, in the context of discussions of the opera, concern for the continued quality of French artistic production: Garnier, "Le Tout-Paris," vi.

40 Bourdieu, *Distinction*, 418f.

41 Bourdieu, *Distinction*, 19.

42 M. A. Deville, *La Philosophie au Théâtre* (Paris, 1883), 46.

43 Bourdieu, *Distinction*, 19.

Epilogue

Background and Impact
of the Librettists

Directors, critics, Tout-Paris: Everyone responsible for monitoring the content of the librettos recognized that opera expressed social or political ideas only when these contradicted their own. A librettist who became aware of such a discrepancy, or who was made aware of it, had to choose between entertaining the prejudices of those who supported his artistic endeavors financially, or persevering with plans that expressed his own social and political outlook. Generally speaking, analysis of the social origins and career patterns of the librettists sheds little light on their works' social and political content. As a result, the background and ideas of the librettists, which might have been expected to lie at the heart of any discussion of the librettos' content, occupy only a peripheral place.

Understanding the mentality and milieu of the librettists tells us more about the motives that led them to write for the market. Both the real and perceived status of the dramatic author changed considerably under the Third Republic; this process accelerated as the century drew to a close. Increasingly important pecuniary rewards made most librettists even more eager for commercial success. All the more striking, in view of the prevailing attitude, are the important exceptions of successful authors such as Zola and Maeterlinck, who wrested from directors the right to challenge their audience's prejudices.

Among the obstacles to systematic analysis of the relationship between the background and opinions of the librettists on the one hand, and the content of their works on the other, is a technical one: It is difficult to isolate the contributions of the individual librettists in the texts of the large number of operas — about half the total — written by two or more authors in collaboration. In some cases, the partners had complementary talents; a dramatist would devise characters and plot, then ask a poet to express the results in verse. Gondinet and Gille divided the labor in this fashion in the case of *Jean de Nivelle*, working together in the same room on the details of the libretto. At the other extreme, the collaboration might represent a mere financial arrangement in disguise: Adolphe d'Ennery is credited as one of three librettists for Massenet's *Le Cid* because the other two writers wanted to borrow a scene from one of his plays.[1] Collaborative authorship was also a means of assimilating the contributions of writers with socio-cultural disadvantages, such as those from small provincial towns, or women. In order to improve their chances of having a work accepted for production, such marginal writers routinely joined themselves to better-connected collaborators.

At the time their librettos were produced, nearly all of the librettists were residents of Paris, or lived in country houses in the immediate environs. The ideal is represented by Charles Nuitter, also archivist of the Opéra, of whom it was said that he had never spent a day outside of Paris in his life. Almost half of Belle Epoque librettists were born in the provinces, but only a handful — Bretons and Alsatians — resisted relocating in the capital in order to launch their careers or follow up initial success. The importance of literary connections contributed to the hegemony of the urban and specifically Parisian cultural milieu by putting small-town immigrants at a disadvantage; they almost invariably sought out partners who were Parisians. Armand Silvestre, a native Parisian poet with close ties to the Midi, specialized in such arrangements: Between 1875 and 1901, a series of five provincial writers placed their first works at the Opéra or Opéra-Comique in collaboration with him. Directors frequently brought manuscripts with potential to Edmond Gondinet to be reworked, knowing that whatever he did would be marketable. He sometimes worked on four or five such plays at a time, for different directors, leaving him little time for original work of his own.[2]

Women librettists also took male collaborators; of four women among the Belle Epoque librettists, only Augusta Holmès, who also composed the music for her opera, acted independently. Maurice Rostand (son of Edmond) and his mother Rosemonde Gérard, who together wrote *La Marchande des Allumettes* (OC-1914), are the best known of these pairs. Since Rostand fails to mention the work in his otherwise highly detailed memoirs,[3] there is reason to believe that Gérard was largely responsible for it. Well-born, and exceptionally well-connected through her husband and in her own right, she had been, before her marriage, a promising poet and *protégée* of Leconte de Lisle. According to the director of the Opéra-Comique, she also enjoyed the particular favor of the radical-socialists who were in power at the time.[4] Although Gérard would not have needed a male collaborator to bring her work to the attention of opera management, he would still have been useful in overseeing rehearsals, where respectable women might have had trouble defending their interests or resolving technical problems. Regardless of their motives, the difficulty of identifying the particular contributions of the women librettists within these partnerships makes it impossible to isolate, with any confidence, evidence of gender-based distinctions within the librettos.

Augusta Holmès' *La Montagne-Noir* (O-1895), though unambiguous in this regard, illustrates the more general problems of relating the content of the libretto to the author's background or outlook. Her libretto is an unfortunate example of the worst type of over-complicated, super-saturated pseudo-*Wagnérisme*. The heroine Yamina, a Moslem woman who has been captured and enslaved by Montenegrin rebels, represents the liberated, voluptuous Eastern woman, in sharp contrast to the submissive Christian drudges who make up the women's chorus. Holmès portrays the latter in so unattractive a light, serving with bent backs and red hands their idle, complaining husbands, that the audience is forced to respond positively to Yamina's sensuousness, her nonchalance, and her independent self-assertiveness. Everything we know about Holmès' unconventional personal life — in particular her disdain for traditional patterns of relations between the sexes — suggests that she sympathized with these qualities in her heroine. Inexplicably, however, she makes the Montenegrin Christian men into the heroes of the piece, and in the last act, identifies Yamina unequivocally with treachery, intoxicated orgies, neglect of duty, and Satanic Islam.

What cannot be determined is whether the internal contradictions in *La Montagne-Noir* reflected the psychology of the author. Holmès may quite possibly have bowed to undocumented pressure from Opéra management to alter some earlier variant of the ending of the opera. The minister of public information, whose patronage of novice French composers helped bring *La Montagne-Noir* to the stage, would also have been in a position to insist on changes in the text. Though reluctant to politicize the Opéra for his own political ends, he may well have intervened to shield Holmès — and the audience — from the scandal of another *Carmen*. In any case, from the version that came to the stage, no unambiguous conclusion can be drawn about the relationship of the libretto's content even to so significant a variable as gender.

The problem of identifying individual contributions to the content of the librettos is compounded by the difficulty of estimating the extent to which librettists subordinated their own ideas to the prejudices of directors, of audiences, or of patrons who could further their career goals. Many poets and playwrights, especially early in the period under discussion, unabashedly approached libretto writing as a means of making money, which would permit them to devote their creative time to more legitimate forms of artistic endeavor. Others, whose social origins and opinions differed substantially from those of their audiences, adopted the attitudes of their clientele as they became more successful. Librettists varied widely in their commitment to the integrity of the art of the libretto, but the accommodating attitude of Meilhac and Halévy, when projections of audience reaction led the director Du Locle to demand fundamental modifications in *Carmen*, represents a typical approach to the librettist's craft. Accustomed to rewriting according to the whims of composers, performers and directors, librettists learned not to take their own efforts too seriously. The relative status of the individual composer and librettists within the partnership, and of the two professions within the artistic community, influenced their attitudes as well. In the case of *Carmen*, playwrights at the summit of success argued for giving the audience what it wanted while the young Bizet, struggling to establish himself, committed himself to innovative artistic principles.

Emile Bergerat and Armand Silvestre were friends and associates of long standing when the impresario Carvalho confronted them with demands for the modification of a recently completed libretto. Though a recent marriage had put him in desperate need of money, Bergerat refused to tamper with the work in accordance with the director's analysis of public taste. This unwillingness to compromise, characteristic of his whole career, had already earned him a reputation as one who was difficult for directors to work with. In his own eyes he was "unfit for the commerce of his art."[5] Bergerat had only one libretto accepted for production by the state opera theatres, and his earnings from theatrical endeavors in general were comparatively small.

His collaborator Silvestre thought of himself primarily as a poet; as such his prospects for commercial success were negligible. Like many writers who would have tolerated no interference with their poetry, he thought of theatre as an inferior but remunerative trade. To Bergerat's qualms, his reaction was: "What difference does it make to you, since dramatic art is the least of the arts? It is only a question of making money."[6] With this attitude, Silvestre continued to be much sought after as a librettist; despite the marginal success of his first efforts, only six of the 104 Belle Epoque librettists had more works accepted for production than he.

Wide variations in style and content within the opus of individual librettists suggest that Silvestre's attitude was more common than Bergerat's. Louis Gallet, the most successful of all Belle Epoque librettists in number of works accepted for production at the Opéra or Opéra-Comique, undoubtedly worked to order, as is illustrated by his own story of how he and Bizet struggled to come up with a scenario acceptable to the baritone Faure, in hopes that he could influence management to accept their opera for production (see above, Chapter II). Gallet's librettos came in a variety of aesthetic and ideological types, ranging from the reactionary, as in his adaptation of Corneille's *Le Cid* for Massenet (O-1885); to the comparatively democratic, in Paladilhe's *Patrie!* (O-1886); to the *vériste*, in *L'Attaque du Moulin* (OC-1893), based on a story by Zola. This versatility is characteristic of nearly all the librettists who had more than one or two librettos accepted for production. There is no sign that their ideas developed consistently over time either. The tendency to jump from one style to another and back again suggests that they had little commitment to any specific point of view or to any particular aesthetic approach, but wrote what the composers asked for, or what they themselves calculated that the audience demanded.

Prosopographical analysis,[7] based on admittedly spotty biographical data, yields no significant pattern of correlation between the librettists' social origins, or the opinions they expressed as adults, and their librettos' content. In only a few cases are the social origins of the librettist's ideas evident in his work. Vincent d'Indy, a descendant of crusaders, filled the libretto of *Fervaal* with inherited anti-democratic political opinions. The few librettists of plebian origins were among the first, after the pioneering work of Bizet, to introduce realistic working-class themes into their operas. *La Troupe Jolicoeur* (OC-1902) by Arthur Coquard, the son of Burgundian peasants, has for its heroine an orphan adopted by a troop of wandering entertainers. In defiance of convention, she does not discover any hidden identity in the last act. Gustave Charpentier, who wrote and composed *Louise*, was a baker's son who needed a scholarship from his native village in order to attend the Conservatoire in Paris. His lifelong interest in the Parisian proletariat — especially the women — is evident not only in his librettos, but in the Conservatoire Mimi Pinson, named after De Musset's character, which he founded for the musical education of working women. He also tried to expand the opera audience to include working people by persuading Carré to open the balconies of the Opéra-Comique to seamstresses and their mothers for a performance of *Louise*, and by encouraging his fellow composers and librettists to turn over their complimentary tickets to working-class patrons.[8]

In sharp contrast stands the case of Octave Lebesgue, a laborer's son apprenticed to a saddler at the age of twelve, who was the most authentically working-class librettist of the period. His nom de plume, Georges Montorgueil, was taken from a well-known republican ditty about the working-class quarter where he grew up. One of his two librettos, for Rousseau's *Leone* (OC-1910), featured working-class characters, but it was a standard *faits divers* piece devoid of democratic sentiments. The other, for Rousseau's *La Cloche du Rhin* (O-1898), was extravagant drivel typical of the operas produced to comply with government orders promoting the works of novice French composers.

The relative frequency with which librettists had librettos accepted by one of the opera houses, and the age at which they first succeeded in doing so, may be taken as crude indicators of the relative importance of various social factors in contributing to the success of the librettists, hence to the formation of their attitudes toward their work. In the estimation of the librettist Francis de Croisset, christened Franz Wiener, "One required, in order to be accepted in pre-war Parisian society, a great fortune or plenty of *esprit*, a good deal of talent, or a great name."[9] The incidence of nobility among librettists — around one in ten — is substantially higher than for the population as a whole, though perhaps not for the educated population. It is much lower than that of the Opéra audience, where one in five subscribers had titles and another ten percent claimed the *particule*. Noble rank as such did not prove particularly advantageous to the librettists in their chosen profession. M.-J.-L.-C.-Robert de la Motte-Ange was a Marquis de Flers descended from a lieutenant of Clovis, but his title was only an embarrassment in the theatrical circles he frequented. Vicomte Henri de Bornier was the penniless nephew of a marquise; his patrimony consisted of old-fashioned Legitimist political opinions and Catholic piety, which only hindered him in his careers as lawyer and librettist.

If high rank was no advantage to the librettist in placing many works at the Opéra or the Opéra-Comique, or in placing them there at an early age, personal connections within the social milieu of the notables, especially when combined with access to artistic circles, did contribute to early success. Jules Barbier and Gaston de Caillevet both made their debuts as librettists when still in their thirties, considerably earlier than average. The former was the son of a sculptor who served as tutor to the Duc d'Orléans and secretary to the Duc d'Aumâle. De Caillevet benefited from the nobility of his father, but more from the enterprise and *esprit* of his mother, the mistress of Anatole France, who maintained one of the most dazzling Belle Epoque salons. She included among her regular guests the writers Hérédia, Loti, Leconte de Lisle, and Marcel Proust. Poincaré and Clemenceau, two of the politicians most avidly interested in opera, and Emile Ollivier, an early partisan of Wagner, were also frequent visitors. In this atmosphere, young de Caillevet was systematically trained as a "Parisian playwright."[10]

Besides the sons and daughters of the nobility, a few other librettists came from families of notables who shared the tastes and habits of the Opéra habitués, and mixed comfortably with them. Gaston Jollivet, the son of an *haut bourgeois* politician killed by revolutionaries in 1848, boasted of dissipating his inheritance in the most fashionable, unproductive way at the races, of fighting a number of meaningless duels — and of hanging around at the Opéra. He criticized that institution for insufficient attention to the opinions of the notables among its clientele; it should be an aristocratic preserve, he felt, whose directors catered to the subscribers of the boxes, on whom the economic foundation of the Opéra depended.[11] The librettists' fathers also included a handful of bankers, one of whom transacted business on an international scale; the editor of *Le Figaro*; and the owner of the most important music publishing house in France. Their sons and daughters who wrote for the Opéra and Opéra-Comique presumably grew up with an intimate understanding of the tastes and prejudices of the clientele whom they later served.

Several other librettists came from families of professionals who would have been at home at the Opéra-Comique; they might have aspired to Opéra boxes once these began slowly to become available in the 1890s, and they might have attended as occasional patrons even earlier. Over all, the proportion of librettists born to the outlook of the audience elites is small; the librettists' fathers are distributed much more evenly within the range of social types encompassed by the term "bourgeoisie." Along with the ten or so librettists of noble descent, four who stemmed from the working class, and the larger number — some fifty, perhaps — who inherited some claim to bourgeois or petit bourgeois status, there were also at least fourteen whose fathers were writers or artists. These writers, along with the substantial proportion who were petit bourgeois, and the smattering from working-class families, clearly distinguish the social origins of the librettists from those of their patrons at the Opéra and Opéra-Comique.

The social status of the the artists and authors among the librettists' parents, whose wealth and mode of life sometimes approached that of the highest bourgeoisie, is difficult to compare with the more conventional backgrounds of the other fathers. Yet the artists' and authors' sons constitute a significant group because they achieved notably greater and earlier success than other librettists. On the average, sons of writers placed their first librettos successfully when still in their mid-thirties, much earlier than librettists from other family backgrounds. They displayed no discernible proclivity for countercultural themes and sentiments, which suggests that among the useful lessons learned from their fathers was a healthy respect for the commercial side of their chosen profession. Along with the connections they made along the way, this enabled them to succeed not only more quickly, but more often, in placing librettos with the directors.

In his discussion of the explanatory factors in the Belle Epoque writers' prospects, mentioned above, De Croisset also stressed the important early years of their literary careers:

> Youth has so much importance in the life of an *homme de lettres*. It is
> such a direct and vital explanation of his work and his times, and

Capus was right in saying, "To define conditions in which a writer makes his debut is in fact to define a whole society."[12]

Several librettists who were not necessarily born and raised in the milieu could have developed a clear sense of the opera audience's traditions and tastes from association with the opera later in life. Eight composers wrote their own librettos, though as a group they were neither prolific nor particularly distinguished. Baron Mermet had success as a composer early in his career, though *Jeanne d'Arc*, chosen as the first work to have its premiere at the new Palais Garnier in 1875, failed completely. D'Indy likewise achieved some recognition as a composer, but more as a scholar and teacher and as an active participant in musical politics. Only Charpentier won both critical acclaim and a popular following for his brilliant success with *Louise*, after which his work was in great demand.

In addition to the composers and Nuitter, the archivist mentioned above, two music publishers, Hartmann and de Choudens, were credited with helping to write librettos that they later published. The complex financial and artistic relationships among composers, librettists, and publishers makes the precise nature of their contributions problematical. Some impresarios also dabbled in writing, despite the policy of the Société des Auteurs et Compositeurs Dramatiques intended to prevent them from producing their own works. When he took over the Opéra-Comique in 1900, Albert Carré immediately revived *La Basoche*, which he and his music director, Messager, had written ten years earlier. Carré also confirmed his reputation for nepotism by reviving the *Contes d'Hoffman* (OC-1881) of his uncle Michel Carré, and by introducing two librettos by Michel Carré *fils*, his first cousin.

For librettists unconnected with the opera, libretto writing was frequently a sidelight to other full-time careers; most of these first entered the work force under the expanding economy of the Second Empire. To be sure, writers for whom finances were not an issue chose to devote themselves exclusively to literature. Of those from the thirteen wealthiest families, among those whose wealth can be reliably estimated, eleven eschewed other employment completely. Writers who did take other employment took slightly longer to achieve success as librettists, on the average, presumably because they had less time to devote to perfecting their craft, associating with more prominent literary figures, keeping abreast of the latest fashions in art, and peddling their wares. But half of those who took real jobs between 1850 and 1870 kept them even after achieving success as writers.

This group, which engaged in a wide variety of careers, included some of the most prolific librettists. Louis Gallet, who had more than twice as many librettos produced during this period as any other librettist, continued his career as hospital administrator while earning hundreds of thousands of francs from nineteen Opéra and Opéra-Comique librettos. Alexandre Chatrian, whose radical political activities had been an obstacle to youthful literary success, signed on as a clerk with the Chemin de Fer de l'Est at an annual salary of Fr.1,500. Forty years later, as the partner of Emile Erckmann, Chatrian's literary career had blossomed, but he was still working for the railway as a *caissier des titres* for Fr.12,000 per year.

The two most popular choices for alternative employment — journalism and the government bureaucracy — both had the potential for significantly altering the outlook of the librettists by contributing to a mentality that discouraged the expression of controversial ideas. The government made a substantial and apparently quite successful effort to control the ideological content of their works by subsidizing writers as members of the "intermittent bureaucracy" described above. Among librettists who supplemented their incomes with other types of employment, by far the largest group — one-third of the total — were full-time journalists. Dismissing the idea that journalism somehow drained writers of their creativity, Emile Zola advised young provincials, in particular, that it would teach them about life and about Paris, and incidentally improve their style. It also taught the librettists among them an approach to the craft of writing that privileged style over substance.[13]

Journalism was similar to the opera in permitting rapid assimilation of young writers into the upper echelons of the Parisian social, political, and intellectual elites. Like the hero of Maupassant's *Bel-Ami*, the future librettist Albert Wolff arrived in Paris almost destitute. He began his literary career as secretary to Alexandre Dumas *père*, a post that nobody held for long since it paid only the nominal sum of thirty francs per month. But valuable literary connections could be formed there; in Wolff's case, these led to a commission to translate the younger Dumas into German. Wolff haunted the offices of *Le Figaro* in search of employment, but his first regular position was with the satirical sheet *Le Charivari*, where he could write up to fifteen articles per month at ten francs per article, if he did odd jobs for the editor's wife on the side. By the eighteen-seventies, when his "Chroniques" were a mainstay of *Le Figaro*, Wolff was earning Fr.60,000 per year from that paper alone. He estimated his total revenue, including the proceeds from drama criticism for a rival paper and various business deals, at Fr.100,000 in a good year.[15]

According to Avenel's history of French journalism, the debut of *Le Figaro* on 2 April 1854 "marks the birth of Second Empire Parisian life, the intellectual style of the period, the blossoming of talents in art and literature."[16] Several future librettists were among the columnists vital to *Le Figaro*'s predominant position amidst the fierce newspaper rivalries of the 'sixties. While Albert Wolff was turning out his "Chroniques," Phillippe Gille contributed the crucial "Echos de Paris" and "Causeries," and Albert Millaud took on the sensitive position of parliamentary reporter. *Le Figaro* succeeded by paying the best journalists exhorbitant wages for exceptional work: In the 'fifties, the future librettist Monselet earned only thirty-five centimes per line there, but by the late 'sixties one of Wolff's colleagues was earning Fr. 500 for only four columns a month.[17]

Le Figaro also benefited many other writers indirectly by engendering large numbers of competitors impressed by and jealous of its success. *L'Evènement*, which hired Emile Bergerat as drama critic in 1872, grew out of a personal quarrel between its founders and the editors of *Le Figaro*. Gaston Jollivet, having squandered his substantial inheritance, took a job at the *Gazette de Paris*, founded by a banker who wanted a front-row seat in the gallery of the Assemblée and a stall for all the theatrical premieres.[18] The founder of the first mass newspaper in France, *Le Petit Journal*, was another journalist with close ties to *Le Figaro*, and the father of the librettist Albert Millaud.

During the era when the librettists were making their way, journalism, like libretto-writing, meant subordinating personal social and political attitudes to the exigencies of the established elites rather than trying to mold the opinions of the latter. The frivolity of *Le Figaro* and its imitators was a highly successful adaptation to the repressive political climate of the Second Empire and the early years of the Third Republic. It colored the outlook of a whole generation of aspiring authors by emphasizing form almost to the exclusion of content, with special aversion to political or serious social commentary. Some observers described the change in Second Empire journalism not as a movement away from politics toward literature, but rather as one that abandoned both politics and literature in favor of mere gossip.[19] Either way, the participation of librettists in this process during the Third Republic put the prospect of adapting librettos to political purposes in opposition to all their habits and assumptions.

Beginning with the liberalization of the Empire in 1868, and especially after the republican triumphs of the late 'seventies, when readers again began purchasing papers according to their political orientation, careers in journalism became less attractive to young men with purely literary talents and aspirations. Those who entered the profession during the 'seventies did so more often as part-time critics, to make a name for themselves while supplementing their erratic incomes. Among the future librettists who reviewed drama during this period was Adolphe Aderer, who introduced the practice of publishing reviews the day following a premiere. Emile Bergerat got his start as art critic for the *Journal Officiel*, without any experience or expertise whatsoever, and later founded his own journal of art criticism.[20] The debilitating moral and intellectual effect that music and drama criticism had on its practitioners has been discussed in an earlier chapter.

Although the potential rewards for literary success were great, many case histories suggest that a period of initial hardship was common. It often determined the librettists' attitudes toward their careers and the price exacted for success. These important differentiating experiences of their formative years, when librettists first tried to cope with the prospect of making a living through literature or otherwise, influenced the content of the repertoire in a number of ways. Fortunately, writers who overcame serious obstacles early in their careers were prone to describing their experiences in great detail later on. Bergerat, encouraged by some early success and against all good advice, decided on a career in literature early in life. His memoirs of Second Empire bohemianism run mostly to the fun of scrounging furniture, of learning how to cook from attractive actresses and artists' models, and of repaying the kindly, indulgent concierge who had been his benefactress when times were hardest.

But young writers faced with the necessity of earning a living varied in the depth of their commitment to literary careers, in their material requirements and expectations, and in their appreciation of the virtues of poverty. The composer/librettist Arthur Coquard described his alternatives to his mentor César Franck in the following terms:

> I am thinking over an irrevocable decision that I must make shortly: either I will be a lawyer for the rest of my life at the Cour de Cassation, honorable, second rate, doing some good around me; or I will throw myself with terrific force of will into an artistic career with the prospect of great struggles, material suffering, preoccupied with my daily bread and a thousand formidable difficulties, but at the same time with the thought that God is calling me to it....[21]

Emile Zola recognized theoretically that a young man with artistic aspirations could live adequately in Paris on Fr.125 a month, and proposed such a budget to his friend Cézanne, still stuck in the provinces. But Zola himself tried and failed to live on Fr.150, the monthly allowance provided by his mother. D'Alméras, pointing out that professional careers were closed to Zola because he had failed his baccalauréat twice, calls him "a bohemian out of necessity, rather than out of conviction."[22] He took a job dispatching parcels for the publisher Hachette, and eventually worked himself up to secretary to the publisher and director of advertising before giving it all up to pursue his writing career full time.

Victorien Sardou, in contrast, though he was willing to give lessons in history, philosophy, or mathematics, and to write articles for revues, minor newspapers, and even dictionaries, turned down posts with the Ministry of Public Instruction and as regent in a provincial secondary school. In fact, he consistently resisted offers of full-time, permanent employment. Many librettists felt that they had little choice; they were forced to eke out an impoverished living from whatever part-time employment presented itself. Adolphe d'Ennery wrote, "When I was twenty years old, I lived in a garret [elsewhere he calls it a 'dark stable'] where I froze in winter and suffocated in summer."[23] He supported himself at various times as a painter, a notary's clerk, a clerk in a novelty shop, and as a part-time journalist.

Experiences such as these brought future librettists into contact with a side of Parisian life that was alien to their bourgeois and aristocratic audiences. If government jobs and journalism had a negative, restraining influence on the librettists' work, the bohemian way of life and the values of the struggling young artists liberated them from the constraints of traditional career aspirations. The librettist Charles Monselet had ties to the romantic bohemia of his best friend Henry Murger, of Gérard de Nerval, Baudelaire, and the Café Momus. Monselet's first contacts with Parisian literary figures, when he arrived from Bordeaux in 1846, yielded a few paltry commissions for literary work from which he earned, during his first month, a total of fifty francs. This disappointed him, even though he had found a *pension* at only forty francs a month, and could have had one even cheaper — only twenty sous a day.[24] After a couple of months in Paris, Monselet had plenty of work, but very little pay; he was ejected from his apartment for non-payment of rent. In order to survive, he was reduced to the meanest, most dangerous sort of literary hack-work: He became a theatre critic. This involved him in a duel with the playwright Emile Augier, and soon afterward a Second Empire roundup of journalists — a general intimidation of writers of a variety of political persuasions — landed him a week in jail. On the other hand, even when food was scarce Monselet was able to attend the theatre several times a week, either in connection with his work, or with the benefit of authors' complimentary tickets from his literary acquaintances.[25]

Eight years after his arrival in Paris, a literary study of Réstif de la Bretonne had given Monselet a certain reputation, but he still had not made any money. For his first book he was to receive Fr. 100 for the first 500 copies sold, and another Fr. 100 after the second 500 copies; it sold 600 copies. Later on, his books earned him the standard rate of approximately one franc per page. In the late 'fifties and the 'sixties Monselet acquired considerable popularity as a humorist; his name on the first issue helped many ephemeral satirical sheets get off to a good start.[26] But if by some standards he was one of the most successful of writers, he made only a modest living. Though Monselet felt at the end of his life that he had worked hard for a very meager return, he had chosen this style of life with his eyes open. He endured its trials the more willingly out of the conviction that a literary career ultimately held considerable potential for riches: "I sense, I see, I believe that there never was a time more favorable to literary success, and through the triple doors of the book, the journal, and the theatre, there is gold that flows unceasingly."[27]

Whether or not they shared Monselet's optimistic assessment of their prospects, many aspiring librettists abandoned other employment during the eighteen-eighties in order to concentrate on literature full time. This exodus from the work force coincided with an increased tendency among younger writers to go directly into literature without taking other employment at all. Between 1850 and 1890, less than one-third attempted to do so; after 1890, more than two out of three took their chances on a literary career directly after completing their education. The general European economic stagnation may have made alternatives to a full-time literary career less rewarding and harder to come by, but there is also evidence that the kinds of literary activity that the librettists engaged in had begun to support increasing numbers of writers, and that more of them were prepared to tolerate a period of bohemian poverty. As bohemianism became more prevalent, it spawned a "truculent" variety, closer to Villon than to Murger in its outlook, and a commercial variety, in both of which the librettists participated.

Maurice Magre, a future librettist who arrived from the suburbs of Toulouse in 1898 with a subsistence allowance from his family of only one hundred francs per month, was not merely serious, but dogmatic about his poverty. "Only a man without a job can live outside of the hypocrisy engendered by the relations of people among themselves," he wrote; others can be saved only by "the wholesome air of poverty." The material deprivation described in Magre's semi-autobiographical, semi-didactic *Conseils à un jeune homme pauvre* contrasts sharply with the quality of life enjoyed by the young Bergerat or Monselet. The tone of the book takes on a tinge of bitterness when Magre describes the sacrifices needed to maintain the indispensable respectable suit, or the embarrassment of having the wrong style of shoes when finally he was invited to his first literary salon.[28]

Noting that a considerably more sober variety of bohemianism had replaced the insouciance of the earlier era, some Third Republic observers attributed the change to the disenchanting effects of the Prussian occupation of Paris, the horrors of the Commune, or the financial scandals of the early 'eighties. The prevailing economic distress probably played its part as well.[29] But the hard-nosed, austere bohemianism of Magre must have been partly the product of his distinctive individual psychology; other descriptions of Montmartre during the same period stress the lively bonhomie of its atmosphere.

At the notorious Chat-Noir nightclub, young artists ridiculed the bourgeoisie and abused public figures in a variety of art forms including poetry, songs, and the famous shadow theatre. According to Maurice Donnay:

> The Tout-Paris ascended to Montmartre; high finance, high society on a spree, the established political world, came to pay a visit to insouciant bohemia and, on certain days, on Friday particularly which had become the chic day, one saw at the Chat-Noir the women of the aristocracy, of the upper bourgeoisie, and also the *demoiselles*, the "*horizontales*."[30]

Friday nights became fashionable when the proprietor began to heap vituperation on prominent members of the audience from non-bohemian circles. The Chat-Noir regulars joined in making visiting provincials the butt of their *blagues*, which they raised almost to the status of an art form. Some of these practical jokes entered into bohemian mythology, to be recounted decades later by anyone with the remotest claim to association with the club.

There was more than a hint of self-advertising in the activities and fancy dress of the bohemians, among whom Jean Richepin was the most flamboyant, because the Chat-Noir was more than just a source of entertainment for slumming society and irreverent pranksters. It brought talented but obscure artists together with patrons and administrators of the arts, providing an institutional base for the advancement of the bohemians' group consciousness and their professional artistic activities. The development of the Montmartre counterculture made it more feasible for aspiring writers to dispense with regular employment and to gamble on being discovered quickly. The Chat-Noir "launched important works and authors, discovered unknown talents, established true vocations," wrote Gheusi, who sometimes read poetry there himself.[31] Maurice Donnay, dramatic author for the internationally renowned Chat-Noir shadow theatre, began a career there that eventually led to the Académie Française. Among the other opera librettists associated with the institution were Coppée and Richepin, also future Académiciens, and Monselet, Lorrain, Saint-Croix, and Haraucourt.

Traces of the librettists' bohemian existence, which differentiated so many of them from their audience, emerge in a significant number of librettos. Among those that extolled the artist's life in contrast to conventional existence were Guiraud's *Piccolino* (OC-1876) and Offenbach's *Contes d'Hoffman* (OC-1881). In Saint-Saëns' *Ascanio* (O-1890), the King of France calls Benvenuto Cellini "a sovereign, more sovereign than I" (I:iv) and a "master who subordinates the universe to his laws!" (V:ii). Charpentier's *Louise*, Coquard's *La Troupe Jolicoeur* (OC-1902) and Missa's *Muguette* (OC-1903) continued the tradition of bohemian opera themes after the turn of the century. The threat represented by the countercultural ideals and values propagated in these librettos was to some extent kept in bounds by assimilating and co-opting bohemianism's more benign aspects into the dominant bourgeois culture. Puccini's *Vie de Bohème*, based on Murger's work, was one of the most popular of all Belle Epoque operas with Parisian audiences; it played for more than 300 Opéra-Comique performances between 1898 and 1914. Ultimately, however, the bohemian librettos contributed to an anti-bourgeois, anti-positivist movement, which, through the medium of theoretical *Wagnérisme*, constituted the librettists' strongest and most direct assault on the cultural hegemony of opera's elites.

The best known of the French works, and by far the most popular in its own day, was Gustave Charpentier's *Louise*, which drew heavily on the composer/librettist's familiarity with Montmartre for its bohemian and working-class local color and for the sentiments expressed by the characters. It is the story of a laborer's daughter, a Parisian working girl who is a seamstress in the luxury trade. She falls in love with a poet who persuades her to leave her family for the joys of the bohemian life in Montmartre. Learning that her departure has made her father ill, she returns to her family. But their abusive domination soon becomes intolerable again, so she runs away for good, even though she realizes it will kill her father.

As in the case of *Carmen*, and for roughly the same reasons, the opera was rebarbative to the Tout-Paris of the premieres. According to one account of the opening, "The bourgeois element in the hall remained lukewarm, not to say glacial."[32] There was still something offensive about the presence of comparatively realistic lower-class characters on the stage of the Opéra-Comique, even though the sentiments they expressed, especially in comparison with those of the bohemians, contained nothing threatening to the bourgeoisie. The seamstresses in Louise's shop are content with their lot; they spend all their time singing and dancing. Louise's father exhibits occasional flashes of bitterness about his advancing age and the impossibility of retirement, but his basic attitude is one of resignation. For him, happiness consists in "the hearth where one rests, where one forgets, in the presence of loved ones, the misfortunes of life" (I:iv). Likewise, an old bent streetsweeper who remembers the time before she lost her looks says, "I have no regrets...I had such a good time" (IIB:ii).

Far from placing the sentiments of the working classes in opposition to those of the bourgeoisie, Charpentier lumps them together in contrast to the libertarian outlook of the Montmartre bohemians. Free love and the denial of authority are central to the emancipated, irreverent style of life enjoyed by the latter, referred to in the opera as "young gods" and "children of harmony." A chorus of gamins and bohemians sings "Scoff at the laws and at the bourgeois...long live the artists! Glory to the anarchists! (III:ii). The hero of the opera urges Louise to reject the traditional values of her family in the following terms:

> Julien: Experience! Ha!ha!ha! Experience, that means routine, tradition, all the oppression of stupid prejudices. Experience puts God himself in bondage! Experience! Cowardly, tyrannical servant of greed standing guard at the threshold of life! Youths driven by passions, all that's ideal, all love, all one's will, all genius shamed, pursued and hunted as if it were ignominious.... Oh, that miserable, odious, infamous, hypocritical, sterile experience!
>
> Louise (simply): So every child has the right to choose for himself the road to happiness?
>
> Julien: Every being has the right to be free! Every heart has the duty to be in love! (III:i)

Though the intrusion of the lower classes into the world of the Opéra-Comique offended the Tout-Paris, the bohemian counterculture was a familiar and accepted part of the bourgeois world.[34] The strong fascination that bohemia exercised on the bourgeoisie, which led them willingly to submit to ridicule at the Chat-Noir, appears also in the reaction of "M. Prudhomme" to Louise. One of Charpentier's biographers describes it this way:

It stirs his blood and excites his imagination. And then the bohemian life, although a bit scandalous, evokes his curiosity more than his anger. . . . The life of the studio, like the life of the student, takes on in his imagination unutterable charms which never lose their appeal, since he can never taste them.[33]

So, despite the initial response of the Tout-Paris, the sentiments expressed in *Louise* found a ready-made sympathetic audience. The cheap seats filled with musicians, artists and would-be artists, students and bohemians, many of whom came again and again; one young man apparently attended all of the first thirty-three performances.[35] *Louise* became a favorite of the regular Opéra-Comique clientele as well, even more quickly than *Carmen*, and established itself as a fixture in the repertoire. Both in Paris and in the provinces, it went on to become one of the most successful of all Belle Epoque operas. It was one of only four to achieve 100 Opéra-Comique performances in its first year, and during the next twenty seasons it passed the impressive total of 500.

While operas such as *Louise* were critical of the established order, some more explicitly than others, and they advertised a very different set of values, their overall effect was not subversive. On the contrary, the social system gained strength and cohesion from the vitality of a counterculture dedicated to free love — and the *blague* — rather than to divisive political action. And when the working women who attended free performances of *Louise* came away talking passionately about free love, so much the better for M. Prudhomme. There was a fine line, however, between sympathetic, romanticized bohemianism, which charmed and seduced its audience, and deviant bohemian values that threatened to subvert the fabric of bourgeois society. Even *Louise* crossed it, in the third act, when she tried to move beyond mere free love to proclaim the right of women to enjoy sex, and even to take the sexual initiative:

Louise: Ah! Once you took the loving virgin, innocent in the springtime of her existence; but today, the loving woman wants in her turn to take her lover!

Louise: Come, oh my poet! Ah! be my conquest! Ah! come die
& beneath my kisses!
Julien: Ah! take your poet! Ah! carry off your conquest! Make me die beneath your kisses. (III:i)

Here the Department of Fine Arts felt obliged to intervene. Censors cut both *Louise's* too aggressive demand for "kisses, Julien, kisses," and the "audacious stage business that accompanied it."[36]

The fundamental ambivalence of the established culture toward the bohemians is revealed in its response to the poet and librettist Jean Richepin, who fashioned a brilliantly successful career out of thumbing his nose at the bourgeoisie. Having grown up in Belleville, a working-class quarter of Paris, he graduated from the prestigious Ecole Normale Supérieure and immediately capitalized on his accomplishment, opening a *frites* stand under the sign:

> FRITES
> JEAN RICHEPIN
> NORMALIEN

The crudity of the poetry that he was writing at the time earned him a month in prison, after which he found work as a sailor and stevedore in Bordeaux and around the Mediterranean. In *Les Etapes d'un Réfractaire*, published in 1871, Richepin roundly condemned social conventions and the people responsible for them. The rich and happy he threatened with revolutionary upheaval: "Oh, you the satiated, you the gorged, you the satisfied, in truth I tremble for you."[37]

Paradoxically, Richepin's disreputable style of life helped to promote his career among some of the most conservative elements in Belle Epoque society. According to his fellow librettist Maurice Rostand:

> His reputation at that time was quite substantial, augmented no doubt by a certain scandal, but supported also by university circles, which backed him with that secret nostalgia of professors who marvelled that one of their own, in frank defiance of the rules, should be permitted to live the tumultuous existence that they had all dreamed of. He wrote correct verse and he went to bed with famous actresses. He piled fiasco on fiasco, in such a way that they were talked about like the successes of other people. He had done a month in prison! And he was an anti-Dreyfusard. This was a "chemineau" [tramp] who finished up in the Académie Française.[38]

Richepin had five relatively successful librettos accepted for production; he drew on his experiences for many of them, but most notably for *Le Chemineau* (OC-1907), set to music by Xavier Leroux. The hero is a vagabond with extraordinary gifts as a healer, peacemaker, and jack-of-all-trades; his primary "occupation is to be happy" (III:xiii) and he suffers when deprived of freedom. "Take advantage of the happiness which chance brings you," he advises his lover, as he refuses either to stay with her or to bring her along on his wanderings (I:vi). In the last act, he abandons her and his child on Christmas Eve, without saying goodbye.

That the anarchist revolutionary of the early 'seventies became an anti-Dreyfusard in the 'nineties should not be surprising. These two opposite poles of the political spectrum — retrograde and avant-garde — united in antipathy for the dominant bourgeois culture. Revolutionaries and bohemians among the librettists found common ground with reactionary Opéra audiences in their mutual rejection of the middle ground. This occurred under the aegis of *Wagnérisme*. Richepin himself wrote a *Wagnériste* libretto, for Massenet's *Le Mage*. As Chapter IV demonstrated, the reactionary *Wagnériste* librettos were attractive to the elite audiences of the Opéra. But socialists and anarchists were also conspicuous among the groups who supported *Lohengrin*. Characterizing themselves as internationalists, the socialists considered chauvinism to be bourgeois. The leader of the internationalist anarchists, "recognizing neither the nation nor art" also presented himself at the general secretariat of the Opéra in order to ask for a ticket.[39] The patriotic left wing, represented by the newspaper *La Bataille*, was *Wagnériste* as well, because, it insisted, the artistic taste of true, socialist workers was more advanced than that of the bourgeoisie. Naturally the socialists referred to Wagner's revolutionary past: He had been on the barricades in Dresden in 1848, and since the 1848 revolutions originated in France anyway, he was practically one of them.[40]

Among the librettists, Vincent d'Indy, the composer/librettist of *Fervaal*, and the author of *Richard Wagner et son influence sur l'art musical français*, was a regular pilgrim to Bayreuth who followed the Master's advice to French composers to explore the legends and folk songs of their own country. This process not only produced *Fervaal*, but stimulated d'Indy's active participation in reactionary, anti-parliamentary French political movements during the eighteen-eighties:

He devoted himself to the increasingly forlorn Legitimist cause. D'Indy's *Wagnériste* opera got a highly favorable review from Alphonse Richaud in the *Revue Socialiste* nonetheless. The radical republican Augusta Holmès likewise took the triumph of the sublime as her theme and featured a bust of Wagner in her salon. It was not the reactionary political message normally associated with *Wagnérisme*, but its critique of bourgeois morality, which appealed to librettists such as Holmès, who was notorious for her unconventional style of life.[41]

Wagnérisme also served to express the librettists' growing antipathy for Third Republic parliamentary government in general. As we have seen, librettists often held republican opinions during the eighteen-eighties and early eighteen-nineties. During the late 'eighties and 'nineties, however, until the Dreyfus Affair re-engaged the active interest of artists and intellectuals in political affairs, the unedifying spectacle of Third Republic parliamentary politics left many librettists disenchanted with the republic that had looked so wonderful during the Empire. Disillusionment, the characteristic sentiment of librettists of all political creeds, manifested itself less in overt hostility toward the regime than in disdain for the whole political process. The very success of the Third Republic fostered this attitude, according to the librettist Maurice Donnay. Describing the beliefs of his fellow bohemians (including a number of librettists) who patronized the Chat-Noir cabaret, he wrote:

> As for domestic politics, I think it is difficult to be more indifferent than we were to the *res publica*. There was no threat to the republic.... Our excuse was that we felt ourselves inserted into a republican system incapable of being reformed.... We didn't read the newspapers.

In one of the *blagues* for which he became famous in *Le Figaro*, the librettist Emile Bergerat systematized this attitude of indifference and abstentionism into a political program called "Zutisme." This was the political — more accurately apolitical — aspect of the system of values and style of life constituting the bohemian subversion of the dominant culture.[43]

Leftists and rightists alike were frustrated by the venality and vacillations of bourgeois parliamentary democracy; they differed in assigning the ultimate blame, but united in condemning the moral bankruptcy of the regime and demanding a renewal of its integrity. Critics from the left, who witnessed deputies truckling to the interests of wealthy financiers, generally denounced the power of money in society and politics. The theatre of Emile Augier, said his fellow librettist Jules Barbier, depicted a bourgeoisie full of gold and pride, "whose stupidity equals their bad faith; unscrupulous parvenus, persuaded that wealth was a substitute for honor."[44] Barbier, subsequently an active Dreyfusard who resigned from the Legion of Honor when Zola was ejected, made it clear that he shared Augier's views, while pointing out that such anti-bourgeois attitudes had led in Augier's case to overindulgence toward the aristocracy.

Rightist librettists tended to concentrate their criticisms of the republic on the debilitating moral effect of parliamentary politics and the *fonctionnaire* mentality. Coppée "hated politics and those who lived by it," while Louis Davyl thought republican leaders were devoid of principle and bent on enriching themselves. The most thorough-going statement of this point of view occurred in Jules Lemaître's *Opinions à Répandre*. He demanded a complete moral regeneration to lift France out of its *fonctionnairisme*, which sapped the initiative and commitment of individual Frenchmen and led to advancement through personal influence rather than merit.[45]

To both sorts of evil — the inordinate influence of big money, and the *fonctionnaire* mentality of the politicians — the *Wagnériste* emphasis on exalted rather than sordid sentiments addressed itself. As the weakness and corruption of the Third Republic began to frustrate writers from a whole range of political persuasions, librettists came to appreciate Wagner's cult of the sublime, and to share his scorn for bourgeois forms of government. The bohemian critique of bourgeois values found a useful theoretical framework in Wagner's prose works, which promoted artists to the status of heroic outsiders destined to bring salvation to decadent French society. Raised to the level of a principle, active repudiation of bourgeois values appeared to them to represent a genuine hope for the future. The various sorts of attraction that *Wagnérisme* had for librettists, in conjunction with the relevance of its ideology to the needs of the reactionary audience, account for the genre's ability to dominate the repertoire of the Opéra for a twenty-year period from the early 'nineties to the outbreak of the Great War.

The responsive chord struck by Wagner's rejection of bourgeois moral and cultural dominance was reinforced, for the librettists, by the appeal that his positive social and political program made to their self-interest and self-esteem. Passages such as the following, translated in the influential *Revue Wagnérienne* as part of Wagner's "Lettre sur la Musique," gave French artists a highly exalted conception of themselves and their occupation: "The arts have provided...the means of making the most elevated and profound goals of humanity intelligible to the assembled people." In another article from the same revue, Houston Stuart Chamberlain likewise referred to "the supreme importance that art can and should have in the life of men and the life of society."[46] Because to the central importance of the *Gesamtkunstwerk* in Wagner's aesthetic system, this grandiose conception of the artist's social function especially enhanced the status of artists connected with the opera. According to the composer and critic Max d'Ollone, Wagner's theoretical works and the philosophy of his dramas had the effect "of interesting many intellectuals in music and opera who found in it new fodder for their intellectual activity and who ceased to treat music as an inferior art because it no longer contented itself, they believed, with expressing emotion, but had 'risen' to the expression of ideas."[47]

At the same time, Wagner's renewed emphasis on the importance of the words among the constituent arts of the opera redounded to the particular prestige of the librettist. During the 1890s, French composers such as Holmès, d'Indy, and Albéric Magnard wrote librettos for their own operas. Composers who chose not to follow Wagner's example in this regard nevertheless insisted on more profound texts and took pains to make them more intelligible. The composer Alfred Bruneau, who revolutionized traditional libretto form by setting prose to music rather than poetry, and who introduced Zola to the opera, wrote that the composer should consider himself the humble servant of the text.[48] Massenet and Charpentier, whose debt to Wagner was less direct, tried to facilitate comprehension by paying particular attention to prosody. Composers and critics alike favored singers capable of conveying words clearly. As a result, the critic and historian of opera Louis Laloy concluded that Wagner had had a greater impact on French librettists than on musicians. He mentioned specifically Jean Richepin and Catulle Mendès, both of them contributing editors to the *Revue Wagnérienne*. Mendès, in particular, with the advantage of literacy in German, was prominent in the dissemination of Wagnerian doctrine in

France. Charles Nuitter and Victor Wilder also translated Wagner's works, besides writing librettos of their own.[49]

Wagner's contention that artists could effect important social changes, and the example of his own theoretical writings, engaged librettists in the debate that dominated *fin-de-siècle* intellectual life, between traditional French positivism and invading idealism. Opera became one of the strongholds of idealism, with the librettos as part of its arsenal, in this battle for the allegiance of the French intelligentsia. Positivist ideas in the Enlightenment tradition had monopolized the mainstream of French intellectual activity, including that of the librettists, through most of the nineteenth century. Its principles have been aptly summarized by Pierre Martino as the belief in progress, in perfectability, in science, and in the methodical application of common sense to all aspects of human existance.

Auguste Comte had provided the most thorough and systematic formulation of its philosophical underpinnings, but the librettists and their circle were more familiar with various attempts to apply positivist principles to history, science, and religion. Gaston Jollivet wrote that he "made the masterpiece of Taine [*Origins de la France Contemporaine*] my bedside reading."[50] The prestige of positivist science and its impact on the public imagination — this was the age of Pasteur and Berthelot — is most evident in the Naturalism of Zola. He claimed to have done for literature what Claude Bernard had recently accomplished for medicine: turning it from an art into a science.[51] In Zola's Naturalism, the physical world predominated and the history of individuals and nations was subject to rigorous determinism.

When carried to its logical conclusion, positivism inevitably entailed the destruction of the old idols, including the church and its moral system. One of the most influential wielders of this philosophic instrument was Renan, whose positivist *Vie de Jesus* repudiated the supernatural. Among the librettists, Renan's chief disciples were Jules Lemaître, author of an important and influential *Revue Bleue* article on him in 1885, and Edmond Haraucourt, whom Renan sponsored for the Legion of Honor. He was also the intellectual guide of the literary group known as the Parnasse, to which the librettists Coppée, Docquois, Dorchain, Mendès, de Regnier, and Silvestre all adhered at various times. Their works were noted for "depicting dead religions and civilizations, hostility to Christianity, enthusiasm for the republic and hatred of the aristocracy, faith in an upcoming regeneration, absolute faith in science."[52]

The positivism of Renan and his disciples paved the way for its own negation, however, by leaving a psychological and cultural void where the supernatural had been. The idealist reaction that overtook France at the end of the century, the theme of H. Stuart Hughes' *Consciousness and Society*,[53] penetrated the milieu of the librettists first in the form of Schopenhauer's cult of pessimism, after which it reinforced their enthusiasm for Wagner. Virtually unknown in France before Ribot's *Philosophie de Schopenhauer* (1874) prompted the translation of his works during the next quarter of a century, Schopenhauer's ideas attracted considerable attention after 1880. At that time, "his name was on every lip; he was commented on from the chairs of philosophy; he was cited in the salons."[54] Among the librettists, both Lemaître and Haraucourt transferred their allegiance from Renan to Schopenhauer. Baillot, in his *Influence de la Philosophie de Schopenhauer en France, (1860-1890)*, says that the latter was the philosopher most often cited in the theatre criticism of Lemaître. He mentions Schopenhauer's influence on Haraucourt as well, and points out that Henri Bataille used quotations from the philosopher's works as aphorisms in his own writings.[55] The dark side of German idealism manifests itself clearly in Bataille's dismal *La Lépreuse*, while the Schopenhauerian conflict between "will" and "representation" shows up in Haraucourt's libretto for the Hillemachers' *Circe* (OC-1907), which ends with a suicide and general despondency.[56] The titles of its three acts are "The Ascendancy of the Flesh," "The Flesh and the Idea," and "The Triumph of the Idea."

If the librettists had any real impact on the development of French intellectual life, it was in their capacity as a sort of intermediate intellectual conduit for transmitting the philosophical idealism of thinkers such as Wagner and Schopenhauer to the social, political and economic elites who comprised the opera audience. Few habitués of the opera read Schopenhauer, or even Bergson, and not many of the librettists did either. But the latter did read and understand the *Wagnériste* critique of positivism, and reproduced this idealist mode of thought in the librettos consumed by their clientele. Positivists from French operatic circles recognized that their dominant position in French intellectual life was threatened by *Wagnérisme*, the most important vehicle for the idealist invasion of this particular milieu. The music critic Lionel de Laurencie wrote that *Wagnérisme* "penetrated into France at the moment when dying Romanticism was giving way to positivist Naturalism, and put our clear, precise, optimistic *mentalité* in conflict with the Germanic *mentalité*, anxious about the future, inoculated with pessimism."[57] Opposition to French liberal thought had indeed been the basis of much of Wagner's theoretical work; he hoped that the idealist principles behind his new music might have widespread beneficial social repercussions by destroying the pernicious French Naturalism which had so thoroughly pervaded modern life.[58]

The range of Wagner's influence can be seen most dramatically in the conversion of Emile Zola. This led to his abandonment of Naturalism, of which he had been the leading spirit, and to new respect for the artistic potential of opera, which he had previously been wont to ridicule: "While [literature] requires thought, [opera] makes it possible 'to abandon oneself with an empty head to easy digestion in a bath of melody,' a sensual pleasure multiplied, in the case of grand operas, by the décors, the staging, and the dances."[59] Readers familiar with the Roujon-Macquart series and his other Naturalist novels are surprised by Zola's librettos. They belong to a lesser-known, idealist phase of his work from the very end of his career, when, as in novels such as *Lourdes*, Zola turned his back on Naturalist precepts. Students of his work have traditionally associated the advent of this idealist posture with the beginning of his liaison with young Jeanne Rozerot. But Jean-Max Guieu, the scholar most familiar with Zola's operatic works, shrewdly and convincingly attributes the change in his approach — and that of other Naturalists such as Daudet and Huysmans — to the influence of *Wagnérisme*.

This operated largely through the *Revue Wagnérienne*, and in the case of Zola, through his young protégé, the *Wagnériste* composer Alfred Bruneau.[60] Though Zola is highly critical of some of the implications of Wagnerian mysticism, especially its exaltation of the virgin over the mother,[61] the general displacement of Naturalism by idealism reveals itself clearly in his operatic works. His characters are frequently symbolic rather than specific, and the action hinges on supernatural as well as natural phenomena. In *Messidor*, for instance, a fortuitous avalanche destroys a factory just as the mob begins its attack, confirming the idea asserted by an old peasant woman that destiny, rather than human action, dispenses justice. It takes a magical necklace, which exposes the guilt of anyone who steals it, to unmask the villain at the end.

The impact of *Wagnérisme* on the artists' perceptions of their distinctive role in society was reinforced by gradual but obvious improvement in the economic position of dramatic writers as a group, and of librettists in particular. Not only could aspiring librettists of the last decade of the century hope to succeed at an earlier age than their predecessors, but the rewards attending success had grown enormously. Through the activities of the Société des Auteurs et Compositeurs Dramatiques, the total royalties distributed to the dramatic authors of France doubled between 1865 and the turn of the century (an era of negligible inflation); in the years before the war they almost doubled again.[62] During the Belle Epoque proper, French dramatic authors believed that they enjoyed prosperity and prestige unmatched in recent history or in any other European country.

"It is the Golden Age," proclaimed the president of the Société des Auteurs et Compositeurs Dramatiques to the 1911 general assembly of that organization.[63] "Of all the countries where people engage in intellectual activity, France is incontestably the one where the profession of dramatic author is the highest and most respected," reported another assembly of the Société.[64] "Who is the dramatic author these days?" asked the critic and librettist Adolphe Brisson. "It is very simple. ... He is the King." This new-found prestige was solidly rooted in economic power. Since the dramatic author had replaced the sculptor as the "*homme à la mode*," he had become "a catch for young women...admired by concierges, landlords, creditors and debtors."[65] In short, Brisson concluded,

> There is nothing else so lucrative. It is the only branch of our career in which the material result is not in proportion to the effort, but superior to it. The journalist, the scholar, the novelist earn a living. The man of the theatre gets rich.[66]

Credit for the enhanced financial status of the dramatic authors goes indisputably to the Société des Auteurs et Compositeurs Dramatiques. It was Beaumarchais who, on the occasion of a performance of *The Barber of Seville* in 1777, first assembled the dramatic authors to investigate the question of literary property. This initiative resulted in a 1791 law declaring that literary and musical works that had not yet fallen into the public domain could not be performed without the express written consent of the authors. They commonly sold their works outright to theatres until 1827 when Scribe organized the Société des Auteurs et Compositeurs Dramatiques. Subsequently, authors began to receive royalties from each performance, but until the Second Empire this right could not be transferred to heirs as could other forms of property.[67]

In 1860, librettists and composers shared equally Fr.500 per performance at the Opéra, weighted according to the length of the pieces on the program. A typical program featuring a three-act opera accompanied by a two-act ballet would have earned the opera librettist half of three-fifths of the total, or Fr.150. In 1871, the Société negotiated with Halanzier, the new Opéra director, for a percentage of the receipts. Librettists and composers shared equally 6 percent of the gross, which averaged about Fr.16,000 per performance after the opening of the Palais Garnier in 1875. According to this schedule, about Fr.288 (= ½ x 6% x ⅗ x Fr.16,000) would have gone to the librettist for his contribution to the typical program described above, almost twice as much as in 1860. By 1890, royalties had increased to 8 percent of the gross at the Opéra, and 12 percent at the Opéra-Comique. Authors also received free tickets worth about Fr.100 per performance. In addition, a librettist who managed to have a total of ten acts produced at the Opéra received a free lifetime pass; ten more acts earned him another one.[68]

Besides negotiating contracts with theatre directors, the Société supervised the collection and distribution of royalties in Paris, in the provinces, and even abroad — anywhere the members' works were produced. It settled disputes among authors by arbitration, provided substantial pensions to retired or indigent members, maintained a medical and pharmaceutical service, and in 1913, secured for all of its members the ultimate perquisite of riding half-price on the railways. Through negotiations with the directors of the Opéra and Opéra-Comique, it also obtained for its members some control over the quality of the production of each new piece or revival. The standard contract between authors and directors gave authors the right to distribute roles for the premiere and second performances, to request extra rehearsals in some circumstances, and to approve décors and costumes.[69] The Société engaged in extensive lobbying activities, especially for improved copyright laws and reciprocal agreements with foreign countries, and for the promotion of provincial theatre through the decentralization of subsidies. Its links with the Department of Fine Arts were so close as to give it semi-official status. That office would not give official approval to any program containing dramatic pieces without the previous consent of the Société. The government recognized it, in other words, as the legal representative of the authors.[70]

The Société was powerful enough to intervene in the internal and external affairs of the Opéra and Opéra-Comique. It moved to suppress the well-established institution of the gala final dress rehearsal, frequented not only by journalists and friends of the principals and management, but by high society as well. On at least two occasions it effectively vetoed candidates for the directorship of the Opéra-Comique, one on the grounds that he was too close a friend of the Opéra director and might unfairly collaborate with him. Likewise, when the director Carvalho was indicted for criminal negligence in the fatal Opéra-Comique fire of 1887, and the prominent librettist Jules Barbier took over temporarily, the Société refused to allow him to take the job on a permanent basis. Barbier's colleagues feared that he would produce the numerous works from which he derived royalties at the expense of works by other librettists, or, if he pledged not to do so, that his collaborators would suffer unfairly. On another occasion, the Société forced the resignation of a musical director. Gheusi commented that the directors of the Opéra and Opéra-Comique were tyrannized much more by the Société than by the government.[71]

This remarkable accumulation of political and economic power, which achieved for the society its unique and envied position, stemmed from its complete and unshakable monopoly of French dramatic production, supported by continued effective defense of its legal position in the courts. The Société imposed its will on recalcitrant directors by denying them all access to its members' plays and librettos. It maintained a closed shop by refusing to allow members' works to be produced at any theatre that produced works by non-members; as a result, its membership included everyone in France who had ever had any play or libretto produced there. In order to become a full member, eligible to participate in the deliberations of the Société, a writer had to have a total of at least five acts accepted at a major theatre, or sometimes fewer in the case of the Opéra. But other members, the *stagiaires*, benefited from contract negotiations, financial and administrative facilities, pensions, and other services.[72]

In 1904, the Société withheld access to its members' works from a theatre trust that it was anxious to break. In response, the librettist Michel Carré *fils* and some *stagiaires* filed suit against the society in order to re-establish the independence of the individual writer in negotiations with theatre impresarios. But the Société won this notable lawsuit as it had every previous one, and soon succeeded in breaking the trust as well. As usual, the organization benefited greatly from the brilliance of its lawyer, Raymond Poincaré, who "doesn't just win the causes that the society confides in him," as the president of the organization put it, "but also interests himself in the existence and future of the society itself, using his experience and foresight."[73] Poincaré's importance to the success of the Société was recognized by the decision to hang his portrait in the executive meeting room along with those of Beaumarchais, Scribe, and the playwright and librettist Victorien Sardou, long-time president of the society during the golden years of the Third Republic. As Poincaré rose to national political prominence, the pressure of ministerial — he was Minister of Public Instruction — and later presidential responsibilities forced him to abandon his leadership of the society's legal office in 1913. But he had already demonstrated how his political influence would continue to serve the organization: When a new licencing law threatened members' control over reproduction of their works on films and discs, Poincaré intervened to appoint the president of the Société to the commission that decided the issue.[74]

The Société showed some concern for the welfare of its less prominent members by promoting the decentralization of French theatre and by requiring directors to introduce new works into the repertoires of the Opéra and the Opéra-Comique. But the greatest proportion of the proceeds secured by the organization went to a rather small number of the most successful authors. Around 1910, it was estimated that as much as two-thirds of the royalties collected by the Société went to only seventy authors out of a total of four hundred members and four thousand *stagiaires*; if this estimate was accurate, these seventy authors earned an average of more than Fr.53,000 each during the year. Only a very small proportion of *stagiaires* earned any royalties at all in any given year; if the remaining revenue went to 350 other members and *stagiaires*, they would have received about Fr.5,400 each. Though this represents only one-tenth of the earnings of a more successful member, it is four or five times as much as the one hundred francs per month allowance that sustained the bohemian librettist Maurice Magre, and at least three times the income of an average Parisian laborer.[75]

Royalties earned from opera librettos varied greatly according to the success of the particular work. For a disastrous failure like *Bacchus* (O-1909), which closed after only five performances, Catulle Mendès and the composer Massenet received no more than Fr.2,500 each. On the other hand, for 376 pre-war performances of *Samson et Dalila*, the most frequently performed of the opéras that had their premieres during the pre-war Third Republic, Ferdinand Lemaire and the composer Saint-Saëns (and their heirs) would have received about Fr.234,000 each, or more than Fr.10,000 per year. Likewise the 1,338 performances of *Carmen* before the war brought Meilhac and Halévy about Fr.230,000 each, and Bizet's heirs twice as much. Meilhac, who also collaborated on the libretto for Massenet's *Manon*, third-most popular of the Belle Epoque *opéra-comiques*, and on Delibes' more ephemeral *Kassya*, must have earned more than Fr.400,000 from these three librettos. Louis Gallet, who wrote or collaborated on nineteen librettos, probably gained over Fr.350,000 for his efforts. Provincial and foreign royalties may have increased these totals by as much as one-quarter to one-third.[76]

There were many more failures than successes, however. Although *opéras* that had premieres between 1875 and the turn of the century averaged sixty-five total performances before the outbreak of the war, less than a third of them achieved that total. Half received fewer than thirty-two performances. This median number of performances, which the librettist might reasonably expect his opera to attain, would have earned him Fr.50,000 in royalties directly from the Opéra, including the value of the author's tickets. Foreign and provincial houses were not likely to invest in any but the most successful Parisian products. At the Opéra-Comique the mean number of performances was ninety-nine, but the median only nineteen. This typical (median) *opéra-comique* would have been worth about Fr.15,000 to its librettists. About half the time these proceeds were distributed among two or more writers working in collaboration.

For the librettist who was not a full-time writer, having a work accepted for production at the Opéra-Comique meant a financial windfall. Median receipts would have amounted to one-and-a-half years' salary for a middle-management railroad executive like the librettist Chatrian. For a poet, the opera libretto was one of a very limited number of ways to earn any money at all from literature. For the average established dramatist, one of the seventy who divided up the bulk of the theatrical royalties, a moderately successful *opéra-comique* libretto represented a third of a year's income. This was a considerable amount of money for not much effort since, according to Emile Zola, a practiced craftsman could turn out a finished product in three weeks.[77] Those who were satisfied with the minimum standard of bohemian existence based on one hundred francs per month had only to sell a typically successful Opéra-Comique libretto every twelve and a half years in order to support themselves. A single typical Opéra libretto would pay for a fifty-year career of opium and unpublished poetry,[78] and any libretto had the potential to be ten times more successful.

To these pecuniary rewards must be added intangibles such as the prestige that attached to writers for the state-subsidized theatres. Having a libretto accepted was an author's entrée to the world of the social and financial elites whose salon was the opera.[79] He (or much more rarely, she) gained access even to the more exclusive backstage area where the cream of society gathered around the *corps de ballet*. If, as the prosopographical data suggest, contact with the right sort of people was crucial to early success as a librettist, success as a librettist was even more definitely a guarantee of introductions to the right people.

The system of rewards offered to successful librettists fostered the assimilation of many into the opera elites where they acquired a taste for luxury that led them to repress their artistic independence. It is impossible to quantify the prevalence of attitudes such as Bergerat's, who preferred poverty or journalism to compromising his artistic integrity, but the large financial resources at the directors' disposal certainly tempted a substantial proportion of them. The evidence suggests that most librettists were more committed to the advancement of their careers than to their art, if indeed they thought of writing librettos as an art at all. Of Catulle Mendès, one who most conspicuously adapted his style from libretto to libretto, it was said that "he lived on such a grand scale and incurred debts of such magnitude that he grasped at every chance of earning a royalty."[80]

Enhanced prestige and financial security enabled other librettists to take a critical stance toward the norms of their society and their art. The capacity of the librettists for introducing idiosyncratic social and political views to their works, and their interest in doing so, increased during the Belle Epoque as a function of their prestige and independence. A more exalted sense of their importance encouraged some of them to assert their opinions more vigorously. Beginning in the eighteen-nineties, librettists such as Zola, Maeterlinck, and Charpentier fought a series of battles with directors for the right to defy audience prejudices in their librettos. In some cases, notably in the operas of Maurice Maeterlinck, idealist librettos featured wholesale critiques of French social mores. Although in the end these librettos failed to overcome the well-entrenched dissociation of opera from social commentary, which kept the audience from recognizing the implicit criticism, these works represent a valiant challenge to the hegemony of bourgeois culture.

The strength of Zola's resistance to directorial authority stemmed from the marketability that his literary renown gave to any theatrical works that he cared to produce. "The name, controversial but resounding, of Emile Zola, the connections of the celebrated novelist in Parisian society, his ties with the press and his combatative ardor, had contributed to opening up the theatres very quickly to the works of Bruneau,"[81] wrote the composer's biographer. Throughout his career, Zola had acknowledged the power of the theatre, which he described as "indirect moralization by the logical and powerful exposition of the truth."[82] But previous failures as a playwright made him reluctant, at first, to take any active role in the adaptation of his stories for the opera. The adulation of the young Alfred Bruneau, combined with Carvalho's determination to inaugurate his Opéra-Comique administration with a "*coup d'audace*," eventually led to a production of *Le Rêve* (OC-1891) with the increasingly engaged cooperation of Zola. Bruneau asked Louis Gallet to write the actual libretto, but Zola corrected it, rewrote several passages, and eventually helped choose the décors and even the cast for the opera. Despite the innovative use of prose rather than poetry in the libretto, *Le Rêve* was a success, and Carvalho encouraged Bruneau to continue setting Zola's works.[83]

During the production of *L'Attaque du Moulin*, which followed two years later, also with a libretto by Gallet, Carvalho fell out with Zola and Bruneau over a costuming issue with political overtones, described in Chapter II. The opera was moderately successful in the form that Carvalho presented it, and Zola, who wrote Bruneau's next libretto on his own, was still very much in demand in the mid-eighteen-nineties. Gailhard of the Opéra eagerly took advantage of the writers' frustration with the Opéra-Comique management; he accepted *Messidor* after hearing the barest outline of the idea. With the Opéra competing with the Opéra-Comique for the right to produce his works, the author gained considerable leverage for staging them according to his wishes, even when the results were likely to be controversial. Like Carvalho, Gailhard found that Bruneau and Zola were uncommonly tenacious in their opinions about production decisions. They objected especially to Gailhard's insistence on a traditional ballet, complete with ballerinas in tutus, which seemed to the authors ludicrous in an opera about an industrial dispute.[84] *Messidor* was quite well received, though it ran for only eleven performances during its first season, in 1897.

Although Gailhard had committed himself to a revival, he reneged when Zola's conspicuous Dreyfusard agitation, besides leading to a conviction for treason, made him persona non grata with the Opéra public. Bruneau's protests to the Department of Fine Arts went unanswered. Victorien Sardou, president of the Société des Auteurs et Compositeurs Dramatiques, promised to arrange "this clear and obvious affair," but outside pressures "intervened even in the very bosom of the Commission des Auteurs Dramatiques." Zola, in exile, expressed the opinion that no state-subsidized theatre would accept his works unless the Dreyfusard cause eventually prevailed.[85] He had important allies, however. The wealthy Jewish *commanditaire* Isaac de Camondo promised to put all of his considerable financial power at the disposal of the author, if he would submit another work for production at the Opéra:

> The way in which *Messidor* has been withdrawn from the theatre bills fills me with indignation and fury. Wishing to make reparations for this injustice without delay, I beg you to reserve your next work for the Opéra, where I am in a position to guarantee it fifty performances.[86]

But Bruneau and Zola were thoroughly estranged from the Opéra, and

Carvalho at the Opéra-Comique had meanwhile consented to produce *L'Attaque du Moulin* with Franco-Prussian War uniforms. In 1901, Zola's *L'Ouragan* had its premiere at the same house under the auspicies of Carvalho's successor, Albert Carré.[87]

Maurice Maeterlinck, who was beyond dispute the most recalcitrant and uncompromising librettist of all, defended his work against not only his director, but his composer as well. He protested bitterly and publicly against comparatively minor modifications of his play *Pélléas et Mélisande* when Debussy and Carré adapted it for the Opéra-Comique. He threatened a law suit, urged the public not to attend, and hoped that it would be a failure. In a letter to *Le Figaro*, Maeterlinck wrote: "They are making arbitrary and absurd cuts which render it incomprehensible; they are keeping what I had intended to suppress or to improve, as I have done in the libretto which just appeared, where it will be possible to see how far the text adopted by the Opéra-Comique differs from the authentic text."[88]

Conflicts over a later Maeterlinck libretto, for *Monna Vanna* (0-1909), did end up in the courts, where his suit established the legal right of the librettist to resist alterations that betrayed his or her intentions: "The right to perform can be ceded like the right to publish, in which case the only privilege retained by the author is that of supervision and surveillance, which extends, in addition, to the right to oppose enterprises that would compromise the integrity of his work, or falsify his thought."[89] Maeterlinck's detractors claimed that his adamant opposition to modifications of his work was in every case intended to pressure impresarios into installing his lover, Georgette Leblanc, in a leading role.[90] Though there is some evidence for this point of view, the fact remains that the librettist who most vociferously defended the rights and prerogatives of the librettist also produced the librettos with the most startlingly unconventional, counterhegemonic ideas.

Pélléas et Mélisande, the first of Maeterlinck's works to appear on the opera stage, contains little of the subversive social doctrine of his later operas. It is significant, however, both in opera history and in the history of ideas, as a sort of existential negation — comparable to Nietzsche's — of Wagner's Romantic negation of bourgeois positivism.[91] As such, it participated in a *fin-de-siècle* intellectual synthesis that superseded nineteenth-century patterns of thought. Maeterlinck and Wagner concurred in denying any significance to the objective existence of physical phenomena. But whereas in Wagner a transcendent reality continually intrudes into the objective sphere — through the magic of the *Ring* and the miracles of *Parzifal* — *Pélléas* just as regularly subverts and breaks down any correspondence between transcendent and material. By reducing the fountain, the ring, even the famous atmosphere, to so many non sequiturs, Maeterlinck demonstrates that objective phenomena cannot be understood as having any necessary relationship with transcendent reality.

When, in the final act, the consulting physician (representing the positivist tradition) suggests that Mélisande might survive, another character points out that everyone in the room is talking in low tones (V:i); this proves to be a more accurate indicator of the heroine's state of health. Thus Maeterlinck insists that reality is not apprehended through its correspondence with the transcendent, or through empirical science, but is instead appropriated by individuals or social groups. In contrast to the ineluctable destiny represented by Wagner's Norns, who determine his characters' fates regardless of their wills, Maeterlinck allows his characters to mold their fates according to their capacities. "If I had loved like you," says Monna Vanna, "I would have said to destiny, 'Get away, I am here....' I would have forced the very stones to take my part" (II:iii).

The political corollaries of Maeterlinck's philosophy appear in *Ariane et Barbe-Bleue* (OC-1907), where militant feminism and solidarity with the underclasses combine to produce self-conscious, systematic resistance to authority.[92] When the existing order is threatening and inexplicable, the heroine asserts as she arrives at Blue-Beard's castle, disobedience is "the primary duty." On the principle that "everything that is permitted teaches us nothing," she opens all the forbidden doors in the castle. Ariane's courage and wisdom lead her to Blue-Beard's imprisoned wives, who had not tried to escape because "everything is shut up tight, and besides it is forbidden" (Act I). She eventually calls on the help of her allies, the powerful armed peasantry, to accomplish their release. Though the liberation, both physical and figurative, of "her sisters" is frustrated ultimately by their own unwillingness to leave their husband (Act II), Ariane wishes them well nonetheless, before leaving to attend to other similar projects.

Just as *Pélléas* is the medieval romance to end all medieval romances, and *Ariane et Barbe-Bleue* the fairy tale to end all fairy tales,

Maeterlinck's third libretto, for Fevrier's *Monna Vanna*, is the last word in Renaissance costume dramas. Like *Ariane et Barbe-Bleue*, it features an exceptionally strong heroine who asserts remarkably advanced principles in the face of conventional restraints. As in *Pélléas*, starving peasantry populate the background. The *condottiere* Prinzevalle is prepared to betray his Florentine employers by raising the siege of Pisa and relieving the famine in exchange for one night with Giovanna, wife of the Pisan despot Guido Colonna. Colonna, who thinks and talks exclusively in romantic conventions, leaves the decision to her, feeling sure that modesty and purity will keep her from going. But she unhesitatingly subordinates personal considerations, including her reputation, to the welfare of the community. "Are you going to kill him and then commit suicide?" asks her husband hopefully. "No," she responds, destroying another of her husband's illusions (I:iii). When Prinzevalle admits to having nursed a secret love for Vanna since their childhood, she reproaches him for demonstrating it in such a cowardly way. Though willing to carry out her bargain, she refuses, out of loyalty to her husband and her marriage vow, to tell Prinzevalle that she loves him, or even that she might have loved him. The night ends in affection and friendship even more beautiful than Prinzevalle imagined love would be.

When his employers discover Prinzevalle's treachery, Vanna offers him refuge in Pisa. Her romantic husband, incapable of accepting her true account of the events, prefers to believe that she seduced the *condottiere* in order to trick him into their hands. Colonna imprisons Prinzevalle, but promises to release him as an act of noblesse oblige if Vanna admits to the seduction. She decides that she can only honor her promise of safe conduct to Prinzevale by falsely confessing to her husband that she had betrayed him (III:ii). When Prinzevale is freed from prison, she deserts the husband who put her in this impossible position, and leaves Pisa as Prinzevalle's lover. In all of this, Vanna maintains perfect respect for her vows and promises, as long as their object is honorable, while demonstrating her complete indifference to convention for its own sake. She exhibits self-sacrifice in the interests of the community, indomitable courage in the pursuit of her principles, and openness to the possibility of friendly relations with the opposite sex.

The audience's reception of *Monna Vanna* represents a remarkable reaffirmation of the tenacity of the dominant culture. In the case of Zola, librettos that were far from antipathetic to the prejudices of the audience had had to be removed from the repertoire because of the author's reputation for muckraking and his aggressive Dreyfusard stance. The intrinsically more subversive radical feminist ideas in Maeterlinck's librettos aroused no controversy or negative critical reaction whatever. Imbued with traditional attitudes toward opera, audiences and critics were prepared to overlook the implications of Maeterlinck's work if at all possible. According to Noël and Stoullig, the public responded warmly to *Monna Vanna* because it is "always amusing to watch a husband deceived and those who are making a fool of him."[93]

Clearly the undermining of traditional operatic conventions in Maeterlinck's fairy tale, medieval romance, and costume drama was too subtle for the audience. Librettists capable of resisting the financial incentives offered for conventional librettos, who could find a composer with a similar outlook and a daring director or a *commanditaire* willing to risk his capital, once they had penetrated the noise and confusion of the hall and the distractions of the music and décor, confronted an audience accustomed to librettos of the most unexacting sort, and thoroughly prejudiced against the intrusion of ideas. Thus, ignorance and misunderstanding constituted the final defense of entrenched social groups against new and challenging ideas. Such is precisely the message of Gustave Charpentier's semi-autobiographical *Julien* (OC-1913), which appeared just before war put an end to the Belle Epoque. The opera is a thoroughgoing critique of *fin-de-siècle* culture; it concludes by ridiculing the idea that artists can be saviors of society.

This sequel to *Louise* begins with a prologue that explores the self-doubts of the hero Julien, who talks more about his art than he actually practices, and of his mistress, Louise, relegated to the demanding but thoroughly unsatisfying role of artist's Muse (P-ii). In the first act, the honor of Julien's reception into a grandiose Temple of Beauty is undercut by lewd and caustic commentary from the acolytes, after which (IC-ii) his calvary begins. The second act deals with his disillusionment with the ordinary people, who respond to his song of eternal love with sarcasm and cries of hate (II-i), and the third portrays the poet's loss of religious faith. Louise appears in these acts respectively as the Goddess of Beauty, as a sexually aggressive working girl, and as the poet's pious grandmother, who expires when he curses her faith. The finale, set in Montmartre, grotesquely parodies the first-act Temple of Beauty scene with the high priest transformed into a carnival barker and Louise as a hideous prostitute. The former personification of Beauty, now "*un peu désenchantée*," can offer the poet only the forgetfulness of absinthe and animal instincts (IVb–i). She laughs at him as the opera ends with the poet crawling in the gutter, pelted with rotten vegetables and the ordure of the street.

NOTES TO THE EPILOGUE

1 Massenet, *My Recollections*, 49. For Gondinet and Gille, Tout-Paris, "La Journée Parisienne," *Le Gaulois* (3/9/1880).

2 Bergerat, *Souvenirs*, 4:78-84.

3 Maurice Rostand, *Confession d'un demi-siècle* (Paris: Jeune Parque, 1948).

4 Gheusi, *Cinquante Ans*, 4:75.

5 Bergerat, *Souvenirs*, 2:7,25; 3:295-302. Cp. 1:59.

6 *Ibid.*, 1:407, 2:25.

7 The most important sources of biographical information for the librettists are *Dictionnaire de biographie française* (Paris: Letouzey et Ane, 1933-1994); Ernst Glaeser, ed., *Biographie Nationale des Contemporains* (Paris, 1878); *Revue Biographique des Notabilités Françaises Contemporaines*, 3 vols. (Paris, 1892-98); G. Vapereau and L. Guitane, *Dictionnaire Universel des Contemporains* (Paris, 1870-73); *Les Archives Biographiques Contemporaines* (Paris, 1906-09); C.E. Curinier, *Dictionnaire National des Contemporains*, 6 vols. (1899-1918); Jules Martin, *Nos Auteurs et Compositeurs Dramatiques* (Paris, 1897); Angelo Mariani, *Figures contemporaines* (Paris, 1894); Henry Carnoy, *Dictionnaire biographique international des écrivains, des artistes etc.*, 4 vols. (Paris, 1902-09); *Qui Etes-vous?* I have not provided individual references to biographical details available in these works. For lists of the librettists' works and references to criticism of them, Hector Talvart et Joseph Place, *Bibliographie des Auteurs modernes de la langue française* (Paris, 1928) and H.P. Thieme, *Bibliographie de la littérature française*, 3 vols. (Paris, 1933).

8 Jules Huret, "Une Idée d'Artistes: Le Peuple au Théâtre," *Le Figaro* (11/19/1900). Cf. Eugenia Herbert, *The Artist and Social Reform: France and Belgium 1885-1898* (New Haven: Yale University Press, 1961), 132. For the Conservatoire Mimi Pinson, Marc Delmas, *Gustave Charpentier et le lyrisme français* (Paris, 1931), 21f.

9 Francis de Croisset, *La Vie Parisienne au Théâtre* (Paris, 1929), 104.

10 The best description of the salon is Jeanne Pouquet, *Le Salon de Mme. Arman de Caillavet* (Paris, 1926).

11 For biographical information, Gaston Jollivet, *Ma Folle Jeunesse* (Paris, 1926) and *Souvenirs*. His criticism of the Opéra management is reported in *l'Autorité* (11/3/1913).

12 Francis de Croisset, *La Vie Parisienne*, 104.

13 Emile Zola, "Etude sur le Journalisme," Oeuvres Complètes, 50:246f. For a comparison of journalism and libretto-writing, Gerhard, *Die Verstädterung der Oper*, 285.

14 Guy de Maupassant, *Oeuvres Complètes*, 28 vols. (Paris, 1921-47), v.13.

15 Toudouze, *Albert Wolff*, 86-117, 284-299, 355ff.

16 Avenel, *Histoire de la Presse Française*, 487. Cf. 483f.

17 Toudouze, *Albert Wolff*, 116.

18 Jollivet, *Souvenirs*, 199. Cf. 85; Avenel, *Histoire de la Presse Française*, 491, 491n., 854.

19 Albert Cassagne, *La Théorie de l'Art pour l'Art en France* (Paris, 1906), 88f.

20 Bergerat, *Souvenirs*, 2:170, 3:74, 106ff., 256, 295.

21 Quoted in Norbert Dufourcq, *Autour de Coquard, César Franck et Vincent d'Indy* (Paris: Librairie Floury, 1952), 23; Bergerat, *Souvenirs*, 1:69-74.

22 D'Alméras, *Avant la gloire*, 188; Denise Le Blond-Zola, *Emile Zola Raconté par Sa Fille* (Paris, 1930), 22-33.

23 Quoted in Duquesnil, *Annales Romantiques*, XI (1914), 60f.

24 André Monselet, *Charles Monselet, sa vie, son oeuvre* (Paris, 1892), 50-54, 59, 90.

25 *Ibid.*, 116-122.

26 *Ibid.*, 180-183, 187.

27 *Ibid.*, 84.

28 Maurice Magre, *Conseils à un jeune homme pauvre* (Paris, 1908). The sum of Fr.100 per month was slightly less than the monthly wage of a Parisian laborer. In 1907, a *machiniste* at the Opéra started at six francs per day. Cp. the wages of male Parisian workers in a variety of trades listed in the *Annuaire Statistique de la France*, 19 vols. (Paris, Imprimerie Nationale, 1878-1899), e.g., 18:230, Tableau 263.

29 Croisset, *La Vie Parisienne*, 93f., 99. Cf. Charles Rearick, *Pleasures of the Belle Epoque* (New Haven: Yale University Press, 1985), 71f.; Jerrold Seigel, *Bohemian Paris: Culture, Politics and the Boundaries of Bourgeois Life, 1830-1930* (N.Y.:Viking, 1986), 132; Weber, *France: Fin de Siècle*, 148. The term "truculent bohemia" comes from d'Alméras, *Avant la gloire*, 103.

30 M. Donnay, D. Bormaud and V. Hyspa, *L'Esprit Montmartrois* (Paris, n.d.), 27.

31 Gheusi, *Cinquante Ans*, 3:43. Cf. Astruc, *Le Pavillon*, 47; Seigel, *Bohemian Paris*, 223ff. For the self-advertising aspect of bohemian behavior, d'Alméras, *Avant la gloire*, 108.

32 Himonet, "*Louise*," 32. On the conservatism of Charpentier's working-class characters, cf. Rey M. Longyear, "Political and Social Criticism in French Opera, 1827-1920," in Robert Weaver, ed., *Essays on the Music of J.S.Bach and other Divers Subjects* (Louisville: University of Louisville, 1981), 250.

33 Seigel, *Bohemian Paris*, 5.

34 Himonet, "*Louise*," 144f.

35 *Ibid.*, 29, 32.

36 Adolphe Jullien, "Revue Musicale," *Feuilleton du Journal des Débats* (2/4/1900), (available also in B.O. Dossier d'artiste/G. Charpentier).

37 Jean Richepin, *Les Etapes d'un Réfractaire* (Paris, n.d.), 235; J.-L. Prim, "La Vie Tumultueuse de Jean Richepin," B.O. Dossier d'artiste/Jean Richepin. Howard Sutton, *The Life and Work of Jean Richepin* (Geneva: E. Droz, 1961), 25, calls the *frites* story apocryphal.

38 Rostand, *Confession*, 42.

39 "'Lohengrin,'" *La Lanterne* (9/23/1891). In *The Reactionary Revolution:The Catholic Revival in French Literature 1870-1914* (London: Constable, 1966), Richard Griffiths likewise notes the similarity between the socialists' and the conservative Catholic writers' objections to bourgeois materialism, 254f. and the *Wagnéristes'* objections as well, 240.

40 "Souvenirs sur 'Lohengrin,'" *La Bataille* (9/15/1891).

41 Alphonse Richaud, *Revue Socialiste* (11/1896), (available also in *Fervaal Devant La Presse*, 111-116); Charles B. Paul, "Rameau, d'Indy and French Nationalism," *Musical Quarterly* 58/1 (Jan. 1972).

42 Maurice Donnay, *Mes Débuts à Paris* (Paris, 1937), 190.

43 Seigel, *Bohemian Paris*, 221; Bergerat, *Souvenirs*, I:45. Cf. Weber, *France: Fin de Siècle*, 143f.

44 Eulogy of Emile Augier by Jules Barbier on behalf of the Société des Auteurs et Compositeurs Dramatiques, *Société:Annuaire*, 1890.

45 Jules Lemaître, *Opinions à Répandre* (Paris, 1901); Adolphe Brisson, "François Coppée," *Portraits Intimes*, 2:337.

46 Houston Stuart Chamberlain, "Le Wagnérisme en 1888 par H.S. Chamberlain," *Revue Wagnérienne* 3 (1887-88), 282; Edouard Dujardin, "Les Oeuvres Théoriques de Richard Wagner," *Revue Wagnérienne* 1 (1885), 65. Dujardin was "founder-director" of the revue.

47 Max d'Ollone, *Le Théâtre Lyrique et le Public* (Paris: La Palatine, 1955), 210.

48 Bruneau, *Musiques de Russie*, 46.

49 Laloy, "L'Opéra," 84; Eckart-Bäcker, *Frankreichs Musik*, 120-139. Cf. Isabelle de Wyzewa, *La Revue Wagnérienne: Essai sur l'Interprétation Esthétique de Wagner en France* (Paris, 1934). Controversies over the production of Wagner's works in France ended up with the courts taking testimony as to the relative merits of various translators' efforts. See "Conclusions: Tribunal Civil de la Seine, Cosima Wagner versus André von Wilder," in *A.N.* AJ XIII (1198). At the same time, scholars such as Octave Fouqué (1882), C.H. Bitter (1884), and Eugène de Bricqueville (1902) revived the longstanding controversy over the proper relationship between librettist and composer with frequent references to the ideas of Rousseau, Rameau, Gluck and Wagner. Critics also regularly addressed this question in their reviews. For the significance of the switch to prose librettos, cp. Combarieu, *Histoire*, 3:557. Cp. Saint-Saëns, "Lettre de Las Palmas." Cf. Bruneau, *A l'Ombre*, 102; *Musiques d'Hier*, 103-108, 111f., 118f. For the changing attitudes of composers see, e.g., Camille Saint-Saëns, *Harmonie et Mélodie* (Paris, n.d.), 187, 261f. For Massenet, Gottfried R. Marschall, "Massenet et la Fixation de la Forme Mélodique Française," Thèse de Doctorat, Université de Paris IV (1978), 21, 25, 46, 110ff., 441, 462. For Charpentier, Eugène Allard and Louis Vauxcelles, "La Musique: Gustave Charpentier" *Le Figaro* (10/28/1900), and Adolphe Adam, "Louise," *Le Temps* (1/30/1900) (both available in B.O. Dossier d'Artiste: Gustave Charpentier).

50 Jollivet, *Souvenirs*, 268; Pierre Martino, *Le Naturalisme Français* (Paris, 1923), 9f., 21.

51 *Ibid.*, 34ff., 42.

52 Martino, *Parnasse et Symbolisme*, 37f.

53 H. Stuart Hughes, *Consciousness and Society*, rev. ed. (N.Y.: Vintage Books, 1977).

54 Martino, *Le Naturalisme*, 45f. Cf. Herbert, *The Artist and Social Reform*, 74f.

55 A. Baillot, *L'Influence de Schopenhauer en France (1860-1900)* (Paris, 1927), 305, 324ff. Cf. Martino, *Parnasse et Symbolisme*, 39f.

56 The dates of these premieres should not be taken as an indication of the longevity of the cult of Schopenhauer in France, because both of these operas took an unusually long time to get to the stage.

57 de Laurencie, *Le Goût Musical*, 25. Cf. *Ibid.*, 336f. Cf. William J. McGrath, *Dionysian Art and Populist Politics in Austria* (New Haven: Yale University Press, 1974), 45. Cp. the review of *Ascanio* (O-1890) in *Le Diogène* (4/30/1890) [available also in *A.N.* AJ XIII (1021),] where the opera is criticized for realism, naturalism and *Wagnérisme* all at once.

58 Ernest Newman, *The Life of Richard Wagner*, 4 vols. (Cambridge: Cambridge University Press, 1976), 2:430-436; Adorno, *Essai sur Wagner*, 200-204; Théodore de Wyzewa, "Le Pessimisme de Richard Wagner," *Revue Wagnérienne* 1/6 (1885).

59 Emile Zola, *Le Naturalisme au Théâtre* (Paris, 1881), 63ff.

60 Guieu, "Le Théâtre Lyrique d'Emile Zola," 27, 105f. Cp. Jacqueline Frichet, "Le Théâtre Lyrique d'Emile Zola," *Les Cahiers naturalistes* 17, No.42 (1971).

61 Bruneau, *A l'Ombre*, 100ff.

62 For the years 1865-67, "Report of the Commission des Auteurs et Compositeurs Dramatiques, E. de Najac, secretary, to the membership, 20 May 1867," B.O. Archives Diverses 11.27. For yearly totals from 1885 to 1914, *Société: Annuaire*.

63 *Ibid.*, 7:304.

64 *Ibid.*, 7:755.

65 Jules Bertaut, *Le Paris d'Avant-Guerre* (Paris, 1919), 215ff.

66 Adolphe Brisson, "L'Auteur Dramatique," *Annales*, 32:vff.

67 Théodore Anne, "Propriété littéraire et artistique: Rapport, loi et observations, 1863," in B.O. Archives Diverses 11.23; Magnen and Fouquet, *Le Théâtre et Ses Lois*, 162.

68 "Conventions faites entre les Auteurs et Compositeurs Dramatiques et MM. Ritt et Gailhard, 26 December 1884," Chapter II, Articles 44, 22, *A.N.* AJ XIII (1189); Dupré and Ollendorff, *Traité de l'Administration*, 2:468; "Conventions faites entre les Auteurs et Compositeurs dramatiques et M. Halanzier, Dir. privilegé de l'Opéra, 19 January 1871," Article 2,

A.N. AJ XIII (446). Included in the gross was the value of complimentary tickets given by management to the press, friends, clients etc.; Martin, *Nos Auteurs*, 600; Louis de Gramont, *L'Eclair* (7/12/1900) [available also in *A.N.* F XXI (1339)]. Beginning in 1909, authors received the value of the tickets from directors instead of the tickets themselves. They had had to sell them to agencies who had paid authors only 58 percent of their nominal value.

69 *Société: Annuaire*, 8:796, 1084, 6:738f., 5:17; *Plaidoirie et Réplique de M. Poincaré*, 109; "Convention entre la Société et MM. Ritt et Gailhard," Article 11.

70 *Plaidoirie et Réplique de M. Poincaré*, 170. Cf. "Chef du Bureau des Théâtres à Président du Comité du 2e Arrondissement de l'Alliance Française, 30 April 1892," *A.N.* F XXI (1332); "Rapport de l'Assemblée Générale de la Société des Compositeurs de Musique [a rival organization], 26 January 1867," *A.N.* AJ XIII (499), 9; *Société: Annuaire*, 3:364, 7:304f., 536f.

71 Gheusi, *Cinquante Ans*, 4:112f., 1:80f.; *Société: Annuaire*, 5:397; *Annales*, 13:145f., 30:102; Victor Wilder, "Le Cas de M. Barbier," *Gil Blas* (12/20/1897) (available also in B.O. Dossier d'artiste/Jules Barbier).

72 *Société: Annuaire*, 7:227-237.

73 *Ibid.*, 7:311. Cf. 6:16f., 274f., 487; *Plaidoirie et Réplique de M. Poincaré*, passim. For theatre trusts, cp. Alphonse Lemonnier, *Les Abus au Théâtre* (Paris, 1895), 7-12.

74 *Société: Annuaire*, 7:1006, 533f.

75 Magnen and Fouquet, *Le Théâtre et Ses Lois*, 36; "Convention entre la Société et MM. Ritt et Gailhard," Chapter IX, Article 61.

76 Gross receipts at the Opéra averaged Fr.15,000 to Fr.16,000 per performance: *Annales*, 33:26n. Cf. H. Moreno, "Semaine théâtrale," *Le Ménestrel* (20 July 1879), 267; "Moyennes comparatives des Recettes." Daily gross receipts at the Opéra-Comique averaged about Fr.5,500 to Fr.6,000. It is difficult to estimate the proportion of foreign and provincial receipts that might have accrued from productions of French operas. About one-fifth of the total theatre receipts of Paris came from the Opéra and Opéra-Comique, but the proportion of provincial theatre receipts deriving from opera would have been substantially lower, since only the largest provincial cities could support theatre on the scale required by opera. According to Gerhard, *Die Verstädterung*, 349, the Darmstädter Hoftheater specialized in works adapted from the French stage after 1871. French opera would have been exported to foreign countries more frequently than other varieties of theatre since it enjoyed an international

reputation and depended less on nuances of language. Adding one-fifth of the total provincial theatre royalties and one-fifth of the total foreign royalties augments the total generated by the opera by 25 to 45 percent.

77 Emile Zola, "Le Drame Lyrique," *Oeuvres Complètes*, 50:149.

78 Librettist Maurice Magre was the author of *Les Soirs d'opium à Paris* (Paris, 1920).

79 An anecdote in Gaston Calmette, "Les Samedis de l'Opéra-Comique," *Le Figaro* (12/3/1885) describes how the librettists Henri Meilhac and Phillippe Gille met with the Prince de Sagan and the impresario Carvalho, at the home of the music editor Durand, to plan the (successful) revival of the Opéra-Comique's subscription series. Both of these librettists had achieved prominence in other spheres — as playwright and journalist respectively — as had many of their colleagues.

80 Harding, *Massenet*, 163.

81 Adolphe Boschot, *La Vie et les Oeuvres de Alfred Bruneau* (Paris, 1937), 18.

82 Emile Zola, "Préface" to *Thérèse Racquin*, *Oeuvres Complètes*, 15:122.

83 Jean-Max Guieu, "Le Théâtre Lyrique d'Emile Zola," 37-42. On the question of prose librettos, Alfred Bruneau, *Musiques d'Hier*, 118f. For Carvalho's motives, *Annales*, 17:119.

84 Bruneau, *A l'Ombre*, 89f.

85 *Ibid.*, 114, 173; Guieu, "Le Théâtre Lyrique d'Emile Zola," 69-72. Cf. Adolphe Boschot, *La Vie et les Oeuvres de Alfred Bruneau*, 18f.

86 Bruneau, *A l'Ombre*, 110.

87 Guieu, "Le Théâtre Lyrique d'Emile Zola," 65; Bruneau, *A l'Ombre*, 56, 80, 109f.

88 *Le Figaro* (4/13/1902).

89 "Cession de droits d'auteur," Magnen et Fouquet, *Le Théâtre et ses Lois*, 70.

90 Pierre Lalo, "La Musique," *Le Temps* (8/4/1908). Carré revived *Ariane et Barbe-Bleue* later in his term of office when Georgette Leblanc was no longer an issue; he called it a masterpiece, and subsidized it with his own resources and those of his investors.

91 Cf. Helmut Schmidt-Garré, "Debussy und Maeterlinck — die Kongruenz ihres Empfindens und die Inkongruenz ihrer Wirkung," *Neue Zeitschrift für Musik*, 130 no.2 (1969), 88.

92 Georgette Leblanc, Maeterlinck's wildly original consort, claims to have been responsible for the startling feminism of his operatic works. Dukas' biographer confirms that the libretto of *Ariane* was based on an episode in her life, and included some of her actual words as well. Her claims are all the more plausible in view of the hopelessly conventional bourgeois attitudes that Maeterlinck manifested in his own relations with women. Favre, *L'Oeuvre de Paul Dukas*, 57. Cf. Georgette Leblanc, *Souvenirs: 1895-1918* (Paris, 1931), 192f.

93 *Annales*, 35:2f.

BIBLIOGRAPHY

ARCHIVAL MATERIAL

France. Archives Nationales:

Dossiers AJ XIII 446, 499, 1006, 1021, 1022, 1098-99, 1187, 1189, 1193, 1194, 1197, 1198, 1202, 1279

Dossiers F XVII 2661, 2662

Dossiers F XXI 957, 997, 1041, 1091, 1330, 1332, 1336, 1337, 1339

Bibliothèque de l'Opéra:

Archives Diverses 11.23, 11.27.

Dossiers d'artistes Jules Barbier, Albert Carré, Carvalho, Gustave Charpentier, Halanzier, Ludovic Halévy, Louis Grammont, Jean Richepin, Rouché, Saint-Saëns, Trépard.

Dossiers d'oeuvres *Manon, Patrie!*

Fonds Rouché.

Opéra Archives 19e. siècle.

Opéra Archives 20e. siècle.

Opéra-Comique Archives. 19e. siècle.

Opéra-Comique Presse 1887.

P.A. 1871-1879, 1900-1927.

PRIMARY SOURCES AND CONTEMPORARY WORKS (1875-1914)

d'Alméras, Henri. *Avant la gloire: Leurs débuts.* Première série. Paris, 1902.

Annuaire Statistique de la France. 19 vols. Paris: Imprimerie Nationale, 1878-1899.

Les Archives Biographiques Contemporaines. Paris, 1906-09.

Avenel, Henri. *Histoire de la Presse Française*. Paris, 1900.

Bataille, Félix-Henri. *L'Enfance Eternelle*. Paris, n.d.

Bellaigue, Camille. *Etudes Musicales*. Paris, 1898.

Benjamin, E. and Buguet, A. *Coulisses de Bourse et de Théâtre*. Paris, 1882.

Bergerat, Emile. *Souvenirs d'un Enfant de Paris*. 4 vols. Paris, 1911-13.

_____. *Théophile Gauthier: Entretiens, souvenirs et Correspondance*. Paris, 1880.

Bernheim, Adrien. *Trente Ans de Théâtre*. 4 vols. Paris, 1903.

Bertrand, Gustave. "Etudes d'Economie Théâtrale: Les Théâtres Lyriques de Paris." *La Revue moderne* (2/1/1866).

_____. *Les Nationalités Musicales*. Paris, 1872.

Binet, A. and Passy, J. "Etudes de Psychologie sur les Auteurs Dramatiques." *L'Année Psychologique* I (1894).

Bitter, C.H. *Die Reform der Oper: durch Gluck und R. Wagner's Kunstwerk der Zukunft*. Braunschweig, 1884.

Bizet, Georges. *Lettres à Un Ami: 1865-1872*. Paris, 1909.

Bois, Jules. "Catulle Mendès librettiste." *Grande Revue* III (1904).

de Bricqueville, Eugène. "L'Evolution du Drame Lyrique." Conférence Faite à l'Institut populaire de Versailles, 6/17/1902. Paris, n.d.

Brisson, Adolphe. *Portraits intîmes*. 5 vols. Paris, 1894-1904.

_____. *Le Théâtre et les Moeurs*. Paris, n.d.

Bruneau, Alfred. *La Musique Française*. Rapport présenté à Monsieur le Ministre de l'Instruction Publique et des Beaux-Arts; Au Nom de la Commission des Grandes Auditions Musicales. Paris, 1901.

_____. *Musiques d'Hier et de Demain*. Paris, 1900.

_____. *Musiques de Russie et Musiciens de France*. Paris, 1903.

_____. *A l'Ombre d'Une Grande Coeur*. Paris, 1932.

Buguet, H. and d'Heylli, G. *Foyers et Coulisses*. Vol. VIII: *L'Opéra*. Paris, 1875.

Calvocaressi, M.-D. "La Critique musicale: ses devoirs, sa méthode." *Courrier musicale* XII no.20 (10/15/1910).

Carnoy, Henry. *Dictionnaire biographique international des écrivains, des artistes etc.* 4 vols. Paris, 1902-09.

Carré, Albert. *Souvenirs de Théâtre.* Paris: Plon, 1950.

_____. *Les Théâtres en Alsace-Lorraine.* Nancy, Paris, Strasbourg, 1919.

Cassagne, Albert. *La Théorie de l'Art pour l'Art en France.* Paris, 1906.

Chamberlain, Houston Stuart. "Le Wagnérisme en 1888 par H.S. Chamberlain." *Revue Wagnérienne* III (1887-88).

La Chronique Musicale 3e année v.IX (July-September, 1876).

Coppée, François. *Souvenirs d'un Parisien.* Paris, 1910.

Couyba, Ch.-M. *Les Beaux-Arts et la Nation.* Paris, 1908.

de Croisset, Francis. *La Vie Parisienne au Théâtre.* Paris, 1929.

Curinier, C.E. *Dictionnaire National des Contemporains.* 6 vols. Paris, 1899-1918.

Daubresse, M. "Notes Brèves sur la Critique Musicale." *Le Guide Musicale* 55e année no.18 (2 May 1909).

Dauriac, Lionel. "A Travers l'Esthétique Musicale: La Critique Musicale au Temps Présent." *S.I.M. Revue Musicale Mensuelle* VI/7 (1910).

David, Jean. *La Subvention de l'Opéra.* Paris, 1879.

Davyl, Louis. *Les Idées de Pierre Quiroul.* Paris, 1883.

Debray, Victor. "A L'Opéra-Comique: La Danseuse de Pompéii." *Le Courrier Musical* 15e année no.22 (15 November 1912).

Debussy, Claude. *Monsieur Croche, Antidilettante.* Paris, 1926.

De Lara, Isidore. *Many Tales of Many Cities.* London, n.d.

Déodat de Sévérac. "La Centralisation et les petites Chapelles musicales." *Le Courrier Musical* 11e année no.1 (1 January 1908).

Deville, M.A. *La Philosophie au Théâtre.* Paris, 1883.

Dinger, Hugo. *Richard Wagner's geistige Entwicklung*. Leipzig, 1892.

Donnay, Maurice. *Mes Débuts à Paris*. Paris, 1937.

_____. *Le Lycée Louis-le-Grand*. Paris, 1939.

_____. *Des Souvenirs...*. Paris, 1933.

_____, Bormaud, D., and Hyspa, V. *L'Esprit Montmartrois*. Paris, n.d.

Dujardin, Edouard. "Considérations sur l'art wagnérien." *Revue Wagnérienne* v.III vi-vii (July-August 1885).

_____. "Les Oeuvres Théoriques de Richard Wagner." *Revue Wagnérienne* I (1885).

Dukas, Paul. *Les Ecrits de Paul Dukas sur La Musique*. Paris, 1948.

Dupré, Paul and Ollendorff, Gustave. *Traité de l'Administration des Beaux-Arts*. 2 vols. Paris, 1885.

Duquesnil. *Annales Romantiques* XI (1914).

Durand, Jacques. *Quelques Souvenirs d'un Editeur de musique*. 2 vols. Paris, 1924-5.

"Enquête sur la Question Sociale au Théâtre." *Revue d'Art Dramatique* Nouvelle Série 3 (2/20/1898).

Escudier. *L'Art Musical* (12 October 1876).

Eymieu, Henri. "De l'Influence de la Critique." *Le Monde Musical* III/60 (10/30/1891).

Fervaal Devant La Presse. Paris, 1897.

Fétis. *Revue et Gazette Musicale de Paris* 42e année nos.3, 46, 47, 51; 43e année no.2.

Finck, Henry T. *Massenet and His Operas*. New York, 1910.

de Flers, Robert. *Revue d'Art Dramatique* (March 1900).

_____. "Meilhac et Halévy: Leur Vie et Leur Carrière." *Conférence* 18 année no.19 (9/15/1924).

Fouqué, Octave. *Les Révolutionnaires de la Musique*. Paris, 1882.

Galabert, Ed. *Souvenirs et Correspondance*. Paris, 1877.

Gallet, Louis. *Notes d'un librettiste*. Paris, 1891.

_____. "Quatre Directeurs de l'Opéra." *Revue Internationale de la Musique* I no.4.

Garnier, Charles. *Le Nouvel Opéra de Paris.* 2 vols. Paris, 1877–81.

_____. *Le Théâtre.* Paris, 1871.

Gauthier, Théophile. *Souvenirs de Théâtre, d'Art et de Critique.* Paris, 1883.

Geispitz, Henri. *Histoire du Théâtre-des-Arts de Rouen, 1882-1913.* Rouen, 1913.

Gheusi, P.-B. *Cinquante Ans de Paris.* 3 vols. Paris, 1940.

Glaeser, Ernst. ed. *Biographie Nationale des Contemporains.* Paris, 1878.

Halévy, Ludovic. *Carnets.* 2 vols. Paris, 1935.

_____. *La Famille Cardinal.* Paris, 1883.

_____. "La Millième Représentation de *Carmen.*" *Le Théâtre* 1905/1 (jan.-juin).

_____. *Notes et Souvenirs.* Paris, 1889.

Haraucourt, Edmond. *Mémoires Des Jours et des Gens.* Paris: E. Flammarion, 1946.

Hellouin, Frédéric. *Essai de critique de la critique musicale.* Paris, 1906.

Hennequin, Emile. *La Critique Scientifique.* Paris, 1888.

Henriet, Frédéric. *Monographie du Spectateur au Théâtre.* Paris, 1892.

Heulhard, A. *Bravos et Sifflets.* Paris, 1886.

_____. "Revue Musicale." *La Chronique Musicale* 1e année v.II; 3e année v.IX (July-September 1876).

Hippeau, Edmond. "Quelques Mots à Propos de 'Sigurd.'" *Revue du Monde musical dramatique et littéraire* 7e année no.18 (10 May 1884).

d'Indy, Vincent. *Richard Wagner et son Influence sur l'Art Musical Français.* Paris, 1930.

Istel, Edgar. *Das Libretto: Wesen, Aufbau und Wirkung des Opernbuchs.* Berlin, 1914.

Jollivet, Gaston. *L'Art de Vivre.* Paris, 1887.

_____. *Ma Folle Jeunesse.* Paris, 1926.

_____. *Souvenirs d'un Parisien*. Paris, 1928.

Jullien, Adolphe. *Paris Dilettante au Commencement du Siècle*. Paris, 1884.

LaFare, A. *Opéra et Comédie-Française: Carnet des abonnés*. Paris, n.d.

Laloy, Louis. "Le Drame Musical Moderne; III: Les véristes français: Gustave Charpentier." *Mercure Musicale* I (1 July 1905).

de La Rounat, Charles. *Souvenirs et poésies diverses*. Paris, 1886.

Larroumet, Gustave. *L'Art et l'Etat en France*. Paris, 1895.

de la Laurencie, Lionel. *Le Goût Musical en France*. Paris, 1908.

Leblanc, Georgette. *Souvenirs (1895-1918)*. Paris, 1931.

Le Blond, Maurice. "Le Théâtre héroique et social." Conférence prononcé au Collège d'Esthétique Modern, 5/11/1901. Paris, n.d.

Lemaître, Jules. *Opinions à Repandre*. Paris, 1901.

Lemonnier, Alphonse. *Les Abus au Théâtre*. Paris, 1895.

Léna, Maurice. "Massenet." Conférences lues aux Concerts historiques Pasdeloup. Paris, 1920.

Léon, Paul. *Du Palais Royal au Palais Bourbon*. Paris: A. Michel, 1947.

Lyonnet, Henry. *Dictionnaire des Comédiens Français*. Geneva, n.d.

Magnen, E. and Fouquet, E. *Le Théâtre et ses Lois*. Paris, n.d.

Magre, Maurice. *Conseils à un jeune homme pauvre*. Paris, 1908.

_____. *Les Soirs d'opium à Paris*. Paris, 1920.

Maillard, Georges. "M. Halanzier-Dufrenoy." *Revue du Monde Musical et Dramatique* 1e année no.2 (11/23/1878).

Malherbe, Ch. *Notice Sur Esclarmonde*. Paris, 1890.

Malliot, A.L. *La Musique au Théâtre*. Paris, 1866.

Maréchal, Henri. *Rome: Souvenirs d'un Musicien*. Paris, 1904.

Mariani, Angelo. *Figures contemporaines*. Paris, 1894—.

Martin, Jules. *Nos Auteurs et Compositeurs Dramatiques*. Paris, 1897.

Massenet, Jules. *My Recollections*. Translated by H. Villiers Barnett. Boston, 1919.

de Maupassant, Guy. *Oeuvres Complètes*. 28 vols. Paris, 1921–47.Vol.13: *Bel-Ami*.

Monselet, André. *Charles Monselet, sa vie, son oeuvre*. Paris, 1892.

Morand, Paul. *1900*. Paris, 1931.

Moreno, H. "Semaine Théâtrale." *Le Ménestrel* 42e année nos. 16 (19 March 1876), 17 (26 March 1876), 38 (20 August 1876); 45e année (16 March 1879), (20 July 1879); 46e année (3 October 1880); 47e année no.15, no.31, no.32; 55e année no.25 (23 June 1889).

Mortier, Arnold (Un Monsieur de l'Orchestre). *Les soirées Parisiennes*. 11 vols. Paris, 1875.

Noël, Edouard and Stoullig, Edmund, eds. *Annales du Théâtre et de la Musique*. 40 vols. Paris, 1875–1914.

Nordau, Max. *Dégénérescence*. Translated by Auguste Dietrich. 2 vols. Paris, 1894.

"Nouvelles Diverses: Paris et Départements." *Le Ménestrel* 48e année no.15 (12 March 1882).

Opéra et Comédie-Française: Carnet des Abonnés, Saison 1892-93. Paris, n.d.

L'Opéra et M. Halanzier: Extraits du Journal "La Presse". Paris, 1877.

Parisis. *La Vie Parisienne*. Paris, 1887.

Paul-Boncour, Joseph. *Art et démocratie*. Paris, 1912.

de Pawlowski, G. "M. Jacques Rouché est nommé de l'Académie Nationale." *Comoedia* (31 October 1913).

Pelissier, Paul. *Histoire Administrative de L'Académie de Musique et de Danse*. Paris, 1906.

Plaidoirie et Réplique de M. Poincaré, Avocat. Paris, 1906.

Pougin, Arthur. *Musiciens du XIXe Siècle*. Paris, 1911.

Proudhon, P.-J. *Du Principe de l'Art et de sa Destination sociale*. Paris, 1865.

Proust, Antonin. *L'Art sous la République*. Paris, 1892.

_____. "Le Ministère des Arts." *Revue Politique et Littéraire* 3e. série, v.III (January-July 1882).

Qui Etes-Vous, 1908-09. Paris, 1909.

Revue Biographique des Notabilités Françaises Contemporaines. 3 vols. Paris, 1892–98.

La Revue Musicale (January 1901–January 1912, March 1929).

"Revue des Théâtres Lyriques." *Revue et Gazette Musicale de Paris*. 42e année no. 3 (17 January 1875).

Reyer, Ernest. *Quarante Ans de Musique*. Paris, 1910.

Richepin, Jean. *Les Etapes d'un Réfractaire*. Paris, n.d.

Rolland, Romain. "Louise." *Rivista Musicale Italiana* no.7 (1900).

_____. *Musiciens d'aujourd'hui*. 2nd. ed. Paris, 1908.

_____. *Paris als Musikstadt*. Translated by Max Graf. Berlin, 1904.

Rostand, Maurice. *Confession d'un demi-siècle*. Paris: Jeune Parque, 1948.

Roujon, Henry. *Artistes et Amis des Arts*. Paris, 1912.

_____. *En Marge du Temps*. Paris, 1908.

Rouxel. *L'Etat et les Théâtres*. Paris, 1877.

_____. "Artistes et Subventions." *Journal des Economistes* 4e série, 6e année no.22 (April–June 1883).

Ruelle, Jules. "Théâtre National de l'Opéra." *L'Art Musicale* XVI no.18 (3 March 1877).

de Saint-Auban, Emile. *L'Idée Sociale au Théâtre*. Paris, 1901.

Saint-Saëns, Camille. *Ecole Buissonière*. Paris, 1913.

_____. *Harmonie et Mélodie*. 6th ed. Paris, n.d.

_____. "Lettre de Las Palmas." *La Nouvelle Revue* (30 March 1897).

Scudo. "Revue Musicale." *Revue des Deux Mondes* XXIII (15 October 1859).

Séché, Alphonse, and Bertaut, Jules. *L'Evolution du Théâtre Contemporain*. Paris, 1908.

Servières, Georges. *La Musique française moderne*. Paris, 1897.

_____. *Richard Wagner jugé en France*. Paris, 1887.

Silvestre, Armand. *Au Pays des Souvenirs*. Paris, 1887.

Société des Auteurs et Compositeurs Dramatiques: Annuaire. 7 vols. Paris, 1887-1915.

Soubies, Albert and Malherbe, Charles. *Histoire de L'Opéra-Comique*. 2 vols. Paris, 1892.

Spoll, E.-A. *Mme. Carvalho: Notes et Souvenirs*. Paris, 1885.

Strauss, Richard, and von Hofmannsthal, Hugo. *Correspondence*. Translated by Hans Hammelmann and Ewald Osers. London: Collins, 1961.

Taine, Hippolyte. *Philosophie de l'Art*. 5th. ed. Paris, 1890.

Theuriet, André. *Souvenirs des Vertes Saisons*. 2nd. ed. Paris, 1904.

Toudouze, G. *Albert Wolff, histoire d'un Chroniquer*. Paris, 1883.

Treich, Leon, ed. *L'Esprit de Robert de Flers*. Paris, 1928.

Vallette, Alfred. "'Pélléas et Mélisande' et la Critique Officielle." *Mercure de France* (July 1893).

Vapereau, G. and Guitane, L. *Dictionnaire Universel des Contemporains*. Paris, 1870-1873.

Villiers de l'Isle Adam. *Chez les Passants*. Paris, 1879.

Wagner, Richard. *Oeuvres en Prose*. Translated by J.G. Prod'homme. Vol.IV: *Opéra et Drame*. Paris, n.d.

_____. *Richard Wagner's Prose Works*. Translated by William Ashton Ellis. 8 vols. N.Y., 1892-99.

Wolff, Albert. *La Gloriole*. Paris, 1888.

de Wyzewa, Isabelle. *La Revue Wagnérienne: Essai sur l'Interpretation Esthétique de Wagner en France*. Paris, 1934.

de Wyzewa, Théodore. "Le Pessimisme de Richard Wagner." *Revue Wagnérienne* I no.6 (1885).

Zadig. "Silhouettes Parisiennes: Jean Richepin." *Revue Bleue* 4e. Série, v.XIII no.2 (13 January 1900).

Zola, Emile. *Le Naturalisme au Théâtre*. Paris, 1881.

_____. *Oeuvres Complètes*. Edited by Maurice Le Blond. 50 vols. Paris, 1927.

_____. *La République et la Littérature*. Paris, 1879.

SECONDARY WORKS

Adorno, Theodor. *Essai sur Wagner*. Translated by Hans Hildebrand and Alex Lindenberg. Paris: Gallimard, 1966.

_____. *Klangfiguren: Musikalische Schriften I*. Berlin: Suhrkamp, 1959.

Althusser, Louis. "Ideology and Ideological State Apparatus: Notes Towards an Investigation," in *"Lenin and Philosophy" and other essays*. Translated by Ben Brewster. 2nd. ed. London: NLB, 1977, 127-186.

Anderson, R.D. *France 1870-1914: Politics and Society*. London: Routledge & Kegan Paul, 1977.

Andrieu, Pierre. *Souvenirs des Frères Isola*. Paris, 1943.

de Anna, Luigi. *Francisque Sarcey: professeur et journaliste*. Florence, n.d.

Arvin, Neil Cole. *Eugène Scribe and the French Theatre, 1815-1860*. Cambridge, Mass., 1924.

Baillot, A. *L'Influence de Schopenhauer en France (1860-1900)*. Paris, 1927.

Barthes, Roland. "Structure du faits divers." *Essais critiques*. Paris: Editions du Seuil, 1964, 188-197.

Becker, Heinz, ed. *Die "Couleur locale" in der Oper des 19. Jahrhunderts*. Regensburg: Bosse, 1976.

_____. "Giacomo Meyerbeer's Mitarbeit an den Libretti seiner Oper." *Bericht über den Internationalen Musikwissenschaftlichen Kongress, Bonn 1970*. Kassel, 1971.

Bekker, Paul. *The Changing Opera*. Translated by Arthur Mendel. New York, 1935.

Bellanger, Claude, et. al. *Historie générale de la presse Française*. 4 vols. Paris: PUF, 1972.

Bellessort, André. *Les Intellectuels et l'Avènement de la Troisième République*. Paris, 1931.

Bernard, Elisabeth. "L'Evolution du Public d'Opéra de 1860 à 1880," *Régards sur L'Opéra*. Paris: PUF, 1976.

Bertaut, Jules. *L'Opinion et les Moeurs*. Paris, 1931.

————. *Le Paris d'Avant-Guerre*. Paris, 1919.

Bissell, C. *Les Conventions du Théâtre Bourgeois Contemporain en France, 1887-1914*. Paris, 1930.

Boschot, Adolphe. *La Vie et les Oeuvres de Alfred Bruneau*. Paris, 1937.

Bossuet, Pierre. *Histoire des Théâtres Nationaux: Les Théâtres et l'Etat*. Paris, n.d.

Bourdieu, Pierre. *Distinction: A Social Critique of the Judgement of Taste*. Translated by Richard Nice. Cambridge, Mass.: Harvard University Press, 1984.

———— and Passeron, Jean-Claude. *Reproduction: In Education, Society and Culture*. Translated by Richard Nice. SAGE Studies in Social and Educational Change. London and Beverly Hills: SAGE Publications, 1977.

Brophy, Brigid. "Figaro and the Limitations of Music." *Music & Letters* 51 (1970), 26-36.

Brown, Frederick. *Theater and Revolution: The Culture of the French Stage*. N.Y.: Viking Press, 1980.

Burde, Wolfgang. "Analytische Notizen zum gesellschaftlichen Gehalt und Standort von Musikwerden." *Zeitschrift für Musiktheorie* II (1974), 20-22.

Carlson, Marvin. *The French Stage in the Nineteenth Century*. Metuchin, N.J.: Scarecrow Press, 1972.

Carner, Mosco. *Puccini: A Critical Biography*. London: Duckworth, 1958.

Clark, Priscilla B. "Stratégies d'Auteur au XIXe siècle." *Romantisme* 17-18 (1977), 92-102.

Clément, Catherine. *Opera: or the Undoing of Women*. Translated by Betsy Wing. Foreward by Susan McClary. Minneapolis: Virago, 1988.

Combarieu, Jules. *Histoire de la Musique*. 3 vols. Paris, 1923.

Crosten, William L. *French Grand Opera: An Art and a Business*. New York: King's Crown Press, 1948.

Curtiss, Mina. *Bizet and His World*. New York: Knopf, 1958.

de Curzon, H. *Léo Delibes: Sa Vie et Ses Oeuvres*. Paris, 1926.

Delmas, Marc. *Gustave Charpentier et le lyrisme français*. Paris, 1931.

Descotes, Maurice. *Le Public de Théâtre et son histoire*. Paris: PUF, 1964.

Dictionnaire de biographie française. Paris: Letouzey et Ane, 1933-94.

Dufourcq, Norbert. *Autour de Coquard, César Franck et Vincent d'Indy*. Paris: Librairie Floury, 1952.

Duvigneaud, Jean. *Sociologie du Théâtre*. Paris: PUF, 1965.

Eckart-Bäcker, Ursula. *Frankreichs Musik zwischen Romantik und Modern: Die Zeit im Spiegel der Kritik*. Regensburg: Bosse, 1965.

Elwitt, Sanford. *The Making of the Third Republic*. Baton Rouge: Louisiana State University Press, 1975.

_____. *The Third Republic Defended*. Baton Rouge: Louisiana State University Press, 1986.

Farmer, Paul. *France Reviews its Revolutionary Origins: Social Politics and Historical Opinion in the Third Republic*. Morningside Heights, New York, 1944.

Favre, George. *L'Oeuvre de Paul Dukas*. Paris: Durand & Cie., 1969.

Ferro, Marc. "Faits Divers, Fait d'Historie: Présentation." *Annales: Economies, Sociétés, Civilizations* IIIe. année no.4 (July–August 1983), 821-826.

Frichet, Jacqueline. "Le Théâtre lyrique d'Emile Zola." *Les Cahiers naturalistes* XVII no.42 (1971).

Fulcher, Jane. *The Nation's Image*. New York: Cambridge University Press, 1987.

Genest, Edmond. *L'Opéra-Comique: Connu et Inconnu*. Paris, 1925.

Georges-Michel, M. *Un Demi-Siècle de Gloires Théatrales*. Paris: A. Bonne, 1950.

Gerhard, Anselm. *Die Verstädterung der Oper: Paris und das Musiktheaters des 19. Jahrhunderts.* Stuttgart, Weimar: Verlag J.B. Metzler, 1992.

Giffard, Pierre. *La Vie au Théâtre.* Paris, n.d.

Goubault, Christian. *La Critique Musicale dans la Presse Française de 1870 à 1914.* Geneva and Paris: Slatkine, 1984.

Gouldner, Alvin W. *The Coming Crisis in Western Sociology.* New York: Basic Books, 1970.

Gourret, Jean. *Ces Hommes qui ont fait l'Opéra.* Paris: Albatros, 1984.

Gramsci, Antonio. *Selections from the Prison Notebooks.* Edited and translated by Quintin Hoare and G.N. Smith. New York: International Publishers, 1971.

Griffiths, Richard. *The Reactionary Revolution: The Catholic Revival in French Literature, 1870-1914.* London: Constable, 1966.

Guichard, Léon. *La Musique et les Lettres en France au Temps du Wagnérisme.* Paris: PUF, 1963.

Guiet, René. "L'Evolution du Genre: Le Livret d'Opéra en France de Gluck à la Révolution 1774-1793." *Smith College Studies in Modern Languages* XVIII (Oct. 1936-July 1937).

Guillais, Joëlle. *La Chair de l'Autre: Le Crime passionel au XIXe siècle.* Paris: O. Orban, 1986.

Halévy, Daniel. *La Fin des Notables.* 2 vols. Paris, 1920.

Halls, W.D. "Les débuts du Théâtre nouveau chez Maeterlinck." *Annales de la Fondation Maeterlinck* III (1957).

_____. *Maurice Maeterlinck: a Study of His Life and Thought.* Oxford: Clarendon Press, 1960.

Hansen, Eric C. *Disaffection and Decadence.* Washington, D.C.: University Press of America, 1982.

_____. *Ludovic Halévy: A Study of Frivolity and Fatalism in Nineteenth-Century France.* Lanham, MD: University Press of America, 1987.

Harding, James. *Massenet.* London: Dent, 1970.

_____. *Saint-Saëns and his Circle.* London: Chapman & Hall, 1965.

Harth, Erica. *Ideology and Culture in Seventeenth-Century France*. Ithaca, N.Y.: Cornell University Press, 1983.

Haskell, Thomas L. "Capitalism and the Humanitarian Sensibility." *American Historical Review* v.90 no.2,3 (April, June 1985) 339-361, 547-566.

Hays, Michael. *The Public and Performance: Essays in the History of French and German Theater, 1871-1900*. Ann Arbor: UMI Research Press, 1974.

Hayward, J.E.S. "The Official Philosophy of the French Third Republic: Léon Bourgeois and Solidarism." *International Review of Social History* v.1 (1961), 19-48.

Herbert, Eugenia. *The Artist and Social Reform: France and Belgium 1885-1898*. New Haven: Yale University Press, 1961.

Himonet, Andre. *'Louise' de Charpentier*. Paris, 1922.

Hughes, H. Stuart. *Consciousness and Society*. Revised edition. New York: Vintage Books, 1977.

Jäckel, Kurt. *Richard Wagner in der französischen Literatur*. Breslau, 1931.

Jameson, Frederic. *The Political Unconscious*. Ithaca, N.Y.: Cornell University Press, 1981.

Jeuland-Meynaud, Maryse. "Légitimité de la Librettologie." *Revue des Etudes Italiennes* Nouvelle Série, XXII (1976), 60-101.

Kivy, Peter. *The Corded Shell: Reflections on Musical Expression*. Princeton, N.J.: Princeton University Press, 1980.

Klein, John W. "The Two Versions of 'Carmen.'" *Musical Opinion* (March 1949), 292f.

Krakovitch, Odile. *Hugo Censuré: La liberté au théâtre au XIXe siècle*. Paris: Calmann-Levy, 1985.

Lalo, Charles. *L'Art et la Vie Sociale*. Paris, 1921.

Laloy, Louis. "L'Opéra," Le Théâtre Lyrique et la Symphonie de 1874 à 1925. Edited by Ladislas Rohozinski. Paris, 1925.

Large, David C., and Weber, William, eds. *Wagnerism in European Culture and Politics*. Ithaca, N.Y.: Cornell University Press, 1984.

Lears, T.J. Jackson. "The Concept of Cultural Hegemony: Problems and Possibilities." *American Historical Review* v.90 no.3 (June 1985), 567-594.

Le Blond-Zola, Denise. *Emile Zola Raconté par Sa Fille*. Paris, 1930.

Leppert, Richard, and McClary, Susan, eds. *Music and Society: the politics of composition, performance and reception*. Cambridge: Cambridge University Press, 1987.

Levin, Miriam R. *Republican Art and Ideology in Late Nineteenth-Century France*. Ann Arbor: UMI Research Press, 1986.

Lhomme, Jean. *La Grande Bourgeoisie au Pouvoir (1830-1880)*. Paris: PUF, 1960.

Lindenberger, Herbert. *Historical Drama: The Relation of Literature and Reality*. Chicago: University of Chicago Press, 1975.

Link, Klaus-Dieter. *Literarische Perspektiven des Opernlibrettos: Studien zur italienischen Oper von 1850 bis 1920*. Abhandlungen zur Kunst, Musik und Literaturwissenschaft, Band 173. Bonn: Bouvier, 1975.

Locke, Robert. *French Legitimists and the Politics of Moral Order in the Early Third Republic*. Princeton: Princeton University Press, 1974.

Lockspeiser, Edward. *Debussy: His Life and Mind*. 2 vols. London: Cassell, 1962.

Longyear, Rey M. "Political and Social Criticism in French Opera, 1827-1920." *Essays in the Music of J.S. Bach and other Divers Subjects*. Edited by Robert L. Weaver. Louisville: University of Louisville, 1981, 245-254.

Lough, John. *Writer and Public in France: From the Middle Ages to the Present Day*. Oxford: Clarendon Press, 1978.

Lukacs, George. *History and Class Consciousness*. Translated by Rodney Livingstone. Cambridge, Mass.: MIT Press, 1971.

McClary, Susan. *Georges Bizet: Carmen*. Cambridge Opera Handbooks. Cambridge and New York: Cambridge University Press, 1992.

McGrath, William J. *Dionysian Art and Populist Politics in Austria*. New Haven: Yale University Press, 1974.

Mahling, Ch.-H. "Selbstdarstellung und Kritik der Gesellschaft in der Oper? Bemerkungen zu Opern von Mozart bis Dessau." *Bericht über den Internationalen Musikwissenschaftlichen Kongress, Bonn 1970*. Kassel, 1971.

_____. "Zur Frage der 'Bürgerlichkeit' der bürgerlichen Musikkultur im 19. Jahrhundert." *Musica* 31 (1977), 13-18.

Manévy, Raymond. *La Presse Française: de Renaudet à Rochefort.* Paris: J. Foret, 1960.

_____. *La Presse de la IIIe République.* Paris: J. Foret, 1955.

Martino, Pierre. *Le Naturalisme Français.* Paris, 1923.

_____. *Parnasse et symbolisme 1850-1900.* Paris, 1925.

Mayer, Arno. *The Persistence of the Old Regime: Europe to the Great War.* New York: Pantheon Books, 1981.

Meyer, Leonard B. *Emotion and Meaning in Music.* Chicago: University of Chicago Press, 1956.

Mornet, Daniel. *Histoire de la littérature et de la pensée française contemporaine, 1870-1925.* Paris, 1923.

Nelms, Brenda. *The Third Republic and the Centennial of 1789.* N.Y.: Garland Pub., 1987.

Newman, Ernest. *The Life of Richard Wagner.* 4 vols. New York: Cambridge University Press, 1976.

d'Ollone, Max. *Le Théâtre Lyrique et le Public.* Paris: La Palatine, 1955.

Paul, Charles B. "Rameau, d'Indy and French Nationalism." *Musical Quarterly* LVIII no.I (January 1972), 46-56.

Perrot, Michelle. "Faits divers et histoire au XIXe siècle." *Annales: Economies, Sociétés, Civilizations* 38 no.4 (July–August 1983), 911-919.

Peter, René. *Le Théâtre et la Vie sous la Troisième République.* Paris, 1945.

Peytel, Adrien. "Jurisprudence: Le Théâtre et Les Auteurs." *Encyclopédie de la Musique.* Paris, 1931.

Pouquet, Jeanne. *Le Salon de Mme. Arman de Caillevet.* Paris, 1926.

Prud'homme, J.G. "Albert Carré, 1852-1938." *Rivista Musicale Italiana* Anno XLIII fasc.3-4, 398-402.

Rearick, Charles. *Pleasures of the Belle Epoque.* New Haven: Yale University Press, 1985.

Robinson, Paul. *Opera & Ideas: From Mozart to Strauss.* New York: Harper & Row, 1985.

Rohozinski, Ladislas, ed. *Cinquante Ans de Musique Française.* 2 vols. Paris, n.d.

Rubsamen, Walter. "Music and Politics in the Risorgimento." *Italian Quarterly* V (1961), 100-120.

_____. "Political and Ideological Censorship of Opera." *Papers of the American Musicological Society, Annual Meeting 1941.*

Rude, Maxime. *Tout-Paris au Café.* Paris, n.d.

Rudorff, Raymond. *Belle Epoque: Paris in the Nineties.* London: Hamilton, 1972.

Salmen, Walter., ed. *Beiträge zur Geschichte der Musikanschauung im 19. Jahrhundert.* Regensburg: Bosse, 1965.

_____, ed. *Der Sozialstatus des Berufmusikers vom 17. bis 19. Jahrhundert.* Kassel: Barenreiter-Verlag, 1971.

Schmidt-Garré, Helmut. "Debussy und Maeterlinck — die Kongruenz ihres Empfindens und die Inkongruenz ihrer Wirkung." *Neue Zeitschrift für Musik* 130 no.2 (1969), 85-88.

Schorske, Carl. *Fin-de-Siècle Vienna: Politics and Culture.* New York: Vintage Books, 1981.

Seager, Frederic H. *The Boulanger Affair.* Ithaca, N.Y.: Cornell University Press, 1969.

Seigel, Jerrold. *Bohemian Paris: Culture, Politics and the Boundaries of Bourgeois Life, 1830-1930.* N.Y.: Viking, 1986.

Servières, G. "Les débuts de Massenet à l'Opéra." *Rivista Musicale Italiana* Anno XXXII fasc.1 (1925), 40-50.

Shattuck, Roger. *The Banquet Years.* New York: Harcourt Brace, 1958.

Silverman, Debora L. *Art Nouveau in Fin-de-Siècle France: Politics, Psychology and Style.* Berkeley: University of California Press, 1989.

Singer-Kérel, Jeanne. *Le Coût de la vie à Paris de 1840 à 1954.* Paris: A. Colin, 1961.

Spies, André. "The French Revolution and Revolutionary Values in Belle Epoque Opera." *Essays in European History* 2 (1996).

_____. "Lohengrin Takes on the Third Republic: Wagner and *Wagnérisme* in Belle Epoque Paris." *Nineteenth Century Studies* 3 (1989).

Stompor, Stephan. "Ein Opernhaus und seine Gattung." *Musikbühne*. Edited by Horst Seeger. Henschelverlag Kunst und Gesellschaft, 1974, 119-143.

Sutton, Howard. *The Life and Works of Jean Richepin*. Geneva: E. Droz, 1961.

Talvart, Hector, et Place, Joseph. *Bibliographie des Auteurs modernes de la langue française*. Paris, 1928.

Thieme, H.P. *Bibliographie de la littérature française*. 3 vols. Paris, 1933.

Watson, David Robin. *Georges Clemenceau*. New York: Evre Metheuen, 1974.

Weber, Eugen. *France: Fin de Siècle*. Cambridge, Mass: Belknap Press, 1986.

Weber, William. *Music and the Middle Class*. New York: Holmes & Meier Publishers, 1975.

Williams, Raymond. *Marxism and Literature*. Oxford: Oxford University Press, 1977.

Williams, Rosalind. *Dream Worlds: Mass Consumption in Late Nineteenth-Century France*. Berkeley: University of California Press, 1982.

Zeldin, Theodore. *France, 1848-1918*. 2 vols. Oxford: Clarendon Press, 1973-1977.

DISSERTATIONS AND THESES

Buteau, Max. "Le Droit de Critique en Matière Littéraire, Dramatique et Artistique." Thèse pour le Doctorat, Université de Paris, Faculté de Droit, 1909.

Chichmanoff, Irène. "Etude critique sur les Femmes poètes en France au XIXe siècle." Thèse de Doctorat, U. Berne, 1910.

Festerling, Wilhelm. "Catulle Mendès Beziehungen zu Richard Wagner." Doctoral dissertation, U. Greifswald, 1913.

Guieu, Jean-Max. "Le Théâtre Lyrique d'Emile Zola." Doctoral dissertation, University of Maryland, 1976.

Guiliani, Elizabeth. "Le Public et le répertoire de l'Opéra à l'époque de J.J. Rousseau." Mémoire de Maîtrise, Université de Paris X, 1970-71.

Marschall, Gottfried R. "Massenet et la Fixation de la Forme Mélodique Française." Thèse de Doctorat, Université de Paris IV, 1978.

Nolte, Nancy W. "Government and Theatre in Nineteenth-Century France: Administrative Organization for Control of the Comédie Française Repertoire." Doctoral Dissertation, University of Akron, 1985.

Pezzer, Raymond de. "L'Opéra devant la loi et la jurisprudence." Thèse pour le Doctorat, Faculté de Droit de l'Université de Paris, 1911.

Sorin, Paul. "Du Role de l'Etat en matière d'Art Scénique." Thèse pour le Doctorat, Faculté de Droit de l'Université de Paris, 1902.

Spies, André. "French Opera During the Belle Epoque: A Study In the Social History of Ideas." Doctoral dissertation, University of North Carolina, 1986.

Sudik, Thomas J. "The French Administration of Fine Arts, 1875-1914." Doctoral dissertation, University of North Carolina, 1979.

Turbow, Gerald Dale. "Wagnerism in France, 1839-1870." Doctoral dissertation, UCLA, 1965.

NEWSPAPER ARTICLES

"Abonnements des Samedis à l'Opéra-Comique." Le Figaro (3 December 1885).

Adam, Adolphe. "Louise." Le Temps (30 January 1900).

Allard, Eugene, and Vauxcelles, Louis. "La Musique: Gustave Charpentier." Le Figaro (28 October 1900).

"Les Beaux-Arts." La XIXe Siècle (14 September 1891).

"Bloc-Notes Parisien." Le Gaulois (31 October 1913).

Calmette, Gaston. "Les Matinées de l'Opéra." Le Figaro (4 January 1892).

Clarétie, Jules. "Paris l'Hiver." *Le Journal* (5 October 1900).

Clisson, Eugène. "M. Bertrand à l'Opéra." *L'Evénement* (1 July 1891).

Conbert. "Le Peuple à l'Opéra." *Paris* (5 January 1892).

"Constans le Goujat." *L'Intransigeant* (19 February 1891).

"Les Coulisses de l'Opéra." *La Vie Parisienne* (13 April 1889).

Le Cri de Paris (9 November 1913).

Le Cri du Peuple (29 May 1887).

Croze, J.L. "La Guerre en Musique." *L'Eclair* (31 October 1913).

Le Diogène (30 April 1890).

"La Direction de l'Opéra." *Les Nouvelles* (30 October 1913).

Drault, Jean. "Le Luxe au Théâtre." *Le Libre Parole* (18 July 1901).

Duhamel, Georges. "Le Souvenir de A.-Ferdinand Hérold." *Mercure de France* (11 January 1949).

Le Figaro (3 December 1885).

Gaucher, André. "La Question d'*Astarté*." *La Liberté* (7 March 1901).

Le Gaulois de Dimanche (14 August 1908).

Gohier, Urbain. "Au Théâtre." *L'Aurore* (13 September 1901).

Gil Blas (31 October 1913).

de Gramont, Louis. *L'Eclair* (12 July 1900).

Hahn, Reynaldo. "Journal d'un Musicien." *Candide* (22 August 1935).

"L'Hebdomadaire." *Le Petit Républicain-Rouen* (8 November 1913).

Huret, Jules. "Le Directeur de l'Opéra-Comique." *Le Figaro* (14 January 1898).

_____. "Un Idée d'Artistes: Le Peuple au Théâtre." *Le Figaro* (19 November 1900).

Jollivet, Gaston. *L'Autorité* (3 November 1913).

Le Journal (14 August 1900).

Le Journal Officiel.

Jullien, Adolphe. "Revue Musicale." *Feuilleton du Français* (15 June 1885).

_____. "Revue Musicale." *Feuilleton du Journal des Débats* (4 February 1900).

Jumelles. "Le Théâtre Meurt." *Le Voltaire* (20 March 1901).

Lalo, Pierre. "La Musique." *Feuilleton du Temps* (4 August 1908).

La Lanterne (31 October 1913).

La Liberté (29 May 1891, 26 August 1900).

Maeterlinck, Maurice. *Le Figaro* (13 April 1902).

"La Matinée d'hier à l'Opéra." *Le Jour* (5 January 1892).

"L'Opéra Démocratique." *La France* (5 January 1892).

"L'Opéra Populaire." *Paris* (5 January 1892).

"Paradoxe sur l'Opéra." *Dépêche de Toulouse* (5 November 1913).

Pedrille. "La Journée d'Hier à l'Opéra." *Le Petit Journal* (4 January 1892).

Reyer, Ernest. "Revue Musicale." *Feuilleton du Journal des Débats* (21 June 1885).

de Saint-Aubin, Emile. "Le Théâtre Social." *Le Soleil* (14 February 1901).

de Saint-Croix, Camille. "Tribune Littéraire: Opéra-Comique." *Le Paris* (8 July 1896).

Spectator. "Derrière la Toile." *Eclair de Montpellier* (8 November 1913).

"Subventions théâtrales." *L'Autorité* (11 July 1900).

Tailhade, Laurent. "Le Théâtre Gratuit." *La Petite République* (11 January 1901).

Le Temps (14 September 1891).

"Tribunal Correctionel de Paris." *Gazette des Tribunaux* (28-29 November 1887).

Vitu, Auguste. "Premières Représentations." *Le Figaro* (8 January 1884).

Wilder, Victor. "Le Cas de M. Barbier." *Gil Blas* (20 December 1897).

OPERA REVIEWS

Carmen (4-16 March 1875):

Le XIXe Siècle, Le Figaro, Le Français, Le Gaulois, La Gazette de France, Le Journal des Débats, Paris-Journal, Le Petit Journal, L'Ordre, La République Française, Le Pays, Le Rappel, Le Soleil, Le Temps.

Jeanne d'Arc (4-12 April 1876):

Le XIXe Siècle, Le Figaro, Le Français, Le Journal des Débats, Le National, L'Ordre, Paris-Journal, Le Pays, Le Rappel, Le Soleil.

Cinq-Mars (7-16 April 1877):

Le Français, La Gazette de France, La Liberté, L'Ordre, Le Petit Journal, Le Rappel, La République Française, Le Soleil.

Polyeucte (8-21 October 1878):

Le XIXe Siècle, Le Français, La France Nouvelle, Le Gaulois, Le Journal des Débats, Le National, Le Pays, Le Petit Journal, Le Rappel.

Suzanne (1-14 January 1879):

Le XIXe Siècle, L'Estafette, Le Journal des Débats, La Lanterne, Le National, La Patrie, Le Petit Journal, Le Petit Parisien, Le Rappel, Le Soir.

La Courte Echelle (11-24 March 1879):

La Civilisation, L'Estafette, Le Figaro, Le Français, La Gazette de France, Le Journal des Débats, Le National, Paris-Journal, Le Soir, Le Temps.

Jean de Nivelle (9-22 March 1880):

La Civilisation, Le Figaro, Le Français, Le Gaulois, La Gazette de France, La Liberté, Le Petit Journal, Le Petit Parisien, La Presse, *La République Française.*

Henri VIII (4–19 March, 1883):

Le XIXe Siècle, Le Français, La Gazette de France, Le Journal des Débats, La Lanterne, Le National, Le Pays, Le Rappel, Le Soleil.

Sapho (28 March - 8 April 1884):

Le Français, La Gazette de France, Le Cri du Peuple, La Justice, La Lanterne, La Liberté, La Patrie, Le Pays, Le Rappel, La République Française, Le Temps.

Le Cid (27 November - 14 December 1885):

La Bataille, Le XIXe Siècle, L'Echo de Paris, Le Figaro, Le Français, Le Gaulois, Le Journal des Débats, La Justice, La Lanterne, Le National, Le Pays, Le Rappel, La République Française.

Patrie! (11–27 December 1886):

L'Autorité, Le XIXe Siècle, Le Français, Le Gaulois, Le Journal des Débats, La Lanterne, Le National, Le Rappel, Le Soleil.

Esclarmonde (15–19 May 1889):

L'Autorité, La Bataille, L'Estafette, Le Figaro, La Gazette de France, L'Intransigeant, Le Journal des Débats, La Lanterne, Le National, Le Petit Parisien, La Presse, La République Française, Le Soleil, Le Temps.

Kassya (24–27 March 1893):

La Bataille, L'Eclair, Le Figaro, Le Gaulois, La Gazette de France, La Justice, La Lanterne, La Liberté, Le Petit Journal, Le Rappel, Le Temps.

Lohengrin (9–25 September 1891):

L'Autorité, La Bataille, Le Cri du Peuple, La Croix, Le XIXe Siècle, L'Echo de Paris, L'Estafette, L'Intransigeant, Le Figaro, Le Gaulois, La Gazette de France, Le Journal des Débats, La Justice, La Lanterne, La Liberté, Le Matin, Le National, Le Paris, La Patrie, Le Pays, Le Petit Journal, Le Petit Parisien, La Presse, Le Rappel, La République Française, Le Soir, Le Soleil, Le Temps, L'Univers.

L'Attaque du Moulin (22–30 December 1893):

La Bataille, L'Intransigeant, Le Journal, La Justice, La Lanterne, La Liberté, Le Matin, La Patrie, Le Petit Journal, Le Petit Parisien, La Petite République, Le Rappel, La République Française.

La Vivandière (1–11 April 1895):

L'Autorité, La Bataille, L'Eclair, Le Figaro, Le Gaulois, La Gazette de France, L'Intransigeant, La Justice, La Liberté, Le Matin, La Patrie, Le Petit Journal, Le Petit Parisien, Le Rappel, Le Temps.

La Habanera (27 February – 3 March 1908):

L'Echo de Paris, Le Gaulois, L'Humanité, Le Petit Journal, Le Petit Parisien, La Petite République, Le Rappel, La République Française, Le Temps.

Index of Names

The librettists and composers of full-length French operas that had premieres at the Opéra and Opéra-Comique bewteen 1875 and 1914 are listed in italics and in bold type, respectively.

INDEX OF OPERAS

Studies in Modern European History

The monographs in this series focus upon aspects of the political, social, economic, cultural, and religious history of Europe from the Renaissance to the present. Emphasis is placed on the states of Western Europe, especially Great Britain, France, Italy, and Germany. While some of the volumes treat internal developments, others deal with movements such as liberalism, socialism, and industrialization which transcend a particular country.

The series editor is:

Frank J. Coppa
Director, Doctor of Arts Program
in Modern World History
Department of History
St. John's University
Jamaica, New York 11439